MEDIUM
RAW

MEDIUM RAW

A Bloody Valentine to the World of
Food and the People Who Cook

ANTHONY BOURDAIN

ecco

An Imprint of HarperCollinsPublishers

HarperCollins books may be purchased for educational, business, or sales promotional use. For information, please write: Special Markets Department, HarperCollins Publishers, 10 East 53rd Street, New York, NY 10022.

FIRST EDITION

Designed by Suet Yee Chong

Library of Congress Cataloging-in-Publication Data has been applied for.

ISBN: 978-0-06-171894-6 (Hardcover)
ISBN: 978-0-06-200903-6 (International Edition)

10 11 12 13 14   OV/RRD   10 9 8 7 6 5 4 3 2 1

To Ottavia

On the whole I have received better treatment in life than the average man and more loving kindness than I perhaps deserved.

—Frank Harris

CONTENTS

I **recognize the men at the bar.** And the one woman. They're some of the most respected chefs in America. Most of them are French but all of them made their bones here. They are, each and every one of them, heroes to me—as they are to up-and-coming line cooks, wannabe chefs, and culinary students everywhere. They're clearly surprised to see each other here, to recognize their peers strung out along the limited number of barstools. Like me, they were summoned by a trusted friend to this late-night meeting at this celebrated New York restaurant for ambiguous reasons under conditions of utmost secrecy. They have been told, as I was, not to tell anyone of this gathering. It goes without saying that none of us will blab about it later.

Well . . . I guess that's not exactly true.

It's early in my new non-career as professional traveler, writer, and TV guy, and I still get the vapors being in the same room with these guys. I'm doing my best to conceal the fact that I'm, frankly, starstruck—atwitter with anticipation. My palms are sweaty as I order a drink, and I'm aware that my voice sounds oddly high and squeaky as the words "vodka on the rocks" come out. All I know for sure about this gathering is that a friend called me on Saturday night and, after asking me what I was doing on Monday, instructed me, in his noticeably French accent, that "Tuh-nee . . . you *must* come. It will be very special."

Since leaving all day-to-day responsibilities at my old restaurant, Les Halles, and having had to learn (or relearn)—after a couple of book tours and many travels—how to deal, once again, with civilian society, I now own a couple of suits. I'm wearing one now, dressed appropriately, I think, for a restaurant of this one's high reputation. The collar on my shirt is too tight and it's digging into my neck. The knot on my tie, I am painfully aware, is less than perfect. When I arrived at the appointed hour of eleven p.m., the dining room was thinning of customers and I was discreetly ushered here, to the small, dimly lit bar and waiting area. I was relieved that upon laying eyes on me, the maître d' did not wrinkle his nose in distaste.

I'm thrilled to see X, a usually unflappable figure whom I generally speak of in the same hushed, respectful tones as the Dalai Lama—a man who ordinarily seems to vibrate on a lower frequency than other, more earthbound chefs. I'm surprised to see that he's nearly as excited as I am, an unmistakable look of apprehension on his face. Around him are some of the second and third waves of Old Guard French guys, some Young Turks—along with a few American chefs who came up in their kitchens. There's the Godmother of the French-chef mafia . . . It's a fucking *Who's Who* of the top tier of cooking in America today. If a gas leak blew up this building? Fine dining as we know it would be nearly wiped out in one stroke. Ming Tsai would be the guest judge on every episode of *Top Chef*, and Bobby Flay and Mario Batali would be left to carve up Vegas between themselves.

A few last, well-fed citizens wander past on their way from the dining room to the street. More than one couple does a double take at the lineup of familiar faces murmuring conspiratorially at the bar. The large double doors to a private banquet room swing open and we are summoned.

There's a long table, set for thirteen people, in the middle of the room. Against the wall is a sideboard, absolutely groaning under the weight of charcuterie—the likes of which few of us (even in this group) have seen in decades: classic Careme-era terrines of wild game, gallantines of various birds, pâté, and rillettes. The centerpiece is a wild boar pâté en croute, the narrow area between forcemeat and crust filled with clear, amber-tinted aspic. Waiters are pouring wine. We help ourselves.

One by one, we take our seats. A door at the far end of the room opens and we are joined by our host.

It's like that scene in *The Godfather*, where Marlon Brando welcomes the representatives of the five families. I almost expect our host to begin with "I'd like to thank our friends the Tattaglias . . . and our friends from Brooklyn . . ." It's a veritable Apalachin Conference. By now, word of what we're about to eat is getting around the table, ratcheting up the level of excitement.

There is a welcome—and a thank-you to the person who procured what we are about to eat (and successfully smuggled it into the country). There is a course of ravioli in consommé (quite wonderful) and a *civet* of wild hare. But these go by in a blur.

Our dirty plates are removed. The uniformed waiters, struggling to conceal their smiles, reset our places. Our host rises and a gueridon is rolled out bearing thirteen cast-iron cocottes. Inside each, a tiny, still-sizzling roasted bird—head, beak, and feet still attached, guts intact inside its plump little belly. All of us lean forward, heads turned in the same direction as our host high pours from a bottle of Armagnac, dousing the birds—then ignites them. This is it. The grand slam of rare and forbidden meals. If this assemblage of notable chefs is not reason enough to pinch myself, then this surely is. This is a once-in-a-fucking-lifetime meal—a *never*-in-a-lifetime meal for most mortals—even in France! What we're about to eat is illegal there as it's illegal here. Ortolan.

The ortolan, or *emberiza hortulana*, is a finch-like bird native to

Europe and parts of Asia. In France, where they come from, these little birdies can cost upwards of 250 bucks a pop on the black market. It is a protected species, due to the diminishing number of its nesting places and its shrinking habitat. Which makes it illegal to trap or to sell anywhere. It is also a classic of country French cuisine, a delight enjoyed, in all likelihood, since Roman times. Rather notoriously, French president François Mitterrand, on his deathbed, chose to eat ortolan as his putative last meal, and a written account of this event remains one of the most lushly descriptive works of food porn ever committed to paper. To most, I guess, it might seem revolting: a desperately ill old man, struggling to swallow an unctuous mouthful of screamingly hot bird guts and bone bits. But to chefs? It's wank-worthy, a description of the Holy Grail, the Great Unfinished Business, the Thing That Must Be Eaten in order that one may state without reservation that one is a true gastronome, a citizen of the world, a chef with a truly experienced palate—that one has really been around.

As the story goes, the birds are trapped in nets, then blinded by having their eyes poked out—to manipulate the feeding cycle. I have no doubt that at various times in history this was true. Labor laws being what they are in Europe these days, it is apparently no longer cost-effective to employ an eye-gouger. A simple blanket or a towel draped over the cage has long since replaced this cruel means of tricking the ortolan into continuingly gorging itself on figs, millet, and oats.

When the birds are suitably plumped up—with a desirable layer of thick fat—they are killed, plucked, and roasted. It is claimed that the birds are literally drowned in Armagnac—but this, too, is not the case. A simple whiff of the stuff is enough for the now morbidly obese ortolan to keel over stone-dead.

The flames in the cocottes burn down, and the ortolans are distributed, one to each guest. Everyone at this table knows what to do and how to do it. We wait for the sizzling flesh and fat before us to quiet down a bit. We exchange glances and grins and then, simultaneously, we place our napkins over our heads, hiding our faces from God, and with burning fingertips lift our birds gingerly by their hot skulls, placing them feet-first into our mouths—only their heads and beaks protruding.

In the darkness under my shroud, I realize that in my eagerness to fully enjoy this experience, I've closed my eyes. First comes the skin and the fat. It's hot. So hot that I'm drawing short, panicky, circular breaths in and out—like a high-speed trumpet player, breathing around the ortolan, shifting it gingerly around my mouth with my tongue so I don't burn myself. I listen for the sounds of jaws against bone around me but hear only others breathing, the muffled hiss of rapidly moving air through teeth under a dozen linen napkins. There's a vestigial flavor of Armagnac, low-hanging fumes of airborne fat particles, an intoxicating, delicious miasma. Time goes by. Seconds? Moments? I don't know. I hear the first snap of tiny bones from somewhere near and decide to brave it. I bring my molars slowly down and through my bird's rib cage with a wet crunch and am rewarded with a scalding hot rush of burning fat and guts down my throat. Rarely have pain and delight combined so well. I'm giddily uncomfortable, breathing in short, controlled gasps as I continue, slowly—ever so slowly—to chew. With every bite, as the thin bones and layers of fat, meat, skin, and organs compact in on themselves, there are sublime dribbles of varied and wondrous ancient flavors: figs, Armagnac, dark flesh slightly infused with the salty taste of my own blood as my mouth is pricked by the sharp bones. As I swallow, I draw in the head and beak, which, until now, had been hanging from my lips, and blithely crush the skull.

What is left is the fat. A coating of nearly imperceptible yet unforgettable-tasting abdominal fat. I undrape, and, around me, one after another, the other napkins fall to the table, too, revealing glazed, blissed-out expressions, the beginnings of guilty smiles, an identical just-fucked look on every face.

No one rushes to take a sip of wine. They want to remember this flavor.

Flashback, not too many years. Close enough in time to still vividly remember the smell of unchanged Fryolator grease, the brackish stank of old steam-table water heating up, the scorched odor of a griddle caked with layers of ancient Mel-Fry.

It didn't smell like ortolan.

I was working a lunch counter on Columbus Avenue. It was a "transitional" phase in my career, meaning I was transitioning from heroin to crack, and I was wearing a snap-front, white polyester dishwasher shirt with the name of the linen service over the left breast pocket, and dirty blue jeans. I was cooking pancakes. And eggs fucking Benedict—the English muffins toasted under the salamander on one side only, half-assed, 'cause I just didn't care. I was cooking eggs over easy with pre-cooked bacon rewarmed on the griddle, and sunny-side ups, and some kind of a yogurt thing with nasty fruit salad and granola in it. I could make any kind of omelet with the fillings available, and the people who sat at my counter and placed their orders looked right through me. Which was good, because if they really saw me, really looked into my eyes, they'd see a guy who—every time somebody ordered a waffle—wanted nothing more than to reach forward, grab them by the hair, and drag a dirty and not particularly sharp knife across their throat before pressing their face into the completely fucked-up, always-sticky waffle iron. If the fucking thing worked anywhere near as inefficiently as it did with waffles, their face would later have to be pried off with a butter knife.

I was, needless to say, not a happy man. I had, after all (as I reminded myself frequently), been a chef. I had run entire kitchens. I had once known the power, the adrenaline rush of having twenty to thirty people working for me, the full-tilt satisfaction of a busy kitchen making food that one could (at least for the time and circumstances) be proud of. When you've known the light caress of Egyptian sailcloth against your skin, it's all the more difficult to go back to poly—particularly when it's adorned with the linen company's logo of a fat, smilingly accommodating chef twirling his mustache.

At what seemed at the time to be the end of a long, absurd, strange, wonderful but lately awful road, there was nothing to be proud of. Except maybe the soup. I made the soup.

It was goulash.

So I was scraping home fries off the griddle with a spatula and I turned around to plate them up next to an order of eggs over hard when I saw a familiar face across the room. It was a girl I knew in college, sitting down at a rear table with friends. She had been, back then, much admired for her fabulousness (it being the '70s and fabulousness having then been the greatest of virtues). She was beautiful, glamorous—in an arty, slightly decadent, Zelda Fitzgerald kind of a way, outrageous, smart as hell—and fashionably eccentric. I think she let me fondle her tit once. She had, since college, become a downtown "personality," poised on the brink of an apparent success for her various adventures in poetry and the accordion. I read about her frequently in the alternative paper of the day. I saw her and tried, instinctively, to shrink into my polyesters. I'm quite sure I wasn't actually wearing a peaked paper cap—but it sure felt like I was. I hadn't seen the girl since school, when I, too, it had appeared to some, had a career trajectory aimed somewhere other than a lunch counter. I was praying she wouldn't see me back there but it was too late. Her gaze passed over me; there was a brief moment of recognition—and sadness. But in the end she was merciful. She pretended not to have seen.

I was ashamed of that counter then, I'm thinking. But not now.

From this rather luxurious vantage point, the air still redolent of endangered species and fine wine, sitting in a private dining room, licking ortolan fat off my lips, I realize that one thing led directly to the other. Had I not taken a dead-end dishwashing job while on summer vacation, I would not have become a cook. Had I not become a cook, I would never and could never have become a chef. Had I not become a chef, I never would have been able to fuck up so spectacularly. Had I not known what it was like to fuck up—*really* fuck up—and spend years cooking brunches in bullshit no-star joints around town, that obnoxious but wildly successful memoir I wrote wouldn't have been half as interesting.

Because—just so we all understand—I'm not sitting here at this table among the gods of food because of my cooking.

Dessert arrives and it's Isle Flotante. A simple meringue, offering up its charms from a puddle of crème anglaise. Everybody roars with delight at this dino-era classic, as old school as it gets. We bask in the warm glow of bonhomie, of our shared appreciation for this remarkable meal. We toast our good fortune with Calvados and Cognac.

Life does not suck.

But the obvious question lingers. I know *I'm* asking it quietly of myself.

What the fuck am *I* doing here?

I am the peer of no man nor woman at this table. None of them—at any time in my career—would have hired me, even the guy sitting next to me. And he's my best friend in the world.

What could my memoir of an undistinguished—even disgraceful—career have said to people of such achievements? And who *are* these people, anyway? Leaning back in their chairs, enjoying their after-dinner cigarettes, they look like princes. Are these the same losers, misfits, and outsiders I wrote about?

Or did I get it all wrong?

MEDIUM
RAW

Selling Out

I **was so supremely naive about** so many things when I wrote *Kitchen Confidential*—my hatred for all things Food Network being just one of them. From my vantage point in a busy working kitchen, when I'd see Emeril and Bobby on the tube, they looked like creatures from another planet—bizarrely, artificially cheerful creatures in a candy-colored galaxy in no way resembling my own. They were as far from my experience or understanding as Barney the purple dinosaur—or the saxophone stylings of Kenny G. The fact that people—strangers—seemed to love them, Emeril's studio audience, for instance, clapping and hooting with every mention of gah-lic, only made me more hostile.

In my life, in my world, I took it as an article of faith that chefs were unlovable. That's why we were chefs. We were basically . . . bad people—which is why we lived the way we did, this half-life of work followed by hanging out with others who lived the same life, followed by whatever slivers of emulated normal life we had left to us. Nobody loved us. Not really. How could they, after all? As chefs, we were proudly dysfunctional. We were misfits. We knew we were misfits, we sensed the empty parts of our souls, the missing parts of our person-alities, and this was what had brought us to our profession, had made us what we were.

I despised their very likability, as it was a denial of the quality I'd always seen as our best and most distinguishing: our otherness.

Rachael Ray, predictably, symbolized everything I thought wrong—which is to say, incomprehensible to me—about the Brave New World of celebrity chefs, as she wasn't even one of "us." Back then, hearing that title applied to just anyone in an apron was particu-larly angering. It burned. (Still does a little.)

What a pitiable fool I was.

But my low opinion of the Food Network actually went back a little further in time. Back to when they were a relatively tiny, sad-sack start-up with studios on the upper floors of an office building on Sixth Avenue, a viewership of about eight people, and the production values of late-night public-access porn. Before Emeril and Bobby and Mario helped build them into a powerhouse international brand. (In those days, such luminaries of the dining scene as Donna Hanover [then Giuliani] and Alan Richman, Bill Boggs and Nina Griscom, would sit around in tiny, office-size rooms, barely enough room for the cameras, showing pre-recorded promo reels—the type of crap they show on the hotel channel when you turn on the tube at the Sheraton.) You know the stuff: happy "customers" awkwardly chawing on surf and turf, fol-lowed by "Chef Lou's signature cheesecake . . . with a flavor that says 'Oooh la-la!'" After which, Alan or Donna or Nina or Bill would take a few desultory bites from a sample of same—which had been actu-ally FedExed from whatever resort or far-flung dung hole they were promoting that week.

I was invited on to cook salmon. I was working at Sullivan's at the time, and flogging my firstborn (and already abandoned by its publisher) book, a crime novel called *Bone in the Throat*. I arrived to find a large and utterly septic central kitchen/prep area, its sinks heaped with dirty pots and pans, refrigerators jammed with plastic-wrapped mystery packages that no one would ever open. Every surface was covered with neglected food from on-camera demonstrations from who knows how long ago, a panorama of graying, oxidizing, and actively decaying food beset with fruit flies. The "chef" in charge of this facility stood around with one finger jammed up his nose to the knuckle, seemingly oblivious to the carnage around him. Cast and crew from the various productions would wander in from time to time and actually pick at this once-edible landfill and eat from it. Once in the studio, cooking on camera was invariably over a single electric burner, which stank of the encrusted spills left by previous victims. For my salmon demonstration, I recall, I had to scrub and wash my own grill pan, after retrieving it from the bottom of a sink as multilayered as the ruins of ancient Troy.

This unimpressive first encounter in no way made me actively "hate" the Food Network. It would be more accurate to say I was dismissive. I didn't take them seriously. How could one?

And, to be honest with myself, I never really "hated" Emeril, or Bobby, or even Rachael, as much as I found their shows . . . ludicrous and somehow personally embarrassing.

My genuine contempt for FN came *later*—after *Kitchen Confidential*. After I was making a nice living making fun of Emeril and Bobby and Rachael. When I went to work for the bastards.

I was still cooking every day and night. The book was on the *New York Times* bestseller list, but a healthy distrust, a strong suspicion that I'd better keep my day job, was still very much the order of the day. This couldn't last, I thought. It was surely a fluke. A flash in the pan. What possible appeal could my story—something I'd written with no larger audience than New York–area line cooks, waiters, and bartenders in mind—have beyond the tristate area? And if twenty-eight years in the restaurant business had taught me anything at all, it was that if things look good today, they will most assuredly turn to shit tomorrow.

While I doubted the longevity of my time in the sun, I was aware that I was putting up some nice numbers for my publisher. I may have been a pessimist, but I was not an idiot. So, striking while the iron is hot, as they say, I went in and pitched a second book and a decidedly fatter advance—quickly, before the bloom was off the rose and I faded inevitably back into insolvency and obscurity. I brashly suggested a book about me traveling all over the world, to all the cool places I'd ever dreamed of going, eating and drinking and getting into trouble. I would be willing to do this—and write about it, I suggested. If my publisher would pay for it.

Shockingly, they were willing to pay for it.

Shortly after that, two unimpressive-looking men walked into Les Halles and asked me if I'd be interested in making television. They had *Kitchen Confidential* in mind, no doubt, a property I had already sold off to Hollywood (to end up as a *very* short-lived sitcom). Undaunted by this news, they expressed interest when I told them I'd be unlikely to find time in any case—as I was about to embark on a year-long bounce around the world to fulfill my childhood fantasies of the exotic East and elsewhere.

I have to tell you that even at this early point, still wearing my kitchen whites, I was already dubious of anyone who claimed to be offering a TV deal. I had very quickly learned that when TV or movie people tell you "we're all big fans over here" or "we're very excited about this project," it usually means nothing more than that they're planning on paying for lunch. I was even more skeptical when they mentioned Food Network as a prime candidate for acquiring the project. This notion alone suggested these two goofs had no idea what they were talking about and no juice with anybody. I'd been savagely trashing the Food Network's principal earners for some time—it was already shtick, part of a stand-up bit that would live on long after I stopped performing it. The fact that these two would even suggest Food Network hinted at problems far beyond the usual lack of imagination. The word "delusional" came to mind.

When, a week later, they called to tell me they'd set up a meeting, I was annoyed. Actively pissed off. No good would come of this. This, I was certain, was a waste of fucking time. I bothered to neither shave nor shower for the meeting.

I ended up with a show titled, like the book, *A Cook's Tour*. Something that necessarily and despite our best efforts quickly evolved into a sort of gonzo-travelogue of vérité footage and thrown together voice-overs. I had assumed my involvement with television would last no longer than the time it took me to write the book. And yet, amazingly enough, the show was picked up for a second season. Even more incredibly, the network, from the beginning, let me do pretty much whatever the fuck I wanted—allowing me to take the show anywhere I pleased, smoke on camera, curse as I needed—and, even more remarkably, along with the camera people/field producers, whom I became increasingly close to over many miles and many months of traveling together—tell stories any way I cared to, making, as it turned out, pretty good television.

I have to admit, I grew to like this life—roaming the globe in search of nothing more than food and kicks. I also came to enjoy the new-to-me process of telling stories with the help of an all-new chest of toys: cameras, editing boards, sound editing—and really creative professionals who knew how to use them. I like making things. And I like telling stories. I like going to Asia. And this TV gig allowed me to do all of those things

I got sucked in—not by fame or money (of which there was precious little). I'd long ago had all the cocaine I'd ever wanted. No sports car was ever going to cure my ills. I became seduced by the world—and the freedom that television had given me—to travel it as I wished. I was also drunk on a new and exciting power to manipulate images and sound in order to tell stories, to make audiences feel about places I'd been the way I wanted them to feel. I was increasingly proud of some of the episodes I and my partners, camera people/producers Chris Collins and Lydia Tenaglia, were making—and how we were making them. I began to appreciate what editors and sound mixers and post-production people can do. Making TV was becoming . . . *fun*, and, in more than a few cases, actually creatively satisfying.

I wrote the book and yet continued filming. The tail now wagged the dog. I was hooked on travel, on seeing the world, and on the terms I was seeing it. Simply put? I didn't want to share. The world had become, on the one hand, a much bigger place, but, on the other hand, it contracted. Like a lot of travelers, I started to turn inward from the view out the window, started to see what was going on out there through an ever-narrowing lens. When I'd set out, I'd see a sunset or a temple and want, instinctively, to turn to my right or to my left and say to somebody, anybody, "Isn't that a magnificent sunset?"

That impulse quickly faded. I felt proprietary about the world. I became selfish. That sunset was mine.

I was on the road for the better part of two years, during which time everything in my life changed. I stopped working as a chef—a job whose daily routines had always been the only thing that stood between me and chaos. My first marriage began to fall apart.

Sitting down in the Food Network's corporate offices back in New York, I was a guy with very different priorities than the ones I'd left my kitchen with. For better or worse, I now had the ludicrous notion that this television thing could be "good" and even, occasionally, "important."

On a recent book tour in Spain, I'd been introduced to Ferran Adrià—and, amazingly, he'd agreed to allow us to shoot him in his workshop *taller* and in his nearly-impossible-to-reserve restaurant, El Bulli. Adrià was already the most important and controversial chef on the planet—and his restaurant the most sought-after reservation.

More significantly, no one to date had ever filmed what he had agreed to show me and my crew: full access to his creative process, to him, his chefs, his favorite restaurants, his inspirations—and, finally, to eat and film the entire El Bulli tasting menu in the kitchen with Adrià himself at the table, explaining things course by course. It had never been done—nor has it since, as far as I know.

But while I was away, something had happened.

Suddenly they weren't so interested in "foreign"-based shows anymore at Food Network. The executives who'd enthusiastically taken us on and supported our more self-indulgent and racy endeavors didn't seem to have the pull they'd once had. Or the interest. When we told them about what Adrià had agreed to do, they were indifferent. "Does he talk English?" and "It's too smart for us" were both mentioned as factors in their eventual refusal to pony up for such an episode—or any episodes outside the United States, it now seemed.

A sour-faced network lawyer became a regular participant at "creative" meetings—subtly setting the agenda and guiding their direction. As warning signs go, this should have been a red alert. The biggest show on the network at that time, it was explained, was something called *Unwrapped*, involving stock footage of cotton candy and Mars Bars being made. Episodes cost about a tenth of what it cost to make our show—and rated, of course, much much higher. On those few occasions when we'd filmed *A Cook's Tour* in America, it was pointed out, particularly when I was seen to put anything barbequed in my mouth, ratings skyrocketed. Why couldn't I confine my wanderings to my own country—to parking-lot tailgate parties and chili cook-offs? All this foreign stuff, what with people talkin' funny and eatin' strange food . . . didn't, it was explained in perfect lawyerese, fit their "current business model."

I knew there was no light at the end of the tunnel the day we were joined by a new hire—the lawyer and the (it would soon be revealed) outgoing execs stood up and said, "Say hello to Brooke Johnson . . .

who we're all *delighted* to have join us from . . . [some other network]."

Ms. Johnson was clearly not delighted to meet me or my partners. You could feel the air go out of the room the moment she entered. It became instantly a place without hope or humor. There was a limp handshake as cabin pressure changed, a black hole of fun—all light, all possibility of joy was sucked into the vortex of this hunched and scowling apparition. The indifference bordering on naked hostility was palpable.

My partners and I left knowing that it was the end of us at Food Network.

Of course, the FN "business model," for which Ms. Johnson was apparently the vanguard, turned out to be a spectacularly successful one. With each incremental dumbing down of their programming, ratings climbed proportionately. A purge of the chefs who'd built the network followed. Mario and Emeril and nearly anybody else who'd committed the sin of professionalism were either banished or exiled, like Old Bolsheviks—seen as entirely unnecessary to the real business of "Food"—which was, they now recognized, actually about likable personalities, nonthreatening images, and making people feel better about themselves.

With every critical outrage—the humiliating, painful-to-watch Food Network Awards, the clumsily rigged-looking *Next Food Net-work Star*, the cheesily cheap-jack production values of *Next Iron Chef America*—every obvious, half-assed knock-off they slapped on the air would go on to ring up sky-high ratings and an ever-larger audience of cherished males twenty-two to thirty-six (or whatever that prime car-buying demographic is). In service to this new, groin-level dynamic, even poor, loyal Bobby Flay was banished from cooking anywhere near as well as he actually could—to face off with web-fingered yokels in head-to-head crab-cake contests—to almost inevitably (and dubiously) lose.

If any further evidence is needed of the inevitability, the supremacy of the Food Network Model—the runaway locomotive of its success, the brutal genius of the Brooke Johnson Five-Year Plan—well, look at the landscape now: *Gourmet* magazine folded, and while the glossy-magazine industry is in dire straits everywhere and distinguished, 180-year-old newspapers are closing down across the country, *Food Network* magazine, *Everyday with Rachael Ray*, and Paula Deen's branded magazines are booming, the Empire of Mediocrity success-fully spreading its tentacles everywhere.

This, I have come to understand, is the way of the world. To re-sist is to stand against the hurricane. Bend (preferably at the hip, ass-cheeks proffered). Or break.

But perhaps you need more visceral evidence of the Apocalypse:

Rachael Ray sent me a fruit basket. So I stopped saying mean things about her. It's that easy with me now. Really. An unsolicited gesture of kindness and I have a very hard time being mean. It would seem . . . ungrateful. Churlish. To be nasty to someone after they sent you a gift of fruit doesn't fit my somewhat distorted view of myself as secretly a gentleman. Rachael was shrewd about that.

Others have taken a more . . . confrontational approach.

So, it's the party following the *Julie & Julia* premiere, and I'm standing there by the end of the buffet, sipping a martini with Ot-tavia, the woman I'd married in 2007, and two friends, when I feel somebody touching me. There's a hand under my jacket and running up my back and I instantly assume this must be somebody I know really well to touch me in this way—particularly in front of my wife. Ottavia has had a couple of years of mixed martial arts training by now, and the last time a female fan was demonstrative in this way, she leaned over, grabbed her wrist, and said something along the lines of "If you don't take your hands off my husband, I'm going to smash your fucking face in." (In fact, I remember that those were her words exactly. Also, that this was not an idle threat.)

In that peculiar slow motion one experiences in car wrecks, in the brief second or so it took for me to turn, I recall that particularly frightening detail: my wife's expression, significant in that it was frozen into a rictus of a grin, paralyzed with a look I'd never seen before. What could be standing behind me that would put this unusual expression on my wife's face—make her freeze like that—a deer in the headlights?

I turned to find myself staring into the face of Sandra Lee.

Ordinarily by now, a woman's hand up my back, Ottavia would have been across the table with a flying tomahawk chop to the top of the skull—or a vicious elbow to the thorax—followed immediately by a left-right combination and a side kick to the jaw as her victim was on the way to the floor. But no. Such are the strange and terrible powers of television's Queen of Semi-Homemade that we, both of us, stood there like hypnotized chickens. The fact that Sandra was standing next to New York's attorney general—and likely next governor—Andrew Cuomo (her boyfriend), added, I thought, an implied menace.

"You've been a bad boy," Sandra was saying, perhaps referring to casual comments I may or may not have made, in which I may have suggested she was the "hellspawn of Betty Crocker and Charles Manson." The words "pure evil" might have come up as well. It is alleged that the words "war crimes" might also have been used by me—in reference to some of Sandra's more notorious offerings, like her "Kwanzaa Cake." Right now, I have no contemporaneous recollection of those comments.

Nor do I have any recollection of how I responded to the feel of Sandra's icy, predatory claws working their way up my spine and around my hips—like some terrifying alien mandibles, probing for a soft spot before plunging deep into the soft goo of my kidneys or liver. Looking back, I imagine myself doing that Ralph Kramden thing: "Homina homina homina . . ."

Actually . . . no. It was closer to *Cape Fear*. Gregory Peck and family mesmerized by the evil Robert Mitchum—standing there in the doorway—a barely veiled menace just skirting the boundaries of acceptable behavior; with every ticking second, you're thinking, "Can I call the police . . . now? . . . How about . . . now?" The menacing would-be intruder not yet crossing the line but letting you know, "I can come in any time I want."

She was probing below my kidney area now, looking my wife directly in the eyes while doing it, too, and saying, "No love handles"—not exactly true, but I don't think accurate meat grading was the point of the exercise. She was letting my wife—and, by extension, me—know that like Mitchum in *Cape Fear*, she could walk right into our living room at any time and do to us whatever unholy and awful things she wished, and there was nothing we could do about it.

"Are your ears red yet?" were her final words as she gave one of my lobes a tug. Then, having had her way with me, she moved on. She'd made her point.

It's Sandra Lee's world. It's Rachael's world. Me? You? We're just living in it.

If this wasn't clear to me then, after Aunt Sandy had turned me inside out, left me shaken and husked, a shell of a man, like the remains of a lobster dinner, it became absolutely clear just last week, when Scripps Howard, the parent company of Food Network, outbidding Rupert Murdoch's NewsCorp, bought *my* network, the Travel Channel—for nearly a billion dollars, putting me right back on Maggie's farm again, so to speak.

I remember now, from a distance, my earlier, dumber self, watching Emeril hawking toothpaste (and, later, Rachael endorsing Dunkin' Donuts and Ritz Crackers) and gaping, uncomprehending, at the screen, wondering, "Why would anybody making the millions and millions of bucks these guys are making endorse some crap for a few million more? I mean . . . surely there's some embarrassment to putting your face next to Dunkin' Donuts—what with so many kids watching your shows—and Type 2 diabetes exploding like it is . . . Surely there's a line not to be crossed at any price for these people, right?"

Later, I asked exactly that question of my fellow chefs—backstage at *Top Chef* one evening, while waiting for the camera crew to set up for the next shot. I was talking with two chefs far more talented, far more creative—and more accomplished than I had ever been—guys with (unlike me) actual reputations to lose. Where does one draw the line, I asked of them? I mean . . . there they were, avidly comparing notes on which airlines gave you more free miles in return for "menu consultation," which products were offering what moneys—and at no point was either of them saying about any particular product: "Burger King . . . not ever . . . no WAY!" or, after considering the question for a moment, "Okay. Mmmm. Lemme think. Astro-Glide? No. I don't care how much money they're offering. I ain't endorsing that!" Like I said, I asked, "Where. Exactly. Is the line for you guys?"

The two of them looked at me like I had a vestigial twin hanging from my neck. Pityingly. They actually mocked me.

"Are you asking, 'How much would I have to pay you to taste a booger?'" said one, as if talking to a child. The two of them resumed their conversation, comparing soft-drink money to frozen pasta dinners, as if I were no longer there. This, clearly, was a conversation for grown-ups, and they considered me too clueless, too dumb, too unsophisticated about the world to be included in the discussion.

They were right. What was I talking about anyway?

The notion of "selling out" is such a quaint one, after all. At what point exactly does one really sell out? To the would-be anarchist— invariably a white guy in dreadlocks, talking about forming a band and "keepin' it real" while waiting for Mom and Dad to send a check— selling out is getting a job.

Certainly, anytime anyone gets up in the morning earlier than one would like, drags oneself across town to do things one wouldn't ordinarily do in one's leisure time for people one doesn't particularly like—that would be selling out, whether that activity involves working in a coal mine, heating up macaroni and cheese at Popeye's, or giving tug jobs to strangers in the back of a strip club. To my mind, they are all morally equivalent. (You do what you've got to do to get by.) While there is a certain stigma attached to sucking the cocks of strangers—because, perhaps, of particularly Western concepts of intimacy and religion—how different, how much worse, or more "wrong," is it than plunging toilets, hosing down a slaughterhouse floor, burning off polyps, or endorsing Diet Coke? Who—given more options, better choices—would do any of those things?

Who in this world gets to do only what they want—and what they feel consistent with their principles—and get paid for it?

Well . . . I guess, *me*—until recently.

But wait. The second I sat down for an interview, or went out on the book tour to promote *Kitchen Confidential* . . . surely that was kind of selling out, right? I didn't know Matt Lauer or Bryant Gumbel or any of these people. Why was I suddenly being nice to them? In what way was I different than a common whore, spending minutes, hours, eventually weeks of my rapidly waning life making nice to people I didn't even know? You fuck somebody for money, it's cash on the barrel. You pick up the money, you go home, you take a shower, and it's gone—presumably having used as much emotional investment as a morning dump. But what about week after week of smiling, nodding your head, pretending to laugh, telling the same stories, giving the same answers as if they'd just—only now—occurred to you for the first time?

Who's the ho now? Me. That's who.

Jesus—I would have given Oprah a back rub and a bikini wax, had she asked me when her people called. Fifty-five thousand copies a minute—every minute Oprah's talking about your book (according to industry legend)? I know few authors who wouldn't. So I guess I knew—even back then—what my price was.

There's that old joke, I've referred to it before, where the guy at the bar asks the girl if she'd fuck him for a million dollars—and she thinks about it and finally replies, "Well, I guess for a million dollars, yeah . . ." At which point he quickly offers her a dollar for the same service. "Fuck you!" she says, declining angrily. "You think I'd fuck you for a *dollar*? What do you think I am?" To which the guy says, "Well . . . we've already established you're a whore. Now we're just haggling over the price."

It's a crude, hateful, sexist wheezer of a joke—but it's as applicable to men as to women. To chefs as to any other craftsmen, artists, or laborers.

What was my problem with my peers—no, my *betters*—grabbing the endorsement dollars left and right: the branded pots and pans, kitchen utensils, ghostwritten cookbooks, commercials for boil-in-a-bag dinners, toaster ovens, California raisins ? I'd turned them all down.

I'd deluded myself for the longest time that there was . . . "integrity" involved . . . or something like that. But as soon as I became a daddy, I knew better.

I'd just been haggling over the price.

There'd never been any question of integrity—or ethics—or anything like that . . . For fuck's sake, I'd stolen money from old ladies, sold my possessions on a blanket on the street for crack, hustled bad coke and bad pills, and done far worse in my life.

I started asking people about this. I needed guidance from people who'd been navigating these murky waters for years.

Among the more illuminating and poignant explanations, one came from—of all people—Emeril. We were guest hosts/roasters at a charity roast of a mutual friend, Mario Batali. In a quiet moment between dick jokes, we talked, as we sometimes do, me asking with genuine curiosity why he continued to do it. He was, at the time, being treated very shabbily by the Food Network—I could see that he'd been hurt by it—and I asked him why he gave a fuck. "You've got a large, well-respected restaurant empire . . . the cookbooks . . . the cookware line"—which is actually pretty high-quality stuff—"presumably you've got plenty of loot. Why go on? Why even care about television anymore—that silly show, the hooting audience of no-necked strangers? If I was you," I went on, "it would take people two weeks to reach me on the phone . . . I'd be so far off the fucking grid, you'd never see me in shoes again . . . I'd live in a sarong somewhere where nobody would ever find me—all this? It would be a distant memory."

He didn't elaborate. He smiled tolerantly, then began listing the number of children, ex-wives, employees (in the hundreds) working for Emeril Inc., establishing for me in quick, broad—and slightly sad—strokes the sheer size of the Beast that had to be fed every day in order for him to be Responsible Emeril—and do right by all the people who'd helped him along the way and who now relied on him, in one form or another, for their living. His success had become an organic, ever-expanding thing, growing naturally larger, as it had to, for to shrink—or even stay the same—would be to die.

Mario has twelve restaurants and counting, watch and clog endorsements, the cookware, the books, the bobblehead doll, NASCAR affiliation, and God knows what else—nothing ever seems to be enough for the man. Above and beyond the fact that he raises millions of dollars for various charities—including his own—he's clearly not in it for the money. Always expanding, always starting new partnerships, trying new concepts. In Mario's case, I think, it's about ego—and the fact that he's got a restless mind. It's not, and never was, enough—or even interesting—to Batali to make money. If that had been the case, he'd have never opened Babbo (or Casa Mono, or Del Posto, or Otto, or Esca); he'd have opened his version of Mario's Old Spaghetti Factories, coast to coast—and been swimming in a sea of cash by now. No.

Mario, I know for a fact, likes to swing by each of his New York restaurants at the end of the night and take a look at the receipts. He's excited by the details. He gets off on successfully filling a restaurant that everyone said was doomed, of bringing the food cost below 20 percent. He likes to do the difficult thing, the dangerous thing—like take a gamble that what America needs and wants right now is ravioli filled with calf brains, or pizza topped with pork fat. For Mario, I'm quite certain, to be ten times richer—twenty times—and NOT take crazy-ass chances on restaurant concepts that no one ever expressed a desire for would mean to expire from boredom.

All Mario enterprises are coproductions. Every restaurant begins with an alliance, a moment of truth, where Don Mario evaluates the creativity and character of another person, looks into their heart, and makes a very important decision. In this way, the success or failure of whatever venture he's embarked on is already determined long before he opens the door. So it's never just business. It's always, always, personal.

Thomas Keller and Daniel Boulud—both with successful, revered, and respected mother-ship restaurants, have talked at various times about the necessity of holding on to talented people; the need to grow with the talents, experience, and ambitions of loyal chefs de cuisine, sous-chefs, and other longtime employees who want and deserve to move up or to have "their own thing." It becomes a simple matter of expand—or lose them.

To some extent, I suspect, what is often the French Michelin star model might be at work here as well: the three-star chef's mother ship simply doesn't and can't ever make as much money as his more casual bistros or brasseries. (Those end up, in very real ways, subsidizing the more luxurious original—or, at the very least, offering a comfortable cushion should costs at the higher-end place rise or revenues decline. You can't start laying off cooks at a three-star every time you have a bad week.)

Gordon Ramsay is maybe the most classic example of the force that keeps well-known chefs constantly, even manically, expanding. In

Ramsay's case, multiple television shows on both sides of the Atlantic coincide with a huge worldwide expansion of hotel-based restaurants. He already has the most successful cooking-competition show on TV with *Hell's Kitchen*. He is a millionaire many, many times over, and yet he keeps expanding—to his eventual peril (the twelve restaurants he opened in the last few years have yet to turn a profit). No matter what your opinion of Ramsay's food, or his awful but wildly popular hit show, or his much better *Kitchen Nightmares* on the BBC, there is no denying that he is a workaholic. There don't seem to be enough hours in the day to contain his various endeavors and enterprises, and yet he goes on.

In Gordon's case, one need only look at his childhood—as described in his autobiography. He grew up poor, constantly on the move, with an untrustworthy and unreliable dreamer of a father. No sooner had his family settled than they would have to move again—often one step ahead of the debt collectors. You *know* What Makes Gordon Run.

Very likely, an impulse similar to that of his onetime mentor and sometimes nemesis, Marco Pierre White. Whatever riches they may have acquired or may yet acquire, there is and always will be the lingering and deeply felt suspicion that come tomorrow, it will all be gone. No amount is enough or will ever be enough, because deep in the bone they know that the bastards could come knocking at any minute and take it all away.

David Chang, whose crazy-ass pony ride to the top of the heap has just begun, feels, I suspect, all of the above motivations: a deadly combination of too few seats at his high-end standard-bearer restaurant, an ever-increasing number of talented loyalists, and a feeling that he'll never be truly good enough at anything.

And then, of course, there's the example of the iconic French Michelin-starred chef, one of the most celebrated and well represented (by sheer number of restaurants) in the world, who, in my presence, said simply:

"Enough bullshit. It's time to make money."

It was vanity that had kept me from being the Imodium guy. Not integrity. I wasn't "keeping it real" declining their offers—and similar ones. I was just too narcissistic and loved myself a little too much to be able to handle waking up in the morning, looking in the bathroom mirror—and seeing the guy from TV who complains about freckling the bowl with loose diarrhea (until Imodium came along to save the day!). I didn't take the cookware gig 'cause I didn't want to find myself in an airport someday, approached by a disgruntled customer of whatever crap central warehouse actually produces that stuff, complaining about my substandard saucepot scorching his paella. I'm the kind of guy who doesn't like to be called on bullshit—unless knowingly bullshitting.

So I didn't take the forty grand a month they offered me to slap my name on a South Beach restaurant, 'cause I figured—even if I *don't* have to actually do anything for the money other than show up once in a while—there's that exposure. I could be on the other side of the world—but if the bartender at this joint, run by strangers, serves one underage girl, one customer gets slipped a roofie, one aggressive rat pops its head up out of the toilet one night and grabs a chunk of somebody's nut-sack, it's gonna be "OUTRAGE AT BOURDAIN RESTAU-RANT" in the tabloids. And that would conflict with my image of myself as somehow above that kind of thing.

But when my daughter came along and I continued to say "no," I knew I wasn't saving my cherry for principle. I'd just been waiting to lose it to the right guy.

2

The Happy Ending

I was born at New York Presbyterian Hospital in New York City in 1956, but I grew up in the leafy green bedroom community of Leonia, New Jersey.

I did not want for love or attention. My parents loved me. Neither of them drank to excess. Nobody beat me. God was never mentioned—so I was annoyed by neither religion nor church nor any notions of sin or damnation. Mine was a house filled with books and music—and, frequently, films. Early in my childhood, my father worked days at Willoughby's camera store in Manhattan—and on weekends would come home with a rented 16-millimeter projector and classic movies. Later, when he became an executive at Columbia Records, I got free records for most of my adolescence. When I was twelve, he'd take me to the Fillmore East to see the Mothers of Invention or Ten Years After or whoever I was listening to that year.

Summers meant barbeques and Wiffle ball games in the backyard.

In school, I was not bullied any more than the next kid—and maybe even a little less. I got the bike I wanted for Christmas. My counselor at camp did not molest me.

I was miserable. And angry.

I bridled bitterly at the smothering chokehold of love and normalcy in my house—compared to the freedom enjoyed by my less-well-looked-after friends. I envied them their dysfunctional and usually empty houses, their near-total lack of supervision. The weird, slightly scary, but enticing stashes of exotica we'd find in their parents' secret places: blurry black-and-white stag films, bags of weed, pills . . . bottles of booze that nobody would notice when missing or slowly drained. My friends' parents always had other, more important things on their minds, leaving their kids to run wild—free to stay out late, to sleep over when and where they saw fit, to smoke weed in their rooms without fear of being noticed.

I was pissed about this. How come *I* couldn't have that? As I saw it, my parents were the only thing standing between me and a life spent taking full advantage of the times.

Much later, standing in some particularly bullshit kitchen, more of a saloon than anything resembling a real restaurant, I wasn't the sort of person to look back in puzzlement and regret, wondering where I might have gone wrong. I never blamed bad choices—like the heroin, for instance—or bad companions for my less than stellar career trajectory. I don't and never did refer to my addiction as my "disease." I'd *wanted* to become a junkie, after all, since I was twelve years old. Call it a character flaw—of which drugs were simply a manifestation, a petulant "fuck you" to my bourgeois parents, who'd committed the unpardonable sin of loving me.

At any given moment, when I'm honest with myself, I can look back and say that, on balance, I'd probably make exactly the same moves all over again. I *know* what brought me to those crummy kitchens, the reeking steam tables, the uncleaned deli-slicer, yet another brunch shift—I did.

Life, even in the bad old days, had been perfectly fair to me. I knew this.

Even when it was McAssCrack's Bar and Grill I was working at, I knew I was pretty lucky. Lucky to be alive, given the precarious business of scoring dope every day in the '80s New York City. Lucky to be in reasonably good health, given what was happening around me—and all the people who came up with me who weren't around anymore. There was even love in my life through it all, however improbable—a criminal partnership of long standing.

As much as I hated standing there in the bad times, pre-poaching eggs for service, letting them slip off the spoon into a bus tub of ice water, I couldn't blame anybody. Like I said, I made my choices. One after the other.

Then again, I could blame my dad, I guess. For all the joy he brought me when he came home with the *Sgt. Pepper* album. Or *Disraeli Gears*. An argument could be made, I guess, that this kind of exposure at an early age could lead one to an appetite for distraction—if not destruction. And maybe nine years old was a little young to see *Dr. Strangelove*—to find out that the world was surely going to end in a nuclear apocalypse (and soon). And that it would be funny when it happened. Perhaps this contributed to the nihilistic worldview I'd adopt later as a world-weary eleven-year-old.

If they ever find me with a crawl space full of dead hookers, I'll be sure to point the finger at Dad—and Stanley Kubrick.

But if we're playing the blame game? Top of the list for "it's all your fault—you made me this way!" goes to two children's classic films: *The Red Balloon* and *Old Yeller*.

What exactly was the message of *The Red Balloon* anyway? Every time our teachers didn't show up, they'd haul out the projector and show us this supposedly heartwarming and inspiring story of a little French boy and his enchanted balloon friend.

But wait a minute. The poor kid is impoverished and clearly unloved. He wears the same clothes every day. Immediately on finding his balloon, he's ostracized by society, banned from public transportation, chastised at school, even ejected from church. His parents are either dead or have abandoned him—as the hideous crone who cruelly throws his balloon out the window at first encounter is clearly too old to be his mom. The boy's schoolmates are a feral, opportunistic bunch who instinctively seek to destroy what they don't understand and can't possess. In fact, nearly every other child in the film is depicted as part of an unthinking mob, fighting viciously among themselves even as they pursue the boy and his balloon through the streets, like a pack of wolves. The boy runs away, is assaulted, separated from his only friend—then reunites with it only to watch it die slowly before his eyes.

The happy ending? Balloons from all over Paris converge. The boy gathers them together and is lifted aloft. He drifts away, dangerously suspended over the city. The end.

Where's the kid going? To an unspecified "better" place—for sure. Or to a fatal drop when the balloons empty of their helium (as we've seen them do just previously).

The message?

Life is cruel, lonely, and filled with pain and random acts of violence. Everybody hates you and seeks to destroy you. Better to opt out altogether, to leap—literally—into the void, escape by any means necessary. However uncertain or suicidal the way out.

Nice, huh? May as well have put a crack pipe in my hand right then. Why wait? Maybe *this* was why I never worked at the French Laundry.

Then there's *Old Yeller*. Even worse. A more cynical and unconscionably bleak message one could hardly imagine.

The story of a boy and his dog. A *Disney* story of a boy and his dog—which, as all children's accumulated experience teaches them, means that *no matter what kind of peril the heroes go through, things will always turn out okay in the end.* This, by the time we sat down in that darkened theater, excited, sticky with Twizzlers, we had come to accept as an article of faith. A contract between kids everywhere, our parents, and the fine people at Walt Disney Studios. This was as powerful a bond as we knew, an assurance that held an otherwise uncertain universe together. Sure, Khrushchev was maybe going to drop the Big One on us, but goddammit, that dog was gonna make it out okay!

So, when Old Yeller gets sick with this rabies thing, little Tony is, naturally, not concerned. Pinocchio, after all, got out of that whale situation no problem. Sure, things looked bad for him, too, for a while, but he figured it out in the end. Bumpy ride with Bambi, what with Mom dying, but that ended okay. Like Mom and Dad never forgetting to pick you up at school, the Happy Ending was a dead cert.

It will be okay. It will turn out fine.

No one will hurt a fucking *dog.*

That's what I'm saying to myself, sitting there between Mom and Dad, staring up at that screen, breath held, waiting for the miracle.

Then they go and blow Old Yeller's fucking brains out.

I sit there stunned. "What do you *mean* there's no cure for rabies? I don't give a *fuck* they hadda put Yeller 'out of his misery'! What about *my* misery, cocksucker! They were supposed to fix things! He was supposed to get *better*!! Don't talk to me about *reality*! I don't care if it's a magical fucking rainbow shining out of a fairy princess's ass makes him better. He's supposed to get *better*!!!"

From that moment on, I looked at my parents and the whole world with suspicion. What else were they lying about?

Life was clearly a cruel joke. A place with no guarantees, built on a foundation of false assumptions if not outright untruths. You think everything's going okay . . .

Then they shoot your fucking dog.

So, maybe *that's* why until I got my first dishwashing job, I had no respect for myself and no respect for anybody else.

I should probably sue.

3

The Rich Eat Differently Than You and Me

I was holed up in the Caribbean about midway through a really bad time. My first marriage had just ended and I was, to say the least, at loose ends.

By "loose ends" I mean aimless and regularly suicidal. I mean that my daily routine began with me waking up around ten, smoking a joint, and going to the beach—where I'd drink myself stupid on beer, smoke a few more joints, and pass out until mid-afternoon. This to be followed by an early-evening rise, another joint, and then off to the bars, followed by the brothels. By then, usually very late at night, I'd invariably find myself staggeringly drunk—the kind of drunk where you've got to put a hand over one eye to see straight. On the way back from one whorehouse or another, I'd stop at the shawarma truck on the Dutch side of the island, and, as best I could, shove a meat-filled pita into my face, sauce squirting onto my shirtfront. Then, standing there in the dark parking lot, surrounded by a corona of spilled sauce, shredded lettuce, and lamb fragments, I'd fire up another joint before sliding behind the wheel of my rented 4×4, yank the top down, then peel out onto the road with a squeal of tires.

To put it plainly, I was driving drunk. Every night. There is no need to lecture me. To tell me what might have happened. That wasting my own stupid life is one thing—but that I could easily have crushed how many innocents under my wheels during that time? I know. Looking back, I break into an immediate cold sweat just thinking about it. Like a lot of things in my life, there's no making it prettier just 'cause time's passed. It happened. It was bad. There it is.

There was a crazy-ass little independent radio station on this particular island—or maybe they broadcasted from another nearby island. I never figured it out. But it was one of those weird, inexplicable little anomalies of expat behavior that you find from time to time if you travel enough: a tiny, one-lung radio station in the middle of nowhere. A DJ whose playlist made no damn sense at all, completely unpredictable selections ranging from the wonderfully obscure to the painfully familiar. From lost classics of garage rock, ancient cult psychobilly hits, and pre-disco funk masterpieces to the most ubiquitously mundane medley of MOR mainstays or parrothead anthems—in a flash. No warning. One second, it's Jimmy Buffet or Loggins and Messina—the next? The Animals' "House of the Rising Sun" or Question Mark and the Mysterians' "96 Tears."

You never knew what was coming up. In the rare moments of lucidity, when I tried to imagine who the DJ might be and what his story was, I'd always picture the kid from *Almost Famous*, holed up, like me, in the Caribbean for reasons he'd probably rather not discuss; only in his case, he'd brought his older sister's record collection circa 1972. I liked to imagine him out there in a dark studio, smoking weed and spinning records, seemingly at random—or, like me, according to his own, seemingly aimless, barely under control, and very dark agenda.

That's where I was in my life: driving drunk and way too fast, across a not very well lit Caribbean island. Every night. The roads were notoriously badly maintained, twisting and poorly graded. Other drivers, particularly at that hour, were, to put it charitably, as likely to be just as drunk as I was. And yet, every night, I pushed myself to go faster and faster. Life was reduced to a barely heard joke—a video game I'd played many times before. I'd light up the joint, crank up the volume, peel out of the parking lot, and it was game on.

Here was the fun part: after making it past the more heavily trafficked roads of the Dutch side, after successfully managing to cross the unlit golf course (often over the green) and the ruins of the old resort (flying heedlessly over the speed bumps), I would follow the road until it began to twist alongside the cliffs' edges approaching the French side. Here, I'd really step on the gas, and it was at precisely this point that I'd hand over control to my unknown DJ. For a second or two each night, for a distance of a few feet, I'd let my life hang in the balance, because, depending entirely on what song came on the radio next, I'd decide to either jerk the wheel at the appropriate moment, continuing, however recklessly, to career homeward—or simply straighten the fucker out and shoot over the edge and into the sea.

In this way, my life could easily have ended with a badly timed playing of Loggins and Messina. On one memorable occasion, as I waited in the brief millisecond of silence between songs, foot on the gas, the cliff edge coming up at me fast, I was saved by the Chambers Brothers. I recognized the "tic-toc" metronome of "Time Has Come Today" and, at the last second, turned away from empty air, laughing and crying at the wonderfulness and absurdity of it all, diverted from what I very much felt to be my just desserts, making (momentarily) some strange and profound sense. Saving my life.

So. That's how I was feeling that year. And that's the kind of smart, savvy, well-considered decision-making process that was the norm for me.

Back in New York, I was living in a small, fairly grim Hell's

Kitchen walk-up apartment that smelled of garlic and red sauce from the Italian hero joint downstairs. As I'd pretty much burned down my previous life, I didn't own much. Some clothes. A few books. A lot of Southeast Asian bric-a-brac. I was seldom there, so it didn't seem to matter. My favorite dive bar, where I was on permanent "scholarship," was right down the street.

I was not seeing anybody regular. I wasn't looking for love. I wasn't even looking for sex. I wasn't in a frame of mind to take the initiative with anybody. Yet, if you brushed up against me in those days, I'd probably go home with you if you asked.

Business took me to England now and again, and one night, surely drunk again, sitting at the bar of a particularly disreputable "club," waiting to meet someone from my publishers, I noticed a very beautiful woman staring at me in the mirror over my shoulder. While this was of moderate interest, it did not cause me to get off my bar stool, wink, nod, wave, or stare back. I had a pretty good sense by now of my unsuitability when it came to normal human interactions. I felt as if I'd had my thermostat removed—was without a regulator. I couldn't be trusted to behave correctly, to react appropriately, or to even discern what normal was. Sitting there, hunched over my drink, I knew this—or sensed it—and was trying to avoid any contact with the world not based on business. But an intermediary—the woman's friend—took matters into her own hands, suddenly at my shoulder insistent on making introductions.

The woman and I got to know each other a little—and from time to time, over the next few months, we'd see each other in England and in New York. After a while, I came to understand that she was from a very wealthy family—that she kept an apartment in New York. That she spent her days mostly traveling to runway shows and buying things with her mother. That she was of British, French, and Eastern European background, spoke four languages beautifully, was smart, viciously funny, and (at least) a little crazy—a quality I usually liked in women.

Okay. She had a problem with cocaine—something I'd moved past. And her T-shirts cost more than the monthly salaries of everybody I ever knew. But I flattered myself that I was the one guy she'd ever met who really and truly didn't give a shit about her money or her bloodline or what kind of muddleheaded upper-class twits she moved with. With the righteousness of the clueless, I saw all that as a liability and behaved accordingly—making the comfortable assumption that when you're *that* kind of wealthy and privileged, the kind her friends seemed to be, you are necessarily simple-minded, ineffectual, and generally useless.

Suffering from the delusion that I was somehow "saving" this poor little rich girl, that surely she would benefit from a week on the beach, enjoying the simple pleasures of cold beer, a hammock, and local BBQ joints, I invited her to join me in the Caribbean over the Christmas holidays.

For the last few weeks, I'd lived friendless and alone down there. In a small but very nice rented villa. The island was largely funky and downscale and charmingly dysfunctional. It was half French, half Dutch—with plenty of social problems, working poor, and a large population of locals going back many generations, meaning there was life and business outside of the tourism industry, an alternate version of the island, where one could—if one so desired—get lost, away from one's own kind. I'd been weeks without shoes, eating every meal with my hands. Who wouldn't love that? I thought.

She came. And for just short of a week, we had a pretty good time. We were both hitting the Havana Club a little hard, for sure, but her presence certainly improved my behavior—my nightly attempts at suicide ended—and I believed that I was good for her as well. She seemed, for a while, genuinely happy and relaxed on the island's out-of-the-way beaches, perfectly satisfied, it appeared to me, with a routine of inexpensive johnnycake sandwiches and roadside pork ribs grilled in sawed-off fifty-five-gallon drums. She took long swims by herself, emerging from the water looking beautiful and refreshed. I thought, surely this is a good thing. Maybe we are good for each other.

We drank at sailor bars, took mid-afternoon naps, mixed rum punches with a frequency that, over time, became a little worrisome. She was damaged, I knew. Like me, I thought—flattering myself.

I identified with her distrust of the world. But as I would come to learn, hers was a kind of damage I hadn't seen before.

"Let's go to St. Barths," she said, one afternoon.

This was an idea that held little attraction for me. Even then, in my state of relatively blissful ignorance, I knew that St. Barths, which lay about ten miles offshore from my comfortably dowdy island, was not somewhere I could ever be happy. I knew from previous day trips that a hamburger and a beer cost fifty bucks—that there was no indigenous culture to speak of, that it was the very height of the holiday season and the island, not my scene in the best of circumstances, would be choked with every high-profile douche, Euro-douche, wannabe, and oligarch with a mega-yacht. I knew enough of the place to know that St. Barths was not for me.

I made obliging, generically willing-sounding noises, fairly secure in the assumption that every rental car and hotel room on the island had been booked solid. A few calls confirmed this to be the case, and I felt that surely she'd drop the idea.

She would in no way, she insisted, be deterred by insignificant details like no place to stay and no way to get there. There was a house. Russian friends. Everything would work out.

It certainly wasn't love that compelled me to abandon all good sense and go somewhere I already hated with somebody I barely knew into circumstances of great uncertainty. It was not a period of my life marked by good decisions, but in agreeing to "pop over" to St. Barths, I'd made a particular whopper of a wrong turn—a plunge into the true heart of darkness. Maybe I saw it at the time as the path of least resistance, maybe I even thought there was indeed some small possibility of a "good time"—but I surely had reason to know better. I *did* know better. But I walked straight into the grinder anyway.

We took a small propeller plane the ten minutes or so across the water, landing at the airport with no ride, no plans, no friends I was aware of, and no place to stay. A famous guy said hello to my friend by the luggage carousel. They exchanged witty banter. He did not, however, offer to let us crash at his place. There were no taxis in sight.

From a comfortable rented villa on a nice island, where—despite my nightly flirtations with vehicular homicide and suicide—I was at least able to swim, eat and drink fairly cheaply, and eventually sleep securely in my own bed, I now found myself suddenly homeless. Worse, my partner, as I quickly discovered, was a spoiled, drunk, and frequently raving paranoid-schizophrenic.

And cokehead. Did I mention that?

Any pretense that mysterious Russian friends with a villa would be there for us had somehow dematerialized somewhere on the flight over. Similar departures from reality would become a regular feature of the next few days. After a long time, we found a taxi to a hotel— where, once the staff laid eyes on my mysterious but increasingly mad companion, a room was hastily made available for a night. A very expensive room.

One of the things I'd forgotten about seriously wealthy people, something I'd noticed during a brief previous exposure in college, was that the old-school, old-money kind of rich people? Those motherfuckers don't pay for shit. They don't carry cash—and even credit cards seem always to be . . . somewhere else, as if whatever small sums as might be needed are beneath notice or discussion. Better *you* pay. And pay I did. Days and nights bingeing on overpriced drinks, bribing bartenders to scoop us up in their private vehicles at end of shift and drive us off into the dark to wherever she thought we might stay that night. One crappy motel-style room after another that cost what a suite at the St. Regis would. More drinks.

By now, I was a prisoner of her escalating and downright scary mood swings and generally bad craziness. She'd turn on a dime from witty and affectionate to hissing, spitting psychotic. One minute we'd be having overpriced mojitos on a lovely beach, the next, she'd be raging at the manager, accusing the busboy—or whoever was at hand—of stealing her cell phone. Fact was, she constantly misplaced her cell phone, her purse, anything of value she had. She'd get sloshed, forgetful, impulsively run off to dance, to search for coke, to say hello to an old friend—and she'd lose track of shit. She'd forget where she'd put things—if she'd ever had them in the first place.

I am not a fan of people who abuse service staff. In fact, I find it intolerable. It's an unpardonable sin as far as I'm concerned, taking out personal business or some other kind of dissatisfaction on a waiter or busboy. From the first time I saw that, our relationship was essentially over. She accused me of "caring about waiters more than I cared about her," and she was right. From that point on, I was babysitting a madwoman—feeling obliged only to get her crazy ass on a plane and back to England as quickly as possible and with as little damage done as could be managed. I'd gotten her here, allowed this to happen, it was impingent on me, I felt, to at least get her back in one piece. This was easier said than done.

People were afraid of her. I noticed this early on.

She *had* mentioned something earlier, back in England, about an ex-boyfriend who'd supposedly "stalked" her. How Mom had had to call some "friends" to "talk to" the fellow in question. How there'd been no problems after that. Somehow I'd blown right past *that* flashing red warning light, too—along with all the others. Now, all I wanted to do was get her on a plane back to London, but it was like reasoning with a wild animal. She didn't want to go. Wouldn't go.

By now, middle of the night, she'd jack the volume on the TV all the way up and flick rapidly back and forth between news stations, raving about oil prices. Strangely, neither neighbors nor management ever dared complain. I went to sleep each night not knowing where we'd sleep the next, if I'd wake up in bed soaked with blood of indeterminate origin, afraid to open my eyes to find out if the girl had cut her wrists—or my throat. I tried, really tried to act as I thought one does with a genuinely crazy person: solicitous, like a gentleman—until one can get 'em safely back in the bughouse. But she'd dragoon people into helping us—strangers and distant acquaintances who seemed to like the idea of chauffeuring around a crazed heiress and giving her cocaine. She crashed parties, jumped lines, scarfed grams at will, a magnet for indulgent enablers, reptilian party-throwers.

"What does she do?" I heard one admiring bystander ask of another as my roomie bounded, gazelle-like, across the dance floor toward the bathroom—there, no doubt, to fill her nostrils.

"Nothing," was the answer. As if this was the proudest profession of all.

Apparently familiar with her rapier wit, her way with a lasting cruel remark, those who knew her from St. Tropez, from Monaco, from Sardinia—wherever fuckwits and fameballs went that year—they cowered at her approach. No one stood up to her.

Maybe it was because they all hated each other. (It seemed the point of the whole exercise.) I soon found out that to move in this woman's poisonous orbit was to willingly attach oneself to a sinister global network of Italian art collectors, creepy Russian oligarchs, horny Internet billionaires, the wrinkled ex-wives of Indonesian despots, princelings from kingdoms that long ago ceased to exist, mistresses of African dictators, former-hookers-turned-millionairesses, and the kind of people who like hanging around with such people—or who make their living doing so. All seemed to have come to St. Barths over the holidays in order to find subtle new ways to say "fuck you" to each other. With a smile, of course.

We spent a somewhat less than romantic New Year's Eve at a party hosted by the Gaddafis. That should tell you something. Enrique Iglesias provided the entertainment. A detail that lingers in the memory like the birthmark on one's torturer's cheek.

Who had the bigger boat, wore the better outfit, got the best table seemed all that mattered. There were decade-old feuds over casual cracks long forgotten by everyone but the principals. They circled each other still—waiting to identify a weakness—looking for somewhere and some way to strike. People jockeyed for position, cut each other's throats over the most petty, nonsensical shit imaginable. This from the people who, it gradually began to dawn on me, actually ran the world.

I was lingering over the buffet on a Dr. No–size yacht with the appropriately Bond-esque name *Octopus*: huge interior docking inside the hull, a six-man submarine, landing space for two helicopters, Francis Bacon originals in the crapper. I looked up from the sushi and got the impression that anybody there—any of the guests dancing, schmoozing, chatting politely at the party—would have watched my throat getting cut without the slightest change in expression.

By the time she lost her wallet for the third and last time, I was ready to dig a hole in the sand and drop her in it—had I thought for a second I could get away with it. But she spoke daily with "Mom." And the option of simply walking out on her, leaving the wallet-less, fund-less, coke-crazy schizo-bitch to her just deserts, broke-ass in a hotel room from which I had every expectation she would be removed at any hour—this, too, I was uncomfortable with.

I also had a very real concern that even were I to do something as measured and sensible as simply walk out on her, what remained of my Caribbean sojourn might end with the arrival of two thick-necked fellows from Chechnya holding a tarpaulin and hacksaws.

I was a bad person in a bad place, with another bad person, surrounded by other, possibly even worse people.

The French, who administered this playground of evil, who serviced its visitors, knew their customers well and catered to them, accommodated them, gouged them, and fucked them over in all the traditional ways—and a few new ones. Sit down for a burger at a beach bar and suddenly the music starts thump-thumping and here come the models with swimwear for sale—or jewelry. It was a bottle-service world—meaning, you pay for the table, not what's on it. Unless, of course, you're like my companion, who had a way of looking confused at the suggestion that *anyone* would pay for *anything*—much less her. Fiftyish men with potbellies hanging out over their Speedos danced with pneumatic-breasted Ukrainian whores—during brunch. Over-groomed little dogs in diamond chokers snapped and barked at one's heels. Waiters looked at everyone with practiced expressions of bemused contempt.

There was, however, one glimmer of light—or inspiration—in all this darkness:

One man on the island understood better than anyone the world my companion moved in. An artist, a genius—a man who stood alone in his ability, the sheer relish with which he fucked the rich. Let's call him, for the purposes of this discussion, Robèrt, the man who took what might be described as the "Cipriani business model" to its most extreme yet logical extension. And a man whose example gave me, in some ways, the strength to endure.

The Criprianis, along with a few other operators and imitators, made, a long while back, a remarkable discovery: that rich international fucktards like to hang out with each other and eat marginally decent Italian food—and are willing to pay outrageous amounts of money for the privilege. Better yet, all the people who want to *look* like they, too, are rich international fucktards will want to get in on the action as well. That's the customer base that dreams are made of. If you go to Harry's Bar in Venice, you get a pretty good plate of food—and the Bellinis are just fine. They just cost a fuck of a lot. But they do treat you courteously and it *is* Venice out the window—and everything's expensive anyway. I'm guessing the Crriprianis figured out that if this model worked in Venice, it would work in New York. That maybe twenty-nine bucks for a bowl of spaghetti with red sauce is perfectly reasonable.

In New York, it is a cruel irony of Italian food that the more ingredients in your spaghetti with red sauce, and the more time and steps spent preparing it—the more it costs to prepare—the less likely it is to be good. (It will also usually be cheaper on the menu.)

Consider, though, a basic, authentic, "just like in Italy" spaghetti *al pomodoro*: a few ounces of good quality dry-cut pasta, a few drops of olive oil, garlic, some tomato, and a basil leaf. This will cost you twenty-nine bucks. And the drink that precedes it will cost at least seventeen.

Essentially, you're paying extra for someone to *not* fuck up your food.

Many who gazed admiringly at the Ciprianis took things a little further, realizing that decent food was in no way necessary. Rich international douchebags and those who love them will happily pay those kinds of prices simply to be jammed into tiny, dollhouse-size banquettes, cheek by Botoxed jowl at Nello—or to poke at faux Chinese food in graveyards of the über-rich, like Mr. Chow and Philippe.

Add to the mix some curiously available Eastern European women who find low-riding ball-sacks distinctly fascinating? You've got yourself a recipe for success.

But Robèrt on St. Barths? He had it *all* figured out. He took the model where it should have been all along, cut things right to their very core nubbin of ugliness: you don't have to have decent food. On the contrary, you can explicitly and with great care and determination, he discovered, serve shit. You don't need a nice room, fancy tablecloths, flowers, or even Russian hookers. You need only a nice location (in this case, a wood-planked beachfront patio deck) and an attitude. Specifically, you need a reputation as an ornery fuck who doesn't give a shit about anything or anybody. Then, like Robèrt, you can not only fuck the rich, you can fuck each and every one of them personally—

one at a time, just bend them over a sawhorse in order, and roger them up the poop chute while they thank you repeatedly.

At his restaurant, for twenty-five euros (about thirty-five bucks then), one gets a few grams of cold, unseasoned, boiled lentils on a very large plate. Lentils. That's it. About two tablespoons of them—with not so much as a carrot chunk or limp dice of onion to distinguish them from what some street kid with a skateboard and a Hacky Sack is eating right now in a parking lot in Portland. Probable food cost to Robèrt? Maybe two cents. Feel free to season with oil and vinegar, though. Provided complimentary.

For the main course, there is the option of chicken or fish. Chicken is one leg, which Robèrt himself (that's him, the scowling, shirtless, and unshaven fellow over there, wearing an apron, shorts, and flip-flops) will personally burn into unrecognizability for you. Nothing less than carbonized will satisfy his exacting standards. Robèrt will take the extra step to ruin your chicken each and every time. People who've had the temerity to step over to the grill preemptively and suggest that, perhaps, this order could be a little less cooked find themselves quickly in the street—next to Madonna.

The fish option is a small, barely cleaned, whole red snapper, prepared with similar attention to detail—which is to say, burned to shit.

Price for these delights of land and sea? Fifty euros (about seventy-five bucks) each.

Add a chilled bottle of the cheapest rosé on the list to stave off the summer's heat, and ameliorate, perhaps, the taste of campfire in your mouth, and you're talking five hundred dollars for lunch. Merci—and fuck you very much.

And yet they line up, they beg, they try and bribe, they conspire, they whisper loudly into their cell phones, to friends in St. Tropez or Punta del Este or Rome, trying to reach someone with influence over the situation—so that they may visibly swan past less favored mortals and sit, triumphant, on the Patio of the Gods.

If, as the man says, "behind every great fortune there is a crime," then, surely, many of these customers have sanctioned every variety of cold-blooded behavior in the interests of a few dollars here and there: relocating African villages, flooding valleys, gouging the infirm, dumping toxins down wells, and knocking off the inconvenient when circumstances require. But for Robèrt, they cheerfully grab their ankles.

And they don't even ask for a reach-around.

It kind of begs the question: *why?*

It's a question I've been wrestling with since early in my career, when I was charged with the care and refilling of the trays and hotel pans at the Rockefeller Center Luncheon Club, where the Masters of the Financial Universe ate every daytime meal at our sorry-ass buffet of the damned. I wondered what might have compelled these people, who singlehandedly decided the fate of nations, the captains of industry, the fabulously wealthy wives of potentates, scions of old European families who didn't even remember where their money came from, why would these people cower in the dreary confines of the lunch club—or fight tooth and nail, clawing over the bodies of their friends to eat truly awful, insultingly priced food on a shabby pool deck, abused by a man of no standing or station, whom, under ordinary circumstances, they would have set the hounds on without a second's thought?

Why, for that matter, tolerate the absurd pretense and prices of Mr. Chow—or Philippe, or Nello, or Cipriani—when there are a hundred better restaurants within a few moments' drive? What my horrible week on St. Barths taught me was that this traveling strata of mega-rich people, all of whom know each other, crave nothing more than the comfort, the assurance, that they're going to the same crummy place as everybody else. Perhaps this explains why they all go to the same lousy beaches—usually narrow, pebbly, and unimpressive stretches of oft-reeking sand that would be unacceptable to any half-seasoned backpacker—and to restaurants that any food nerd with a Web site and a few bucks would walk sneeringly by.

Try arguing the virtues of Nello on chowhound.com, or a similar online meeting ground for knowledgeable food nerds, and prepare to get pilloried. So, why would people who can afford to eat anywhere obligingly allow themselves to be charged outrageous amounts of money for food that's, on its very best day, mediocre?

A clue came to me on St. Barths as I lay on a chaise lounge, half drunk in the moonlight, various Gaddafis and their guests frolicking in the background. Perhaps it's that they're so ugly, these "beautiful" people. They wear the same ugly clothes, designed by the same misogynistic old queens—who must privately piss themselves with laughter seeing their older, richer clientele squeezing into these outfits . . . leading one to the observation that the style-makers themselves, the people who decide what the world will wear next year, who's pretty, what's "hot" and what's "not," are uniformly hideous beyond the lurid imaginings of Cub Scouts round a campfire. Just look at the guest judges on *Project Runway* or *America's Next Top Model*—or at the front row of any fashion show—and you'll get the idea: a dumpier, less attractive, more badly dressed bunch of customers would be hard to find outside a suburban Dress Barn. Rick James—in the '70s—could never have gotten away with what Karl Lagerfeld wears every day. He'd have been hooted off the stage. If Donatella Versace showed up at your door selling Amway products, you'd slam it and double-lock it—before calling the neighbors to warn them.

As I looked around the beach, I saw, in the jaundiced light of my unhappiness, the full extent of the horror of this Island of Dr. Moreau I'd willingly marooned myself on. The full spectrum of plastic surgeries gone wrong—right there in the open, curiosities of the flesh, which at a lesser income level would have been confined to the carnival sideshow: mouths that pulled to the side, lips plumped beyond credibility, cheeks filled with golf ball–like lumps, and foreheads frozen so tight you could play snare drum on them. Identical noses . . . eyes that refused to blink and could barely even close . . .

And there was my date for the night, in her thousand-dollar plain white T-shirt. Searching—once again—for her cell phone.

It makes sense that restaurant operators—and Robèrt—would prey on these people. They should. They are, after all, in the business of desire—of figuring out what fulfills their clients' wants and needs. What they want on St. Barths—as elsewhere, I'm guessing—is to feel secure among others of their ilk. Secure that they've chosen the right place—the place everybody else in their set will choose. Secure that, if nothing else, everyone else in attendance will have bought into the shared illusion. Where no one will point out the obvious: that they're too old and too ugly to be wearing what they're wearing. That the surgery didn't help. That they can't—and shouldn't, in fact—dance, ever again. That they're eating food that the cleanup guy, who's going to sweep up after closing, wouldn't touch with rubber gloves and andirons. That the rest of the people on this planet, if enough of them knew who they really were—and how they'd made their money— would have their heads quickly on pikes.

In the end, I walked away.

After she lost her cell phone for the fourth time, I saw her drunkenly survey the room, eyeballing other partygoers for suspects. I watched as her insane gaze finally settled on the entourage of a prominent gangster rapper who'd taken over the VIP section of the tented restaurant patio. Specifically on two very large women, thick-necked and unfriendly-looking to begin with, both wearing midnight sunglasses— either of whom could easily have taken me in a fair fight. In the kind of slow-motion approach that so often precedes disaster, I watched as my companion confronted the two women, accusingly demanding to know where her cell phone was.

The music was playing—very loud. So I didn't hear their reaction.

But assuming they responded with "What the fuck do I want with your cell phone, bitch?" and "You're accusing us 'cause we're black!," they would have been demonstrating impeccable logic. Utterly disgusted, I now no longer cared if, in the weeks to follow, I was found in a culvert, with my feet sawed off. I no longer cared if there'd be a price to pay later for escape. It was all just too awful to bear—much less look at—anymore. I needed to get out now. I'd had enough. Let her dig her own crazy ass out of this ever-building shit storm.

I pulled her over and said as much—then lurched out of the restaurant and down the road. I packed my bag, arranged with the front desk for her to have two more nights at the hotel, should she need to, and then walked the mile or so to the airport, where I spent the night on a bench. I took the first flight out and landed on my old, familiar—and decidedly more friendly—island ten minutes later.

I retrieved my rental car from the long-term parking and drove gratefully home, where I quickly curled up in the fetal position and slept like the dead for twenty-four hours.

I stayed home, avoiding bars, brothels, and even beaches for the rest of my time on the island. I'd had enough. Somewhere along the line, I'd stared Evil in the face and it had frightened me to my core. I don't know whether it was something I saw on St. Barths—or in the mirror during the worst year of my life—but something had to change. I knew that now.

4

I Drink Alone

People call me "chef." Still.

Walking down the street, I'll hear somebody call that out and my head still swivels to see who's talking to me. Nine years now since I last took up a pan in anger and I still whip around automatically to that title. Of course, it's no longer true. I am not a chef. Still, it usually makes me happy when I hear that.

There's something wonderful about drinking in the afternoon. A not-too-cold pint, absolutely alone at the bar—even in this fake-ass Irish pub. It's new, built to look like old. Erin Go Bragh bullshit with its four flat screens silently flashing sports crawls for games I don't care about. The generic Irish bric-a-brac they deliver by the truck-load. Empty moving vans roaming the Irish countryside right now, I imagine, waiting for old Missus Meagher to drop dead into her black pudding so they can buy up the contents of her curio shelves. All of it shipped straight off to a central clearing house, where it's divvied up between Instant Irish Pubs in New York, Milwaukee, Singapore, and Verona.

I've been at this bar before, of course. We all have. Yet I'm strangely, indefensibly happy here. Even the stink of Lysol from the too-clean floor, the fruit flies hovering over the garnish tray do not distract me from a general feeling of well-being.

The food, were I silly enough to ask . . . well, I know what's on the menu without looking. Fried zucchini sticks, fried mozzarella, surely there's calamari in red sauce. Look deeper and there will be indifferently prepared shepherd's pie; a French dip with salty "gravy" made from canned base; a burger with a limp pickle, an unripe tomato slice, and Simplot Classic frozen French fries. "Bangers and mash" will be an Italian sweet sausage—and there might be a gummy approximation of Irish stew, containing too-lean lamb bits and lots of potatoes.

And what of the seafood options? You are on your fucking own there, boyo.

The bartender is Irish. Jumped a student visa about ten years ago but nothing for him to worry about.

The cook, though, is Mexican. Some poor bastard at ten dollars an hour—and probably has to wash the dishes, too. La Migra take notice of *his* immigration status—they catch sight of his bowl cut on the way home to Queens and he'll have a problem. He *looks* different than the Irish and the Canadians—and he's got Lou Dobbs calling specifically for his head every night on the radio. (You notice, by the way, that you never hear Dobbs wringing his hands over our border to the North. Maybe the "white" in Great White North makes that particular "alien superhighway" more palatable.) The cook at the Irish bar, meanwhile, has the added difficulty of predators waiting by the subway exit for him (and any other Mexican cooks or dishwashers) when he comes home on Friday payday. He's invariably cashed his check at a check-cashing store; he's relatively small—and is unlikely to call the cops. The perfect victim.

The guy serving my drinks, on the other hand, as most English-speaking illegal aliens, has been smartly gaming the system for years, a time-honored process everybody at the INS is fully familiar with: a couple of continuing education classes now and again (while working off the books) to get those student visas. Extensions. A work visa. A "farm" visa. Weekend across the border and repeat. Articulate, well-connected friends—the type of guys who own, for instance, lots of Irish bars—who can write letters of support lauding your invaluable and "specialized" skills, unavailable from homegrown bartenders. And nobody's looking anyway. But I digress . . .

Bushmills or Jameson, Celtics or Rangers, don't mean a thing here. This is a nondenominational Irish bar. No difference, no raised eyebrows. Few Irish, now that I think about it. And the Guinness, of course, blows.

The owner's got ten or twelve of these bars and they all look the same and they all have names like Paddy McGee's or Seamus O'Doul's or Molly whatever—none of whom exist or ever existed.

But I am happy here just the same.

Among the pool table, the jukebox, the inevitable dartboard, the moosehead, toy trains, Yankee banners, the photos of Irish authors who never came here and whom nobody here ever read. You want to talk Joyce or Behan? A Yeats's bust may sit dust-covered on a shelf, but start spouting lines from *The Second Coming* and you can just fuck off down the street, ya prat.

Who drinks here?

Office workers, jackets off, tie still on—or the reverse: jacket on, tie off. Restaurant help, nipping out for a drink, coming off a shift, fortifying themselves for the shift to come. Beaten down by life. Not broken, mind you, not beaten down like a coal miner or an out-of-work steel worker—just . . . dissatisfied with the way things have turned out. Not quite ready to go home just yet. Picture just a little too clear to get on the train at this precise moment. Better, it has been decided, to fuzz things a little around the edges before moving back into their other lives.

I feel right at home here—until Gnarls Barclay's "Crazy" comes on the sound system, which brings me right back to Beirut—as it always does—and I'm pretty sure nobody else at this bar is feeling the same way I am right now. Not like I'm talking post-traumatic stress or anything, I mean it wasn't *that* bad (for me), I mean a sudden sadness, a sense, an awareness of dislocation . . . that image of a Mediterranean, European, Arab city on the sea . . . rockets coming in from the horizon, floating lazily above the airport, then dropping with a delayed bang. The smell of burning jet fuel. More than anything else, the song makes me feel separated from what might, in another life, ten years ago, have otherwise been my drinking buddies at the bar.

I'll never be a regular at this bar. Or any bar. Not even a "writers' bar." If you've ever even spent ten minutes in one of those—a bunch of bitter, snowy-haired, bilious fucks with gin-blossomed noses and ballooning guts talking too loud and laughing too hard and secretly hating each other—you'll reconsider ever putting another word to paper. As much as I admire the work of good writers, I've found that hanging out with more than one of them at a time is about as much fun as being thrown into a cage full of hungry but toothless civet cats.

"You're not a chef," says the kid at the bar—another bar, a "chefs' bar," this time, late at night. I'm probably on a book tour and out for drinks with the kitchen crew from my hotel. Is it Portland? Seattle? Vancouver? Who remembers?

"You're not a chef!" he repeats, giving me the stink-eye, unsteady on his feet. "You don't even cook!"

The others with me, fresh off a long shift in the kitchen, shrink back a little, uncomfortable with the situation. They like me fine. I did write *Kitchen Confidential*, after all, but let's face it, the kid is right.

He's drunk and he's angry and, like a lot of people who own well-thumbed, food-splattered, water-damaged copies of that book—or who've borrowed a copy from the guy who works next to them—he feels betrayed. I'm a heretic now, having abandoned him and everyone like him, repudiated the One True Church of the Working Cook.

Look at me and my nice fucking jacket, standing there all famous and shit.

"Fuck you," he says. "You don't even cook. You're not *one of us* anymore." Far from being offended (though I am hurt), I want to give him a big hug. Another drink or two and I just might.

I don't cook. I'm not a chef. The chefs and cooks who are better than I used to be—better than I ever was—they know this and don't need to say it. They certainly don't need to say it to my face, like this kid, pressing me up against the bar now with the force of his rage and hurt. He will channel these feelings, appropriately, into a demand that I do a shot of tequila with him. Or two.

Which is a relatively friendly and diplomatic solution to an awkward situation.

It's the guys who are most like me who feel most disappointed in me. The hackers, the wake-up-every-fucking-day-and-drag-your-ass-into-pretty-much-one-place-same-as-the-other-to-make-food-you-don't-particularly-like-for-people-you-like-even-less. The ones who smell of fryer grease and burned salmon fat.

When I decline the offer of a third shot, he will at least have had the satisfaction of proving me a pussy. Which will be a victory of sorts.

And when, eventually, he sags to the side in his booth, his comrades in arms looking on tolerantly, and slips into unconsciousness, I will still be thinking about what he said, that he was right.

5

So You Wanna Be a Chef

I am frequently asked by aspiring chefs, dreamers young and old, attracted by the lure of slowly melting shallots and caramelizing pork belly, or delusions of Food Network stardom, if they should go to culinary school. I usually give a long, thoughtful, and qualified answer.

But the short answer is "no."

Let me save you some money. I was in the restaurant business for twenty-eight years—much of that time as an employer. I am myself a graduate of the finest and most expensive culinary school in the country, the CIA, and am as well a frequent visitor and speaker at other culinary schools. Over the last nine years, I have met and heard from many culinary students on my travels, have watched them encounter triumphs and disappointments. I have seen the dream realized, and—more frequently—I have seen the dream die.

Don't get me wrong. I'm not telling you that culinary school is a bad thing. It surely is not. I'm saying that *you*, reading this, right now, would probably be ill-advised to attend—and are, in all likelihood, unsuited for The Life in any case. Particularly if you're any kind of normal.

But let's say you're determined. You're planning on taking out a student loan and taking on a huge amount of debt. In many cases, from lenders associated with—or recommended by—your local culinary school. Ask yourself first: is this culinary school even any *good*? If you're not going to the Culinary Institute of America, Johnson and Wales, or the French Culinary Institute, you should investigate this matter even more intently, because the fact is, when you graduate from the Gomer County Technical College of Culinary Arts, nobody hiring in the big leagues is going to give a shit. A degree from the *best* culinary schools is no guarantee of a good job. A degree from anywhere less than the best schools will probably be less helpful than the work experience you could have had, had you been out there in the industry all that time.

You're about to take on $40,000 to $60,000 in debt training for an industry where—if you are lucky—you will, for the first few years, be making $10 to $12 dollars an hour. In fact, if you are really, *really* lucky—one of the few supremely blessed with talent, ability, and great connections deemed worthy enough to recommend you to one of the great kitchens of Europe or New York for your post-school apprenticeship—you will essentially be making *nothing* for the first couple of years. You will, once living expenses are factored in, probably be *paying* for the experience.

Should you be fortunate enough to be among the one-in-a-million young cooks taken on at a famous and respected restaurant like Arzak, in Spain (for example), this will truly be time and money well spent. If you perform well, you will return home never again needing a résumé. In this case, the investment of all your time and money and hard work will have paid off.

But the minute you graduate from school—unless you have a deep-pocketed Mommy and Daddy or substantial savings—you're already up against the wall. Two nearly unpaid years wandering Europe or

New York, learning from the masters, is rarely an option. You need to make money NOW. If that imperative prevails, requiring that you work immediately, for whomever will have you—once you embark on a career dictated by the need for immediate cash flow, it never gets any easier to get off the treadmill. The more money you get paid straight out of school, the less likely you are to ever run off and do a *stage* in the great kitchens of the world. Time cooking at Applebee's may get you paid—but it's a period best left blank on the résumé if you're planning on ever moving to the bigs. It may just as well have never happened. Country clubs? Hotel kitchens? These are likely employers straight out of school—and they promise a pretty decent, relatively stable career if you do well. It's a good living—with (unlike most of the restaurant business) reasonable hours and working conditions—and most hotels and country clubs offer the considerable advantage of health insurance and benefits. But that sector of the trade is like joining the mafia. Once you enter the warm fold of their institutional embrace, it's unlikely you'll ever leave. Once in—rarely out.

If it matters to you, watch groups of chefs at food and wine festivals—or wherever industry people congregate and drink together after work. Observe their behaviors—as if spying on animals in the wild. Notice the hotel and country club chefs approach the pack. Immediately, the eyes of the pack will glaze over a little bit at the point of introduction. The hotel or country club species will be marginalized, shunted to the outside of the alpha animals. With jobs and lives that are widely viewed as being cushier and more secure, they enjoy less prestige—and less respect.

You could, of course, opt for the "private chef" route upon graduating. But know that for people in the industry, the words "private" and "chef" just don't go together. To real chefs, such a concept doesn't even exist. A private "chef" is domestic help, period. A glorified butler. Somewhere slightly below "food stylist" and above "consultant" on the food chain. It's where the goofs who wasted a lot of money on a culinary education only to find out they couldn't hack it in the real world end up.

How old are you?

Nobody will tell you this, but I will:

If you're thirty-two years old and considering a career in professional kitchens? If you're wondering if, perhaps, you are too old?

Let me answer that question for you:

Yes. You are too old.

If you're planning on spending big bucks to go to culinary school at your age, you'd better be doing it for love—a love, by the way, that will be, almost without a doubt, unreciprocated.

By the time you get out of school—at thirty-four, even if you're fucking Escoffier—you will have precious few useful years left to you in the grind of real-world working kitchens. That's if you're lucky enough to even get a job.

At thirty-four, you will immediately be "Grandpa" or "Grandma" to the other—inevitably much, much younger, faster-moving, more physically fit—cooks in residence. The chef—also probably much younger—will view you with suspicion, as experience has taught him that older cooks are often dangerously set in their ways, resistant to instruction from their juniors, generally slower, more likely to complain, get injured, call in sick, and come with inconvenient baggage like "normal" family lives and responsibilities outside of the kitchen. Kitchen crews work best and happiest when they are tight—when they operate like a long-touring rock band—and chances are, you will be viewed, upon showing up with your knife roll and your résumé—as simply not being a good fit, a dangerous leap of faith, hope, or charity by whoever was dumb enough to take a chance on you. That's harsh. But it's what they'll be thinking.

Am I too fat to be a chef? Another question you should probably ask yourself.

This is something they don't tell you at admissions to culinary school, either—and they should. They're happy to take your money if you're five foot seven inches and two hundred fifty pounds, but what they don't mention is that you will be at a terrible, terrible disadvantage when applying for a job in a busy kitchen. As chefs know (literally) in their bones (and joints), half the job for the first few years—if not the entirety of your career—involves running up and down stairs (quickly), carrying bus pans loaded with food, and making hundreds of deep-knee bends a night into low-boy refrigerators. In conditions of excruciatingly high heat and humidity of a kind that can cause young and superbly fit cooks to falter. There are the purely practical considerations as well: kitchen work areas—particularly behind the line—being necessarily tight and confined . . . Bluntly put, can the other cooks move easily around your fat ass? I'm only saying it. But any chef considering hiring you is thinking it. And you will have to live it.

If you think you might be too fat to hack it in a hot kitchen? You probably are too fat. You can *get* fat in a kitchen—over time, during a long and glorious career. But arriving fat from the get-go? That's a hard—and narrow—row to hoe.

If you're comforting yourself with the dictum "Never trust a thin chef," don't. Because no stupider thing has ever been said. Look at the crews of any really high-end restaurants and you'll see a group of mostly whippet-thin, under-rested young pups with dark circles under their eyes: they look like escapees from a Japanese prison camp—and are expected to perform like the Green Berets.

If you're not physically fit? Unless you're planning on becoming a pastry chef, it is going to be very tough for you. Bad back? Flat feet? Respiratory problems? Eczema? Old knee injury from high school? It sure isn't going to get any better in the kitchen.

Male, female, gay, straight, legal, illegal, country of origin—who cares? You can either cook an omelet or you can't. You can either cook five hundred omelets in three hours—like you said you could, and like the job requires—or you can't. There's no lying in the kitchen. The restaurant kitchen may indeed be the last, glorious meritocracy—where anybody with the skills and the heart is welcomed. But if you're old, or out of shape—or were never really certain about your chosen path in the first place—then you will surely and quickly be removed. Like a large organism's natural antibodies fighting off an invading strain of bacteria, the life will slowly push you out or kill you off. Thus it is. Thus it shall always be.

The ideal progression for a nascent culinary career would be to, first, take a jump straight into the deep end of the pool. Long before student loans and culinary school, take the trouble to find out who you are.

Are you the type of person who *likes* the searing heat, the mad pace, the never-ending stress and melodrama, the low pay, probable lack of benefits, inequity and futility, the cuts and burns and damage to body and brain—the lack of anything resembling normal hours or a normal personal life?

Or are you like everybody else? A normal person?

Find out sooner rather than later. Work—for free, if necessary—in a busy kitchen. Any kitchen that will have you will do—in this case, a busy Applebee's or T.G.I. Friday's or any old place will be fine. Anybody who agrees to let your completely inexperienced ass into their kitchen for a few months—and then helpfully kicks it repeatedly and without let-up—will suffice. After six months of dishwashing, prep, acting as the bottom-rung piss-boy for a busy kitchen crew—usually while treated as only slightly more interesting than a mouse turd—if you still *like* the restaurant business and think you could be happy among the ranks of the damned? Then, welcome.

At this point, having established ahead of time that you are one fucked-up individual—that you'd never be happy in the normal world anyway—culinary school becomes a very *good* idea. But choose the best one possible. If nothing else, you'll come out of culinary school with a baseline (knowledge and familiarity with techniques). The most obvious advantage of a culinary education is that from now on, chefs won't have to take time out of their busy day to explain to you what a fucking "brunoise" is. Presumably, you'll know what they mean if they shout across the room at you that you should braise those lamb necks. You'll be able to break down a chicken, open an oyster, filet a fish. Knowing those things when you walk in the door is not absolutely necessary—but it sure fucking helps.

When you do get out of culinary school, try to work for as long as you can possibly afford in the very best kitchens that will have you—as far from home as you can travel. This is the most important and potentially invaluable period of your career. And where I fucked up mine.

I got out of culinary school and the world seemed my oyster. Right away, I got, by the standards of the day, what seemed to be a pretty good paying job. More to the point, I was having fun. I was working with my friends, getting high, getting laid, and, in general, convincing myself that I was quite brilliant and talented enough.

I was neither.

Rather than put in the time or effort—then, when I had the chance, to go work in really good kitchens—I casually and unthinkingly doomed myself to second- and (mostly) third- and fourth-tier restaurant kitchens forever. Soon there was no going back. No possibility of making less money. I got older, and the Beast that needed to be fed got bigger and more demanding—never less.

Suddenly it was ten years later, and I had a résumé that was, on close inspection, unimpressive at best. At worst, it told a story of fucked-up priorities and underachievement. The list of things I never learned to do well is still shocking, in retrospect. The simple fact is that I would be—and have always been—inadequate to the task of working in the kitchens of most of my friends, and it is something I will have to live with. It is also one of my greatest regrets. There's a gulf the size of an ocean between adequate and finesse. There is, as well, a big difference between good work habits (which I have) and the kind of discipline required of a cook at Robuchon. What limited me forever were the decisions I made immediately after leaving culinary school.

That was my moment as a chef, as a potential adult, and I let it pass. For better or worse, the decisions I made then about what I was going to do, whom I was going to do it with and where, set me on the course I stayed on for the next twenty years. If I hadn't enjoyed a freakish and unexpected success with *Kitchen Confidential*, I'd still be standing behind the stove of a good but never great restaurant at the age of fifty-three. I would be years behind in my taxes, still uninsured, with a mouthful of looming dental problems, a mountain of debt, and an ever more rapidly declining value as a cook.

If you're twenty-two, physically fit, hungry to learn and be better, I urge you to travel—as far and as widely as possible. Sleep on floors if you have to. Find out how other people live and eat and cook. Learn from them—wherever you go. Use every possible resource you have to work in the very best kitchens that will have you—however little (if anything) they pay—and relentlessly harangue every possible connection, every great chef whose kitchen offers a glimmer of hope of acceptance. Keep at it. A three-star chef friend in Europe reports receiving month after month of faxes from one aspiring apprentice cook—and responding with "no" each time. But finally he broke down, impressed by the kid's unrelenting, never wavering determination. Money borrowed at this point in your life so that you can afford to travel and gain work experience in really good kitchens will arguably be better invested than any student loan. A culinary degree—while enormously helpful—is only helpful to a point. A year working at Mugaritz or L'Arpège or Arzak can transform your life—become a direct route to other great kitchens. All the great chefs know each other. Do right by one and they tend to hook you up with the others.

Which is to say: if you're lucky enough to be able to do the above, do not fuck up.

Like I said, all the great chefs know each other.

Let me repeat, by the way, again, that I did none of the things above.

It's a little sad sometimes when I look out at a bookstore audience and see young fans of *Kitchen Confidential,* for whom the book was a validation of their worst natures. I understand it, of course. And I'm happy they like me.

But I'm a little more comfortable when the readers are late-career hackers and journeymen, like I was when I wrote the book. I like that they relate to the highs and lows, the frustrations and absurdities, that they, too, can look back—with a mixture of nostalgia and very real regret—on sexual liaisons on cutting boards and flour sacks, late-night coke jags, the crazy camaraderie that seems to come only in the busiest hash-house restaurants—or failing ones. I wrote the book for them in the first place. And it's too late for them anyway.

But the young culinary students, thousands and thousands of them—new generations of them every year, resplendent in their tattoos and piercings—I worry that some of them might have missed the point.

At no point in *Kitchen Confidential,* that I can find, does it say that cocaine or heroin were *good* ideas. In fact, given the book's many episodes of pain, humiliation, and being constantly broke-ass, one would think it almost a cautionary tale. Yet, at readings and signings, I am frequently the inadvertent recipient of small packets of mysterious white powder; bindles of cocaine; fat, carefully rolled joints of local hydro, pressed into my palm or slipped into my pocket. These inevitably end up in the garbage—or handed over to a media escort. The white powders because I'm a recovered fucking *addict*—and the weed 'cause all I need is one joint, angel dust–laced by some psycho, to put me on TMZ, running buck-naked down some Milwaukee street with a helmet made from the stretched skin of a butchered terrier pulled down over my ears.

Smoking weed at the end of the day is nearly always a good idea—

but I'd advise ambitious young cooks against sneaking a few drags mid-shift at Daniel. If you think smoking dope makes you more responsive to the urgent calls for food from your expeditor, then God bless you, you freak of nature you. If you're anything like me, though, you're probably only good for a bowl of Crunchberries and a *Simpsons* rerun.

On the other hand, if you're stuck heating up breakfast burritos at Chili's—or dunking deep-fried macaroni at TGI McFuckwad's? Maybe you need that joint.

Treating despair with drugs and alcohol is a time-honored tradition—I'd just advise you to assess honestly if it's really as bad and as intractable a situation as you think. Not to belabor the point, but if you look around you at the people you work with, many of them are—or will eventually be—alcoholics and drug abusers. All I'm saying is you might ask yourself now and again if there's anything else you wanted to do in your life.

I haven't done heroin in over twenty years, and it's been a very long time as well since I found myself sweating and grinding my teeth to the sound of tweeting of birds outside my window.

There was and is nothing heroic about getting off coke and dope.

There's those who do—and those who don't.

I had other things I still wanted to do. And I saw that I wasn't going to be doing shit when I was spending all my time and all my money on coke or dope—except more coke and dope.

I'm extremely skeptical of the "language of addiction." I never saw heroin or cocaine as "my illness." I saw them as some very bad choices that I walked knowingly into. I fucked myself—and, eventually, had to work hard to get myself un-fucked.

And I'm not going to tell you here how to live your life.

I'm just saying, I guess, that I got very lucky.

And luck is not a business model.

6

Virtue

There is no debating that it's "better" to cook at home whenever—and as often as—possible.

It's cheaper, for sure. It's almost always healthier than what you might otherwise be ordering as takeout—or eating at a restaurant. And it is provably better for society.

We know, for instance, that there is a direct, inverse relationship between frequency of family meals and social problems. Bluntly stated, members of families who eat together regularly are statistically less likely to stick up liquor stores, blow up meth labs, give birth to crack babies, commit suicide, or make donkey porn. If Little Timmy had just had more meatloaf, he might not have grown up to fill chest freezers with Cub Scout parts.

But that's not what I'm talking about.

I'm interested in whether we *should* cook as a moral imperative—as something that every boy and girl should be taught to do in school and woe to him or her who can't. I'm talking about pounding home a new value, a national attitude, the way, during the JFK era, the President's Council on Physical Fitness created the expectation that you *should* be healthy if you were a kid. That you *should*, no, you *must* be reasonably athletic. That at the very least you must aspire to those goals, try your best—that your teachers, your schoolmates, and society as a whole would help you and urge you on. There would be rigorous standards. Your progress would be monitored with the idea that you would, over time, improve—and become, somehow, better as a person.

With encouragement, of course, came the unstated but implied ugly flip side: negative reinforcement. If you couldn't keep up, you were, at best, teased and, at worst, picked on.

So, I'm not suggesting we put kids who can't cook into the center of a hooting circle of bullies and throw a fat rubber ball at them until they cry—which was the traditional punishment for perceived crimes of "spazdom" back in my time.

But I do think the idea that basic cooking skills are a virtue, that the ability to feed yourself and a few others with proficiency should be taught to every young man and woman as a fundamental skill, should become as vital to growing up as learning to wipe one's own ass, cross the street by oneself, or be trusted with money.

Back in the dark ages, young women and girls were automatically segregated off to home-economics classes, where they were indoctrinated with the belief that cooking was one of the essential skill sets for responsible citizenry—or, more to the point, useful housewifery. When they began asking the obvious question—"Why *me* and not *him*?"—it signaled the beginning of the end of any institutionalized teaching of cooking skills. Women rejected the idea that they should be designated, simply by virtue of their gender, to perform what would be called, in a professional situation, service jobs, and rightly refused to submit. "Home ec" became the most glaring illustration of everything wrong with the gender politics of the time. Quickly identified as an instrument of subjugation, it became an instant anachronism. Knowing how to cook, or visibly enjoying it, became an embarrassment for an enlightened young woman, a reminder of prior servitude.

Males were hardly leaping to pick up the slack, as cooking had been so wrong-headedly portrayed as "for girls"—or, equally as bad, "for queers."

What this meant, though, is that by the end of the '60s, *nobody* was cooking. And soon, as Gordon Ramsay has pointed out rather less delicately a while back, no one even remembered *how*.

Maybe we missed an important moment in history there. When we finally closed down home ec, maybe we missed an opportunity. Instead of shutting down compulsory cooking classes for young women, maybe we would have been far better off simply demanding that the men learn how to cook, too.

It's not too late.

Just as horsemanship, archery, and a facility with language were once considered essential "manly" arts, to be learned by any aspiring gentleman, so, perhaps, should be cooking.

Maybe it's the kid in the future who can't roast a chicken who should be considered the "spaz" (though, perhaps, not made the recipient of a dodgeball to the head when he bungles a beurre blanc). Through a combination of early training and gentle but insistent peer pressure, every boy and girl would leave high school at least prepared to cook for themselves and a few others.

At college, where money is usually tight and good meals are rare, the ability to throw together a decent meal for your friends would probably be much admired. One might even be reasonably expected to have a small but serviceable list of specialties that you could cook for your roommates.

Cooking has already become "cool." So, maybe, it is now time to make the idea of *not* cooking "un-cool"—and, in the harshest possible ways short of physical brutality, drive that message home.

Let us then codify the essentials for this new virtue:

What specific tasks should every young man and woman know how to perform in order to feel complete?

What simple preparations, done well, should be particularly admired, skills seen as setting one apart as an unusually well-rounded, deceptively deep, and interesting individual?

In a shiny, happy, perfect world of the future, what should *every* man, woman, and teenager know how to do?

They should know how to chop an onion. Basic knife skills should be a must. Without that, we are nothing, castaways with a can—but no can-opener. Useless. Everything begins with some baseline ability with a sharp-bladed object, enough familiarity with such a thing to get the job done without injury. So, basic knife handling, sharpening, and maintenance, along with rudimentary but effective dicing, mincing, and slicing. Nothing too serious. Just enough facility with a knife to be on a par with any Sicilian grandmother.

Everyone should be able to make an omelet. Egg cookery is as good a beginning as any, as it's the first meal of the day, and because the process of learning to make an omelet is, I believe, not just a technique but a builder of character. One learns, necessarily, to be gentle when acquiring omelet skills: a certain measure of sensitivity is needed to discern what's going on in your pan—and what to do about it.

I have long believed that it is only right and appropriate that before one sleeps with someone, one should be able—if called upon to do so—to make them a proper omelet in the morning. Surely that kind of civility and selflessness would be both good manners and good for the world. Perhaps omelet skills should be learned at the same time you learn to fuck. Perhaps there should be an unspoken agreement that in the event of loss of virginity, the more experienced of the partners should, afterward, make the other an omelet—passing along the skill at an important and presumably memorable moment.

Everyone should be able to roast a chicken. And they should be able to do it well.

Given the current woeful state of backyard grilling, a priority should be assigned to instructing people on the correct way to grill and rest a steak. We have, as a nation, suffered the tyranny of inept steak cookery for far too long. There's no reason that generation after generation of families should continue to pass along a tradition of massacring perfectly good meat in their kitchens and backyards.

Cooking vegetables to a desired doneness is easy enough and reasonable to expect of any citizen of voting age.

A standard vinaigrette is something anyone can and should be able to do.

The ability to shop for fresh produce and have at least some sense of what's in season, to tell whether or not something is ripe or rotten might be acquired at the same time as one's driving license.

How to recognize a fish that's fresh and how to clean and filet it would seem a no-brainer as a basic survival skill in an ever more uncertain world.

Steaming a lobster or a crab—or a pot of mussels or clams—is something a fairly bright chimp could do without difficulty, so there's no reason we all can't.

Every citizen should know how to throw a piece of meat in the oven with the expectation that they might roast it to somewhere in the neighborhood of desired doneness—and without a thermometer.

One should be able to roast and mash potatoes. And make rice—both steamed and the only slightly more difficult pilaf method.

The fundamentals of braising would serve all who learn them well—as simply learning how to make a beef bourguignon opens the door to countless other preparations.

What to do with bones (namely, make stock) and how to make a few soups—as a means of making efficient use of leftovers—is a lesson in frugality many will very possibly *have* to learn at some point in their lives. It would seem wise to learn earlier rather than later.

Everyone should be encouraged at every turn to develop their own modest yet unique repertoire—to find a few dishes they love and practice at preparing them until they are proud of the result. To either respect in this way their own past—or express through cooking their dreams for the future. Every citizen would thus have their own specialty.

Why can we not do this? There is no reason in the world.

Let us then go forward. With vigor.

7

The Fear

You knew things were going to get bad when Steve Hanson, without warning or visible regret, announced that he was going to shut down his restaurant, Fiamma. A few months of unsatisfactory receipts, true—but they'd recently won a very effusive three stars from the *New York Times*; the chef, Fabio Trabocchi, had been getting a lot of favorable attention and a lot of goodwill from the blogs and the food press. It was just before Christmas, no less, and there was every reason in the world—in an ordinary year—for an owner to find reason to believe things would get better, to hang on. But not this year. Hanson had examined the numbers, glanced at the headlines, taken a quick but hard look at the future—and decided he didn't like what he saw. He shut the doors on Fiamma and another of his restaurants, the Times Square Ruby Foo, in the same week.

Whatever people might think of Steve Hanson's restaurants, no one has ever credibly accused the man of being stupid. Evil, perhaps. Unlikable, probably. But even his detractors won't deny his intelligence.

If Hanson was choosing this moment, and this time—before the holiday season, no less—to drop the hammer on his show pony, arguably the *best* of his restaurants, the one all the opinion-makers actually *liked*, this *meant something*. This was a warning sign. To seasoned restaurant insiders, this was a blood-chilling indicator that things were not just bad—but that they were going to get a whole helluva lot worse.

In a business that lives and breathes dreams, delusions, superstition, and signs, where everybody, from the busboy to the owner, is always trying to figure out what it all might mean—Why are we busy today? Why not yesterday? When will we be busy again?—everybody scrambled to battle stations, trying to figure out what it all could mean, and what they could do to stop it, hopefully before "it" (whatever "it" was) happened.

The year 2008 was the *annus horribilis*, as they like to call such times, the year of the Disaster—The Fear. The stock market plunged, retirement funds became worthless, the rich became poor, the gainfully employed jobless, the eminently respectable suddenly targets for indictment. In a flash, thousands of loud, over-testosteroned men flush with cash and eager to play "whose dick is bigger?"—the secret-sharers, the hidden backbone of the fine-dining business—vaporized into an oily cloud, possibly/probably never to return. What "it" meant in real terms was that, nearly overnight, sales were dropping in the neighborhood of 30 percent. Or worse. Most chefs you talked to admitted to 15 to 18 percent. A few more honest ones would grudgingly admit to upwards of 30—while trying to keep the concern out of their voices. This was fixable. No reason to panic, they insisted. To admit how bad things were—and how absolutely petrified with fear many of them were—was bad luck. The accumulated wisdom of the restaurant business dictates that admitting such things, publicly accepting reality, is bad ju-ju. It only makes things worse, spreads the fear, worries creditors—and, worst of all, frightens away potential customers.

But it was worse than that.

It wasn't just that sales were down at the medium-range and up-market restaurants in town—it was *which* sales were down. It's one thing to take in $20,000 in receipts on a given night. It's another thing if most of that money represents *food* sales. What a lot of people won't tell you is that, for many full-service fine-dining restaurants (the kind with elaborate service, freshly changed floral arrangements, "chef's tables," and a private dining room), the prevailing business model before the crash was the reliance on the "whale customer," the regular patronage of the kind of customers who'd spend a few hundred dollars on a meal—and ten *thousand* (or more) on wine. The percentages on wine are generally excellent—and it requires relatively little in the way of labor or equipment. The margin on food, however, is razor-thin in the best of times—even when the prices on the menu appear to be outrageously expensive. The best ingredients cost a LOT of money. The quality and sheer number of personnel needed to handle those ingredients also require a lot of money. And by the time those ingredients are trimmed down, cooked off, sauced, garnished, and accompanied by the kind of bread, butter, and service one would expect them to keep company with—there's not a lot of profit left over.

The many in the finer of the fine-dining rooms of New York were, in some sense, being subsidized by the few who spent big dollars on wine. A few years back at Veritas, a bar customer was pointed out to me. He'd blown through as much as $65,000 in *one month*, giving out tastes to fellow oenophiles and strangers alike at the bar. That kind of customer can help a chef be a little more generous with the truffles.

Another worrisome feature of what was happening on Wall Street was the little-appreciated fact that, tucked away out of view of regular customers, was an entire revenue stream of corporate customers, organized groups of high rollers, dropping big, expensable Monopoly money on a dependable basis. It had been a perfect arrangement: thousands and thousands of dollars in business from people who didn't want to be seen spending it—conducted mostly out of view of a public for whom the sight of bankers and brokers enjoying themselves had never been attractive. Better yet, these masters of the universe usually had set or limited menus that could be cranked out relatively quickly and easily by kitchen staff. Half the work at minimal effort and premium prices. This was a blue-chip relationship for high-end restaurants, which could, around the holidays, amount to millions of dollars in revenue. Much of it conveniently spent on wine and liquor. That's as close to free money as it gets. Though you could never tell from the dining room, many more restaurants than are ever willing to admit it were designed and built from the get-go to do this kind of two-tracked business. They simply could not survive, operating the way they had before, without it.

Suddenly, overnight, that whole economy was in doubt. What was once a gusher turned into a dribble. When your customers are getting called out in the newspapers for eating at restaurants like yours, that is not an environment conducive to your interests. If a company wasn't currently making a profit for its shareholders, it was now a liability to be seen holding expensive corporate retreats—much less throwing a truffle dinner at Daniel. CEOs who were being vilified for flying private jets and grilled in front of congressional committees for their profligate spending and the obscene scale of their bonuses—they sure didn't want to get busted eating at Masa.

There was panic.

In the blink of an eye, hidebound attitudes and behaviors, which had only yesterday been so deeply ingrained as to be instinctive, completely reversed overnight.

Suddenly, everywhere you went, people were uncharacteristically . . . polite.

Velvet ropes disappeared.

Hostesses who only last week would look right through you with blank, model stares now became as welcoming as your beloved granny: almost painfully accommodating and eager to please. Phones that used to ring forever were picked up on the first toll. A civility bordering on desperation replaced studiously affected contempt. Tables became available where once there had been no possibility of there *ever* being a table.

Even walk-ins were treated with courtesy in the hope that any accrued goodwill might pay off later.

"I'm so sorry we can't accommodate you today but . . . how about next Thursday?" replaced the curt rebuff.

Chefs who hadn't been near their dining rooms, much less their kitchens, in some time suddenly returned—and even made a point of cooking.

Tom Colicchio was among the fastest to grab hold of the situation. Rightly seeing his television celebrity as an asset, he quickly put it to work in the service of his restaurant and announced "Tom Tuesdays" at Craft—where he, himself, stood there for all to see and cooked a special menu.

Half-price specials, half portions, à la carte options appeared where they'd once been unthinkable. Soon, you could order off the menu—individual dishes—in the cocktail waiting area at Per Se, where, previously, the only option had been the full ride through a tasting menu—and only in the dining room. Prices dropped, specials changed to less pricey, less intimidating creations. The words "two for one," "free bottle of wine," "half-price," and even "early bird dinner" began appearing on menus, signs, and Web sites. Comfort-food classics like fried chicken started appearing at weekly special-event dinners held late at night—at places where such quotidian fare would not, under ordinary circumstances, be expected.

But these were not ordinary times—and everyone knew it.

Many customers, particularly of fine-dining restaurants—the kind of people who invested in stocks and bonds—had lost as much as half their net worth in a matter of days. They could hardly be counted on to have the same priorities—to behave as before. Sure, it was not unreasonable to hope that there was still room for restaurants and menus and a level of dining directed at the luxury market—people willing to pay top dollar for the very best. They'd always be there. But there would also be, restaurateurs quickly surmised, plenty they would no longer be willing to pay for.

"I may have money to pay for this white truffle fettuccine," one imagined them to say, "but fuck me if I'm paying for the restaurant to buy that flower arrangement over there!"

That gap would need to be filled. By ordinary customers. We'd better start being nice to them, went the feeling. Pronto.

If there's a new and lasting credo from the Big Shakeout, it's this: People will continue to pay for quality. They will be less and less inclined, however, to pay for bullshit. The new financial imperatives—accompanied, perhaps, by some small sense that ostentatiously throwing a lot of money around unnecessarily might not be *cool* right now—dovetailed perfectly with the rising hipness of the more casual Momofuku and L'Atelier fine-dining models (which had been around for some time), as well as other, more mysterious forces, long simmering under the surface and just now bubbling to the top to be acknowledged and identified. Wiser heads saw this shift as presenting opportunities.

A lot of restaurants closed. And, as always, a lot of restaurants opened to take their places. Industry boosters will point to those aggregate numbers as a means of minimizing the severity of what happened. But who among them will survive? Who will still be standing a year from now? Two?

In the middle of the worst period of crisis, when everyone was predicting the End of Opulence, Chris Cannon and Michael White bravely opened up the *very* opulent Marea on Central Park South. True, the room is ultra-swank. The prices for the food—which unapologetically courts (and deserves) four stars—are expensive. But what's interesting is the wine list. It's cheap. Or, shall we say, unusually focused on moderately priced, lesser known boutique wines and cult wines of Italy. You pay a lot of money for dinner at Marea—but, significantly, you do *not* get gouged on wine. In fact, if anything, you are gently steered toward more sensible choices.

As the prices of raw ingredient continued to rise—and pressure on customers tightened—chefs were caught in the middle. Even traditional "must-have" dishes like salmon and sirloin steak were becoming so expensive to serve that many couldn't make money on them. And customers still wanted organic and sustainable—yet affordable at the same time.

David Chang suggested a way forward in an article in *Esquire*, predicting an inevitable move toward an entirely new expectation of the ratio between protein and vegetables or starch on plates of the future—more along the lines of the Asian model. A concentration on not only "lesser" cuts of meat, like neck, shoulder, and shank—but a lot less meat altogether. A future scenario where meat and bone would be used more as flavoring agents than as the main event, Chang proposed, would not necessarily be a bad thing. That would be more affordable, and would force chefs to be more creative and less reliant on overkill, on bulk, to make their point—and it would be better for a population increasingly at risk of growing morbidly obese.

Hard times, he seemed to be saying, might actually help push us in a direction we were already coming to think we wanted to go—or that we *should* be going but hadn't yet actually gotten around to.

Belt-tightening implies a bad thing. But it also means you're getting thinner.

Serendipitously enough, many chefs have been wanting to go in that direction for decades. They'd *never* loved selling salmon or halibut or snapper anyway—because they were boring. They'd always liked smaller, bonier, oilier fishes, for instance, not because they were cheaper but because they believed them to be good. Now, perhaps, was the time to strike. For every chef struggling to convince their restaurant's owner to put mackerel or (God forbid) bluefish on the menu, now they had a very compelling, even unassailable argument: we just can't *afford* to sell salmon. So, indeed, there *was* light, maybe, in the darkness.

If ever a time called for braised beef shoulder or round or flank steak—this was it.

Something else was happening, too. As young investment bankers moved from the banquette to the unemployment line, they were being replaced by a whole new breed of diner. Jonathan Gold, who's right about everything (except the virtues of Oki Dog), said in an *LA Times* roundup of 2009 that there were "more high profile LA area restaurant openings in the last year or so than we saw in the previous five," but "something truly new was going on that *may fundamentally change the way we look at restaurants*" (italics mine).

"While nobody was paying attention, food quietly assumed the place in youth culture that used to be occupied by rock 'n' roll—individual, fierce and intensely political." He points to the Kogi truck, which broadcasts its location on Twitter, and similar mobile operations, the advent of "pop-up" restaurants, and the general "hipness" now associated with street food, ethnic, "authentic," or "extreme." For a young man with indie aspirations and a modest disposable income, there is now a certain cachet involved in hunting down a shoebox-size Uiger noodle shop in the cellar of a Chinese mall in Flushing.

It ain't a counterculture, however, unless you're "against" something. And the first thing to go, I hope, will be bullshit. Of that, there is *so* much to spare. Money may be less abundant but bullshit we've still got plenty of.

It's not that there will, or should, be a tearing down of everything old—as with many revolutions. If this is the advent of a "movement," it will, unlike all previous movements, move in many different—even opposing—directions. It's the Great Fragmentation, a reflection of what's been happening with television audiences, the music business, and print media for some time. Hopefully, the restaurant business, unlike media conglomerates, will be better suited and faster on its feet to deal with these new historical imperatives. They will have to be.

In the months following the crash, as restaurants were closing and belts tightening, there were a few ominous signs: sales of candy skyrocketed—as did sales at many fast-food chains. Fear and uncertainty, it appeared, led many to rush for the familiar—an infantile urge to grab some of what one *knew*: cheap, familiar tastes—in the same old wrapper. At least Twizzlers hadn't changed. Old Ronald and the Colonel were still there. I wonder, though, how long that will last.

Maybe people will *have* to start cooking again. To save money, and because the cold reality is that people without jobs have more time for that sort of thing.

If any good comes out of all the pain and insecurity, I can only hope that the Asian-style food court/hawker center is one of them. This institution is way overdue for an appearance (on a large scale) in America. Scores of inexpensive one-chef/one-specialty businesses (basically, food stalls) clustered around a "court" of shared tables. When will some shrewd and civic-minded investors (perhaps in tandem with their city governments) put aside some parking lot–size spaces (near commercial districts) where operators from many lands can sell their wares? Sharing tables, as in classic fast-food food courts? Why, with our enormous Asian and Latino populations, can't we have *dai pai dong*—literally, "big sign street," the Chinese version of the indigenous food court, like they do in Hong Kong—or hawker centers, like in Singapore or Kuala Lumpur? Or "food streets," like in Hanoi and Saigon? The open-to-the-air "wet" taco vendors and quesadilla-makers of Mexico City?

Food preparation areas could be enclosed, as they are in Singapore, so food handling and sanitation issues can hardly be an unsolvable impediment: Singapore is the most rigorously nanny of nanny states—with the most vibrant hawker culture.

The hawker center could be an answered prayer for every hard-pressed office worker in a hurry, every blue-collar worker on a budget, every cop on a lunch hour, as well as obsessive foodies at every income level. "Authenticity"; artisanship; freshness; incredible, unheard-of variety—and for cheap? All under one roof? This, let us hope, is at least part of our future—whatever happens.

As for what else lies in store? Who knows. Gold is clearly on to something. What this means, and how bad it's going to get for fine dining at the very top, is a matter of debate. As Eric Ripert says, there will always be room for Hermès. The very best, something people who can afford such things *know* took time and the expert work of many hands to achieve. But what about the other guys? The still very expensive but not quite as good? Will anybody give a fuck about the Versaces of the restaurant business ten years from now?

Gordon Ramsay's example might be instructive. In the last few years, buoyed by his successful television programs—and his reputation as a Michelin-starred chef—he opened twelve new restaurants around the world. All of them have lost money. He narrowly avoided bankruptcy.

Chefs looking to Las Vegas for a brighter future, a final payday, or a "Next Step" have, it appears, misplaced their hopes. That party has moved on.

And Dubai, which briefly presented itself as the new Valhalla for chefs, has revealed itself as the mostly empty, half-built construction site it always was. It is remarkable that the geniuses of high finance are still unable to see what any small-business owner would immediately have recognized: they've been building a lot of structures out there—and selling a lot of land. But nobody has actually *moved in* yet. And, by the way, it's a fucking desert. So, it's doubtful that Dubai can be counted on to be handing free money over to chefs anymore . . . Chefs and restaurateurs will have to go back to their original business model: sell people *food* they like and make money doing it.

If you're looking for bellwethers, a big fat canary in a coal mine, you might look hard at what happens in Miami—with the multimillion-dollar renovation of the Fontainebleau Hotel and its associated businesses (including the very fine Scarpetta restaurant). Bar and "lounge" business—which has also been a stolid underwriter of restaurant bottom lines—will probably be seeing some major changes. This is a town that has traditionally thrived on bottle service: the selling of a twenty-dollar bottle of vodka for five hundred dollars (with accompanying rights to a chair). How long that sort of douche-oriented economy survives is questionable. While there will always be douchebags, how long there will be enough rich douchebags willing to spend that kind of money for, basically, nothing is something I'd be worried about down there—and at any restaurants that double as "lounges."

For that kind of money, one can afford to do a lot of drinking at home.

I'm just hoping that, in the future, a night out doesn't mean you curl up with a gallon jug of Wolfschmitz or a box of wine, turn on the TV, and watch people cooking things on screen that you, yourself, won't be cooking anytime soon.

On the other hand, this would mean that whatever happens, there will always be work in food porn.

8

Lust

Heavenly wine and roses sing to me when you smile
—Lou Reed, "Sweet Jane"
(the slow, best version)

It's Christmastime in Hanoi again and the Metropole Hotel is lit up like an amusement park. In the courtyard, a monstrous white tree with bright red ornamental balls towers over the swimming pool. The decorative palms shine blindingly bright with a million tiny bulbs. I'm on my second gin and tonic and planning on having a third, settled back in a heavy rattan chair and feeling the kind of sorry for myself that most people would be very content with. There's incense in the air, buffeted about by the slowly moving overhead fans: a sickly-sweet odor that mirrors perfectly my mixed feelings of dull heartache and exquisite pleasure.

I often feel this way when alone in Southeast Asian hotel bars—an enhanced sense of bathos, an ironic dry-smile sorrow, a sharpened sense of distance and loss.

Today, this feeling will disappear the second I'm out the door.

Once I'm away from the sight of the other lone Western travelers, each, I imagine, with their own weltschmerz-loaded back story, their own unfulfilled longings, sitting there with their Gerald Seymours and their Ken Follets next to unringing cell phones. After strolling ever so slightly tipsy yet confident through the lobby, the service staff in *ao dai*s and traditional Annanite headgear address me (as they do all the guests) in French: *"Bon soir, Monsieur . . . Ça va?"* I'm through the doors, and suddenly the air fills with the roar of a thousand motorbikes and those feelings are gone, replaced by a giddiness, a familiar rush of overwhelming glee at being back in the country I'm crazy in love with.

The only way to see Hanoi is from the back of a scooter. To ride in a car would be madness—limiting your mobility to a crawl, preventing you from even venturing down half the narrow streets and alleys where the good stuff is to be found. To be separated from what's around you by a pane of glass would be to miss—everything. Here, the joy of riding on the back of a scooter or motorbike is to be part of the throng, just one more tiny element in an organic thing, a constantly moving, ever-changing process rushing, mixing, swirling, and diverting through the city's veins, arteries, and capillaries. Admittedly, it's also slightly dangerous. Traffic lights, one-way signs, intersections, and the like—the rough outlines of organized society—are more suggestions than regulations observed by anyone in actual practice. One has, though, the advantage of the right of way. Here? The scooter and the motorbike are kings. The automobile may rule the thoroughfares of America, but in Hanoi it's cumbersome and unwieldy, the last one to the party, a woolly mammoth of the road—to be waited on, begrudgingly accommodated—even pitied—like the fat man at a sack race.

Linh is driving—and I've finally, after many hours and many times as his passenger, given up on the strictly Western practice of hanging on. Nobody else does. Not the three-year-old child whipping past me, standing in front of his father and mother. Not grandma, riding side-saddle behind her son-in-law and daughter over there, or the hundreds of thousands of young men and women, chatting on cell phones or exchanging comments from the backs of other bikes. Somehow we all manage to stay aboard without gripping our drivers around the waist or shoulders—or even bracing ourselves from the back. Somehow it all works; we manage to move quickly—sometimes very quickly—through space, together and apart, without flying from our seats or colliding with each other. Thousands, millions of us, a moving conversation of words, glances, gestures, and the shrill honks of our horns with an ever-changing cast of characters snaking through Hanoi's Old Quarter, around its lakes, weaving through crosscurrents, breaking over and around the bigger, sadder four-wheel vehicles like stones in a river, barely noticing the souls trapped glumly and impatiently inside.

Is anyone in this city over thirty?

It seems not. Statistically, it is said that nearly 70 percent of the population are under that age, and, if the streets of Hanoi (or any city in Vietnam, for that matter) are any indicator, that number seems even higher. Nobody among them remembers the war. They weren't even alive for it. Much like our post–World War II baby boom, they must have gone straight home from the battlefield and done an awful lot of fuckin' around here. Everyone—*everyone*, it seems—is young and either on the way to eat, returning from eating, or eating at this very minute, absolutely choking the sidewalks on low plastic stools, filling the open-to-the-street shop houses, slurping noodles or nibbling on delicious-looking bits, drinking *bia hoi*, the fresh beer of Hanoi, with varying degrees of joy and seriousness of intent.

My old favorite, *bun cha*—juicy hunks of pork served in room-temperature, sweet-and-sour green papaya juice—are grilling over charcoal by the curb; bowls of *bun oc*, the bright, reddish, steaming mix of snails, noodles, and crab roe–infused broth are recognizable from the hunks of fresh tomato on top as I sweep by. Sizzling crepes; *banh mi* sandwiches—crunchy baguettes overloaded with headcheese, delightfully mysterious pâté, pickles, and, often, a fried egg; *bun bo Hue*—a sort of heartier, more highly testosteroned version of *pho* (noodles heaped with slices of beef and pork); slabs of blood cake—and nearly every delicious goddamn thing you can think of. Tiny electric-red slices of chili peppers, crunchy sprouts, Thai basil, roughly yanked cilantro, mint, green banana slices, wedges of lime everywhere. Everywhere.

Parties of ten, twenty Vietnamese cluster around and hover over hot pots of beef parts and whole fish.

Or they just ride.

If you're in a car, you're fucked for any of this. Most neighborhoods have no room for your spaceship to touch down. At best, you can glide slowly by, face pressed to the glass, or—if you care to torture yourself—open the window for a moment, let your nostrils fill with the complex admixture of a thousand and one delights, most of them unavailable to you. Sure, you can park a few blocks away, maybe—but then you may as well have walked. For the scooters and motorbikes, however, there's the convenience of *valet parking*. Oh, yes. Since nearly every available square foot of sidewalk is packed with tables, there is precious little space for bikes. But not to worry, because every little *com*, coffee shop, street stall, and eatery has a kid outside who will helpfully take your scooter and helmet, scrawl an identifying mark with chalk on the seat, and find some way to jam it in between the scores of others out front. It's the only way the system works. When you're done? He will helpfully extract it and have it ready for departure.

Some things never get old. Some things are just . . . classic. You never lose appreciation for them. Your enthusiasm may wax and wane ever so slightly, but you always come back. Whether it's the Rolling Stones' "Let It Bleed" or doing it doggie-style, good is simply . . . good.

There may be other things in life, but you can pretty much spend eternity considering the matter of the former—or latter—and you'd be hard-pressed to improve on either of them.

I feel exactly like this with Hanoi-style *pho*. I may love the Southern versions of this spicy noodle soup fiercely, and appreciate—even need—from time to time the difference, the rougher, spicier, less subtle charms of Saigon's often cloudier, more assertive sisters. But I wouldn't marry any of them.

Using sexual metaphors to describe food is a practice blithely, even automatically employed by most food writers—yours truly being a frequent perpetrator. But it seems particularly appropriate when describing *pho* in Hanoi—even though it's usually a morning routine, as opposed to a late-night, post-bar, fall-into-sloppy-embrace kind of a thing. Visiting a popular *pho* shop, particularly later in the morning, after the first waves of hungry people on their way to work have been through, resembles nothing so much as the set of a porn shoot.

Here, as there, the landscape of desire is strewn with crumpled tissues, the spent expressions of human lust. Short pink plastic trash baskets overflow with little white paper balls, wet tumbleweeds are littered everywhere. Walk three feet up to the counter and they will cling embarrassingly to the soles of your feet, trail back to your table as if you are hurriedly exiting a peep-show booth. Unlike with sex, however, this walk of shame comes *before* touchdown. For one's efforts, after a long wait on line, the handover of a few *dong* (the unfortunate name for Vietnam's unit of currency), a jostle, and a squeeze in between strangers at a low table on a sidewalk, one is rewarded with perfection.

Broth—usually (but not absolutely always) the savory-sweet extraction of many beef bone, heavy on the marrow. Not too dark—definitely not too light. Chances are, there are three or four enormous pots of the stuff going now behind the counter, steam rising to the ceiling, the proprietor ladling the stuff straight off the top. Locals will tell you it's all about the broth. If the broth isn't right, the best ingredients in the world aren't going to save it. Rice noodles. And they'd better be right, too. Too soft, too old, or too cooked? It's shit. Too chewy? Same. Handmade and cooked to order—or at least in constantly on-going batches, please. Classically, in Hanoi, the meat component is beef—and beef tendon, but preferences vary as to the exact mix. The counter behind the glass of my favorite place in the Old Quarter is stacked with pre-boiled beef shoulders: the perfect balance of lean and fat; and many prefer this—and only this: sliced ever so thinly onto the surface of their broth, where it wilts and relaxes and nearly dissolves into sublime tenderness. Some purists, however, insist entirely on raw beef, sliced at exactly the right degree of thinness and at the very last minute, added to the broth on the way out, so that the customers can "cook" it lightly themselves in the hot broth of their bowl by simply tossing it gently with their noodles. I, like many locals, prefer a mix of raw and cooked. The unattractive-sounding tendon, cooked properly by a master *pho*-maker, should be the best thing in the world—even for the uninitiated. Rather than being rubbery or tough, as one would expect of tendon, it should have just enough bite, just enough resis-tance, dissolving into fatty, marrow-like substance after just a few chews—a counterpoint to the wispy, all-too-brief pleasures of the beef. There're usually very few of the slender, translucent little tubes in one's bowl, and if you're unhappy to discover one on your spoon, then they're doing it wrong.

You complete *pho* at the table—and unlike with many similar dishes, where everybody's got their own way of doing things, in Hanoi there seems to be an accepted orthodoxy. A dot or two of chili paste, a tiny drizzle of chili sauce, a generous squeeze of lime, toss lightly with chopsticks in the right hand—and spoon with the left. Ideally, one wants a perfect marriage of beef, broth, and noodle in each mouthful. Slurping is encouraged. As is leaning down into your bowl. As is lift-ing the bowl to near your mouth.

There will be a generous plate or basket of greens, herbs, and sprouts next to a bowl of *pho*—usually Thai basil, mint, and cilantro—and one adds as needed, periodically incorporating elements of freshness and crunch and a welcome bitterness to one's mix, and one can pick idly at the occasional leaf as well, as kind of a palate cleanser.

I am hardly an expert on this subject, by the way—merely an enthusiast. But this is what I have observed and been told, over time. What is not debatable is that a perfect bowl of Hanoi *pho* is a balanced meeting of savory, sweet, sour, spicy, salty, and even umami—a gentle commingling of textures as well: soft and giving, wet and slippery, slightly chewy, momentarily resistant but ultimately near-diaphanous, light and heavy, leafy and limp, crunchy and tender. There—and nearly not there at all. Were this already not enough to jerk a rusty steak knife across your grandma's throat, empty her bank account, and head off to Hanoi, consider the colors: bright red chilies; the more subdued, richer-red toasted-chili paste; bright green vegetables; white sprouts. Pinkish-red raw meat, turning slowly gray as it cooks in your bowl, the deep brown colors of the cooked meat, white noodles, light amber broth. Nearly all God's colors in one bowl.

This is a sophisticated and deceptively subtle thing, Hanoi *pho*. I do not pretend to fully understand and appreciate its timeless beauty. Here, describing *pho* as more like love than sex would be more accurate—as there is simply not enough time on this planet, I think, to ever truly *know* it. It is an unconditional kind of love, in that it doesn't matter where you enjoy it—elevated only a few feet off a dirty street corner or at the sleekly designed counter of an overdecorated lounge. It contains, like the man said, "multitudes."

Sometimes I think I should feel a little guilty about writing stuff like the above.

It's porn. Albeit food and travel porn.

I had it, I lived it—and, chances are, most of the people reading this have not.

It seems ungracious to share some experiences. Though I'm sure it's difficult to accept, my parents brought me up to believe that showing off was a bad thing, a sign of generally bad manners. (I'm not saying those values took hold, just that I might have heard them mentioned.)

Some things I've seen, some experiences at tables and counters around the world, I feel a little bad telling people about. I may not hesitate to put them on TV at every opportunity—but that's . . . *different* somehow, in that it's somebody *else*, the evil camera people, the editors, doing the telling. This conveniently lets me off the hook.

But writing about sights and sounds and flavors that might otherwise be described as orgiastic—and doing it in a way that is calculated to inspire prurient interest, lust, and envy in others . . . that raises more questions in my mind as to . . . I don't know . . . the moral dimension.

Sitting here, choosing words, letter by letter, on the keyboard with the explicit intention of telling you about something I did or something I ate and making you as hungry and miserable as I can—surely that's *wrong*.

But fuck it.

Who doesn't like a good wank now and then?

Imagine . . .

There's a roast goose in Hong Kong—Mongkok, near the outskirts of the city, the place looks like any other. But you sink your teeth into the quickly hacked pieces and you know you're experiencing something special. Layers of what can only be described as enlightenment, one extraordinary sensation after another as the popils of the tongue encounter first the crispy, caramelized skin, then air, then fat—the juicy, sweet yet savory, ever so slightly gamey meat, the fat just barely managing to retain its corporeal form before quickly dematerializing into liquid. These are the kinds of tastes and textures that come with year after year of the same man making the same dish. *That* man—the one there, behind the counter with the cleaver—hacking roast pork, and roast duck, and roast goose as he's done since he was a child and as his father did before him. He's got it right now for sure—and, sitting there at one of the white Formica tables, Cantonese pop songs oozing and occasionally distorting from an undersized speaker, you know it, too. In fact, you're pretty goddamn sure this is the best roast goose on the whole planet. Nobody is eating goose better than you at this precise moment. Maybe in the whole history of the world there has never been a better goose. Ordinarily, you don't know if you'd go that far describing a dish—but now, with that ethereal goose fat dribbling down your chin, the sound of perfectly crackling skin playing inside your head to an audience of one, hyperbole seems entirely appropriate.

It's nighttime in Puebla and there are a taco lady and her husband standing behind a cart, one naked lightbulb dangling overhead, serving *tacos de lengua*, strips of beef tongue, seared with onions on a griddle. When the edges of the tongue are browned and the air fills with deliciousness, she scrapes them off the hot metal with a spatula, drops them into soft, still-warm corn tortillas, double layered—and quickly drags a spoon of salsa verde across them. She sprinkles them with fresh cilantro and a little raw, chopped onion and hands them over on a paper plate so thin it barely supports their weight without buckling. You quickly shove one of the tacos into your mouth, wash it down with a big pull from a can of cold Tecate—which you've previously rubbed with lime and jammed into a plate of salt, encrusting the top—and you can feel your eyes roll up into your head.

Standing there in the dark, stray dogs cowering expectantly just outside the corona of light from the one bulb, you've got all sorts of scary, blissed-out expressions flashing across your face. A father, mother, and two kids sit on kitchen chairs that the couple has dragged out into the street for their customers—and you hope that the kids, catching a look at you in the weird light, aren't frightened by what they see.

. . .

It's a fucking Everest of shellfish, an intimidating, multilevel tower of crushed ice and seaweed, piled, heaped—festooned with oysters from nearby Belon, and slightly farther away Cancale. There are periwinkles, whelks, palourdes, two types of gargantuan crabs—their claws reaching angrily for the sky over the carcasses of many lobsters, a tangle of meaty claws—their large bodies surrounded by the smaller ones, beady-eyed prawns and langoustines scattered about like the victims of a bus crash. What's striking is that everyone in this small café has an identical mountain range of seafood in front of them: the older couple at the table next to you, tiny figures at the next table, silently cracking and slurping their way through an ungodly amount of seafood—they look too feeble for the kind of damage they're doing, but *mais non*, the waiters scurry to keep up with the ever-filling discard bowls of empty shells. The elegant-looking woman eating by herself, the large table of Parisians— down for the weekend—they've ordered *more*. Everyone is drinking wine—whites and rosés—and, with incongruous delicacy, smearing local butter on little slices of the thin but dense brown bread before re-turning to the carnage that ensues when they grab a hold of a lobster tail and yank, with one jerking movement, tailmeat from the shell—one brutal movement—or gnash and suck their way through the broken carapace of a spider crab, dripping eggs and back fat onto their hands without care. This, too, is a good place to be. You will be in need of a nap after this. A small hotel by the port, perhaps. Pillows a little too hard, a redundant bolster, and sheets that smell slightly of bleach. The people around you, however, will be going out for dinner.

First thing in the morning in Kuching, Borneo: a hangover so bad you don't and can't even look anyone in the eye so certain are you that you said or did something truly awful after a night of *langkau*—the local rice whiskey—and (to the best of your recollection) fucking *tequila*. (And whose great idea was *that*, anyway?) You're oblivious to the view of the river, and the sights and smells of morning, focusing only on the chipped white bowl of steaming *laksa* coming your way—the promise of relief. The smell hits you first as the waiter deposits it in front of you with a clunk you feel in your pineal gland: a rich, fiery, hearty, spicy steam of fish and coconut gravy. You dig in with chopsticks and spoon, slurp your first mouthful of noodles—a powerful hit of *sambal* grabbing hold of you, exorcising the Evil. Ensuing mouthfuls bring shrimp, cockles, and fish cake . . . more spicy-sweet gravy . . . more noodles. It burns. It burns so good. You're sweating now, the poison leaving your pores, brain kick-starting . . . something that might just be hope secreting from somewhere in your shriveled, sun-dried, terribly abused cortex.

It's another one of those *agriturismos*. They're all over Italy, little mom-and-pop joints, for the most part thrown up quickly in farmhouses, private homes, on picnic tables under the trees—serving out of hearths, field kitchens. This one's in Sardinia, and what's on your plate is the simplest thing in the world: *spaghetti alla bottarga*—pasta, tossed quickly with local olive oil (through which a clove of garlic and a hot pepper have briefly been dragged) and the local salt-cured mullet eggs, which are the specialty of the region. There's no explaining why this is so good. It just . . . is. The salty and frankly fishy flavor of the eggs cuddles up to more subtle taste of the durum pasta—the tiniest notes of heat from the pepper—and the sharp yet lush tang of freshly pressed extra-virgin olive oil. You wash this down with a sneakily compelling *Cannonau*—the local red whose rough charms have lately got a serious hold on you. You don't care about the big Bordeauxs anymore. The high-maintenance Burgundies with their complex personalities. The Baron Rothschild could back his car up to the door, trunk full of monster vintages, he's drunk and offering them for free—and you would decline. Here? Now? Mopping olive oil and a few errant fish eggs from the bottom of your plate, swilling this young and proudly no-name wine, there is *nothing* you would rather be drinking.

When you ask the proprietor where the wine comes from, he points to an old man sitting in the corner reading a soccer magazine, a cigarette dangling from his lips.

"It came from him," he says.

The salarymen are getting boisterous in Shinjuku district, their workaday personalities filed away till tomorrow, rapidly being replaced—with every beer, every reciprocally poured sake—with their *real* personalities. Drunk—they're loud, friendly, angry, maudlin, horny. Over yakitori—lovingly grilled bits of artisanal chicken bits—you are particularly well placed to observe Japan's uniquely kooky national schizophrenia. A man with a headband carefully turns skewers of sizzling poultry over glowing charcoal in a metal trough. Someone gives you another beer—an oversized bottle of Sapporo in an undersized glass. The room is filled with smoke from the dripping chicken fat flaring up on the coals, from many cigarettes. You can barely see the men at the tables, sitting or leaning cross-legged in their stocking feet, some of them slumped over, falling to the side, red-faced and sweating. The thick smoke hanging in the air obscures their upper halves. Now and again, one group or another, sitting by a window, will open it for a few minutes and try to air the place out.

You're sitting at the counter, the wooden cup in front of you bristling with naked, recently gnawed skewers—a hedgehog display of dead soldiers. You've had the soft bone (breast cartilage), knee bone, thigh, chicken meatballs dipped in raw quail egg. There have been many orders of chicken hearts; chicken livers; Kobe beef tongue—little, uniformly sized bits impaled neatly on bamboo and slowly turned until

perfectly cooked, salty and slightly redolent of the handmade charcoal, garnished with sea salt—or red pepper. You've had many skewers
of chicken skin—threaded and wrapped tightly around the slivers of
bamboo, then slowly grilled until crispy, chewy, and yet still soft in
the center. But now it's all about ass. You got the last six of them and
you're pretty pleased with yourself about that. That fatty protuberance
of rich skin, each one containing fatty nubbins of flavorful, buttery
meat divided by a thin layer of cartilage—it's the single best piece of
meat and flesh on the chicken. And, of course, there's only one of them
per animal, so supply is limited. The man fighting a losing battle with
verticality across from you, his head teetering on one elbow, then sliding down his forearm from time to time, recovering just before his head
bounces off the counter—he's looking at your chicken asses and he's
angry. You don't know what he's griping about to the chef—who's heard
it all before—but you suspect that he's complaining that the lone gaijin
in the room got the last pieces of ass. You buy him a sake.

At the deli on Houston Street, they haul the pastrami steaming out of
a giant warmer and slice it thickly by hand. It's moist and so tender
you wonder how the guy gets his knife through without mashing it.
He piles the dark pink meat between too-fresh rye bread smeared
with the bright yellow mustard indigenous to these parts. Later, at the
table, the bread gives way, crumbling beneath the weight and wetness
of the pastrami. You push the salty, savory flesh around your plate
with a wedge of dill pickle, wash it down with a Dr. Brown's. The
salty, peppery, savory, spicy, and sour cut just right by the sweetness
of the soda.

Fifty miles out of Prague, the halved carcass of a freshly killed hog
hangs, still steaming in the cold, from what looks like a child's swing

set. It's a wet, drizzling morning and your feet are sopping and you've been warming yourself against the chill by huddling around the small fire over which a pot of pig parts boils. The butcher's family and friends are drinking slivovitz and beer, and though noon is still a few hours off, you've had quite a few of both. Someone calls you inside to the tiled workspace, where the butcher has mixed the pig's blood with cooked onions and spices and crumbs of country bread, and he's ready to fill the casings. Usually, they slip the casing over a metal tube, turn on the grinding machine, cram in the forcemeat or filling, and the sausages fill like magic. This guy does it differently. He chops everything by hand. A wet mesa of black filling covers his cutting board, barely retaining its shape—yet he grabs the casing in one hand, puts two fingers in one open end, makes the "V" sign, stretching it disturbingly, and reaches with the other—then buries both his hands in the mix. A whirlwind of movement as he squeezes with his right hand, using his palm like a funnel, somehow squirting the bloody, barely containable stuff straight into the opening. He does this again and again with breathtaking speed, mowing his way across the wooden table, like a thresher cutting a row through a cornfield, a long, plump, rapidly growing, glistening, fully filled length of sausage engorging to his left as he moves. It's a dark, purplish color through the translucent membrane. An assistant pinches off links, pins them with broken bits of wooden skewer. In moments, they are done.

Back in the cold backyard, you're on your fifth slivovitz when the sausages arrive in a cloud of vapor, straight from the pot. Everybody's damp and a little drunk; hard country people with rough hands and features for whom a mist of cold rain is apparently no obstacle to a meal. There is goulash, mopped with crusts of bread, and there are blood soup and many sausages. The whole of the pig is very well represented. But it's the blood sausage that sings—or, more accurately, spurts. You cut into it with your knife and it explodes across the plate like a Hollywood bullet hitting a skull—and again you think of Zola, the greatest of food pornographers, that wonderful scene in the charcuterie, our tragically absurd hero starving in the midst of ridiculous bounty. His in-laws stirring blood and spices for *boudin noir*, filling their glass display case with enticingly described delights he is unwelcome to try. It smells here like that room must have: blood and onions, paprika and a touch of nutmeg, notes of sweetness, longing . . . and death. The woman at the end of the table with a face like a concrete pylon sees you close your eyes for a second, appreciating, and she smiles.

Six o'clock in the morning is when the *pains raisins* come out, and already the customers are lining up in the dark outside this tiny Parisian *boulangerie* waiting for the first batch. The baguettes are ready—piping-hot from the brick oven, fabulously, deliberately ugly and uneven in shape, slashed crudely across the top. They're too hot to eat but you grab one anyway, tearing it open gingerly, then dropping two fingers full of butter inside. It instantly melts into liquid—running into the grooves and inner spaces of white interior. You grab it like a sandwich and bite, teeth making a cracking sound as you crunch through the crust. You haven't eaten since yesterday lunch, your palate is asleep and just not ready for so much sensation. The reaction is violent. It hurts. Butter floods your head and you think for a second you're going to black out.

On 59th Street, at a fancy Italian joint and fortified with Negronis, you're ready for a good meal—but you're not ready for the little *cicchetti* that arrive unexpectedly at the table: little pillows of sea urchin roe sitting atop tiny slices of toasted bread. Wonderful enough, one would think, but the chef has done something that goes beyond mischievous, possibly into the realm of the unholy: melting onto each plump orange egg-sac is a gossamer-thin shaving of *lardo*, the lightly cured and herbed pork fat made in marble caverns in the mountains of Tuscany, slowly curling around its prey, soon to dissolve. You hurry to put it in your mouth, knowing it's surely a sin against God—and are all the happier for it. It's too much. Way too much. Beyond rich . . . beyond briny-sweet. Beyond decency. You call the waiter over and ask for more.

This prawn comes from particularly deep waters, you are told by the man tending the coals. Special waters. He makes the charcoal himself—two different mixes. The grills are of his own design as well—gleaming, spotlessly clean metal squares, each raised and lowered to specifically selected heights by the turn of a wheel. He puts almost nothing on what he cooks. Sea salt. A spritz of Spanish olive oil from a pump bottle. He's smiling as he places the prawn in front of you and you eat the tail first, stripping away the shell and taking it in two bites. But then comes the head, twisted free and waiting for you. You raise it to your mouth and suck out the soup of hot brains, squeezing it like a toothpaste tube. Silence for a moment, then, from outside, you hear the sheep bleating faintly in the hills. The man smiles, pleased you've properly appreciated his prawn. He has something else. He removes another small pile of burning coals from one of the wood-burning ovens and places it beneath one of his jury-rigged grills, lowers the grid all the way, fans the embers. He produces another device of his own making—a sauté pan that looks more like a strainer than any known cooking vessel—sprays it lightly with oil. He heats it for a few seconds over the glowing coal, then quickly—quickly, but delicately—drops in a handful of tiny, translucent baby eels, sprinkles them with a few granules of salt while he makes them leap once, twice in the pan. In seconds, they are off the fire and into a bowl. They are, you fully appreciate (at this time of year, anyway), the rarest of the rare of God's edible creatures. Each linguine-thin eel has swum here all the way from the Sargasso Sea, upriver into northern Spain—to be caught live. The man has killed them only minutes ago, poisoning them with tobacco. During the two or three weeks you can get them (in the unlikely event you can get them at all), they sell for upwards of a thousand dollars a kilo. They are barely cooked. They don't need to be—they shouldn't be cooked more. Twirled on a fork and lifted to the mouth, they whisper secrets. This, you tell yourself, is a flavor one shouldn't speak of.

Sichuan hotpot is where you find out some very dark things about yourself. You look around at the others in the crowded, painfully bright dining room in Chengdu, wiping the backs of their necks with cold napkins, their faces red and contorted with pain. Some of them hold their stomachs. But they plow on, as you do, dipping chopsticks loaded with organ meats, fish balls, and vegetables into the giant woks of dark, sinister-looking oil. It's like that Victorian brothel in London you've read about, the one that had a spanking machine—could paddle forty customers at a time. There's that kind of consensual perversion going on here. As if we are, all of us—though strangers to one another—bound by an awful compulsion we share. The liquid boils and bubbles like witch's brew opaque, reddish brown distillate of the mind-blowingly excessive amounts of dried Sichuan chilies bobbing and roiling up throughout. The oil is cooking down, reducing by the minute and growing yet more powerful. You drag a hunk of tripe through the oil; it disappears below the surface, where it shrinks, then hardens like an aroused nipple; and then you remove it from the hell-broth and into your mouth. The heat from the dried peppers nearly lifts your head off—but there is something else. Tiny black flower peppers, floating discreetly alongside their more aggressive cousins, have an eerie numbing effect, first on your tongue—and then your entire head. There's the by now familiar floral dimension: you smell it everywhere in this part of China—it's in the air . . . But now it comes on strong, comes to the rescue; like an ice cube applied to abused flesh, it counteracts the pain and burn of way more hot pepper than any man can or should reasonably bear. Sweating through your shirt, resisting the urge to double over in pain, you begin to understand.

Pain—followed by relief.

Burn, followed by a pleasing, anesthetizing numbness. It's like being spanked and licked at the same time. You were, after many years on this planet and what you thought had been a full and rich life, pretty sure you didn't go for such things. The film *9½ Weeks* left you unmoved. At no point in your youthful misadventures would the offer of even playful discomfort have appealed—even if the person offering was a German supermodel in ass-less latex chaps.

Pain, you were pretty sure, was always bad.

Pleasure was good.

Until now, that is. When everything started to get confused.

9

Meat

I believe that the great American hamburger is a thing of beauty, its simple charms noble, pristine. The basic recipe—ground beef, salt, and pepper, formed into a patty, grilled or seared on a griddle, then nestled between two halves of a bun, usually but not necessarily accompanied by lettuce, a tomato slice, and some ketchup—is, to my mind, unimprovable by man or God. A good burger can be made more complicated, even more interesting by the addition of other ingredients—like good cheese, or bacon . . . relish perhaps, but it will never be made better.

I like a blue cheese burger as much as the next guy—when I'm in the mood for blue cheese. But if it's a burger I want, I stick to the classics: meat—and bun.

I believe this to be the best way to eat a hamburger.

I believe that the human animal evolved as it did—with eyes in the front of its head, long legs, fingernails, eyeteeth—so that it could better chase down slower, stupider creatures, kill them, and eat them;

that we are designed to find and eat meat—and only became better as a species when we learned to cook it.

We are not, however, designed to eat shit—or fecal *coli*-form bacteria, as it's slightly more obliquely referred to after an outbreak. Tens of thousands of people are made sick every year by the stuff. Some have died horribly.

Shit happens, right? Literally, it turns out. That's pretty much what I thought anyway—until I read recent news accounts of a particularly destructive outbreak of the pathogen O157:H7. What I came away with was a sense of disbelief, outrage, and horror—not so much at the fact that a deadly strain of *E. coli* found its way into our food supply and made people sick but at the way other, presumably healthy burgers are made—the ones that *didn't* make anybody sick. I was well aware—I mean, I assumed—that your frozen pre-made burger patty—the one intended for institutional or low-end, fast-food use; your slender and cheap, pre-packaged supermarket disk—was not of the best-quality cuts. But when I read in the *New York Times* that, as standard practice, when making their "American Chef's Selection Angus Beef Patties," the food giant Cargill's recipe for hamburger consisted of, among other things, "a mix of slaughterhouse trimmings and a mash-like product derived from scraps" and that "the ingredients came from slaughterhouses in Nebraska, Texas and Uruguay, and from a South Dakota company that *processes fatty trimmings and treats them with ammonia to kill bacteria*" (italics my own), well . . . I was surprised.

By the end of the article, I came away with more faith in the people who process cocaine on jungle tarpaulins—or the anonymous but hardworking folks in their underwear and goggles who cut inner-city smack—than I had in the meat industry. I was no less carnivorous, but my faith had been seriously damaged. A central tenet of my belief system, that meat—even lesser-quality meat—was essentially a "good" thing, was shaken.

Call me crazy, call me idealistic, but you know what I believe? I believe that when you're making hamburger for human consumption, you should at no time deem it necessary or desirable to treat its ingredients in ammonia. Or any cleaning product, for that matter.

I don't think that's asking a lot—and I don't ask a lot for my fellow burger-eaters. Only that whatever it is that you're putting in my hamburger? That laid out on a table or cutting board prior to grinding, it at least resembles something that your average American might recognize as "meat."

Recall, please, that this is *me* talking. I've eaten the extremities of feculent Southern warthog, every variety of gut, ear, and snout of bush meat. I've eaten raw seal, guinea pig. I've eaten bat. In every case, they were at least identifiable as coming from an animal—closer (even at their worst) to "tastes like chicken" than space-age polymer.

An enormous percentage of burger meat in this country now contains scraps from the outer part of the animal that were once deemed sufficiently "safe" only for pet food. But now, thanks to a miracle process pioneered by a company that "warms the trimmings, removes the fat in a centrifuge and treats the remaining product with ammonia," we don't have to waste perfectly good "beef" on Fluffy or Boots.

"An amalgam of meat from different slaughterhouses" is how the *Times* describes what's for dinner when you dig into "American Chef's Selection Angus Beef Patties"—but what the fuck does that mean?

Meat-industry spokesmen, when rushed to television studios to counter the blowback from the latest incident of *E. coli*–related illness, usually respond with expressions of sympathy for the victims, assurances that our meat supply is safer than ever—and the kind of measured, reasonable noises that go over well when faced with hyperbolic arguments against meat in general. But they are very cautious when pressed on the specifics. When asked to describe the kind of scraps used in a particular brand of hamburger, they will invariably describe the trimmings as coming from premium cuts like sirloin, rib, and tenderloin. Which is, of course, technically true.

But what *parts* of those cuts? "Sirloin" and "rib" sections and "primal cuts" sound pretty good—but what we're largely talking about here is the fatty, exposed outer edges that are far more likely to have come in contact with air, crap-smeared hides, other animals, and potential contaminants. The better question might be: Please tell me which of these scraps you would have been unable to use a few years ago—and exactly what do you have to do to them to make them what you would consider "safe"?

In another telling anomaly of the meat-grinding business, many of the larger slaughterhouses will sell their product only to grinders who agree to *not* test their product for *E. coli* contamination—until after it's run through the grinder with a whole bunch of other meat from other sources.

Meaning, the company who grinds all that shit together (before selling it to your school system) often can't test it until *after* they mix it with meat they bought from other (sometimes as many as three or four) slaughterhouses. It's the "Who, me?" strategy. The idea is simply that these slaughterhouses don't want to know—'cause, if they find out something's wrong, they might have to actually do something about it and be, like, accountable for this shit, recall all the product they sold to other vendors.

It's like demanding of a date that she have unprotected sex with four or five other guys immediately before sleeping with you—just so she can't point the finger directly at you should she later test positive for clap. To my way of thinking, *before* you slip into the hot tub at the *Playboy* mansion is probably when your companions would like you to be tested. Not after.

It should be pointed out, I guess, that McDonald's and most other fast-food retailers test the finished products *far* more frequently than the people who sell the stuff to them—and much more aggressively than school systems. Which, while admirable (or at least judicious on their part), seems somehow wrong.

Meat-industry flacks point to the tiny percentage of their products that end up having to be recalled—or turn out to be problematic. But we eat a *lot* of beef in this country. However small that percentage, that's still a lot of fucking hamburger.

I don't want to sound like Eric Schlosser or anything. I'm hardly an advocate for better, cleaner, healthier, or more humane—but you know what? This Cargill outfit is the largest private company in America. A hundred and sixteen *billion* dollars in revenue a year. And they feel the need to save a few cents on their low-end burgers by buying shit processed in ammonia? Scraps that have to be whipped or extracted or winnowed out or rendered before they can put them into a patty mix? Mystery meat assembled from all over the world and put through one grinder—like one big, group grope in moist, body-temperature sheets—with strangers?

I believe that, as an American, I should be able to walk into any restaurant in America and order my hamburger—that most American of foods—*medium fucking rare*. I don't believe my hamburger should have to come with a warning to cook it well done to kill off any potential contaminants or bacteria.

I believe I shouldn't have to be advised to thoroughly clean and wash up immediately after preparing a hamburger.

I believe I should be able to treat my hamburger like food, not like infectious fucking medical waste.

I believe the words "meat " and "treated with ammonia" should never occur in the same paragraph—much less the same sentence. Unless you're talking about surreptitiously disposing of a corpse.

This is not Michael Pollan talking to you right now—or Eric Schlosser, whose zeal on this subject is well documented. I don't, for instance, feel the same way about that other great American staple, the hot dog. With the hot dog, there was always a feeling of implied consent. We always *knew*—or assumed—that whatever it was inside that snappy tube, it *might* contain anything, from 100 percent kosher beef to dead zoo animals or parts of missing Gambino family. With a hot dog, especially New York's famous "dirty-water hot dog," there was a tacit agreement that you were on your own. They were pre-cooked, anyway, so how bad could it be?

The hamburger is different. It's a more intimate relationship. Unlike the pre-cooked German import, the hot dog, the hamburger—or ground beef—has been embraced as an expression of our national identity. The backyard barbeque, Mom's meatloaf—these are American traditions, rights of passage.

Is it too much to feel that it should be a basic right that one can cook and eat a hamburger without fear? To stand proud in my backyard (if I had a backyard), grilling a nice medium-rare fucking hamburger for my kid—without worrying that maybe I'm feeding her a shit sandwich? That I not feel the need to cross-examine my mother, should she have the temerity to offer my child meatloaf?

I shouldn't have to ask for this—or demand it—or even talk about it.

It's my birthright as an American, God damn it. And anybody who fucks with my burger, who deviates from the time-honored bond that one has come to expect of one's burger vendor—that what one is eating is inarguably "beef" (not necessarily the best beef, mind you, but definitely recognizable as something that was, before grinding, mostly red, reasonably fresh, presumably from a steer or cow, something that your average Doberman would find enticing)—anybody selling burgers that can't even conform to that not particularly high standard is, in my opinion, unpatriotic and un-American, in the truest, most heartfelt sense of those words.

If you are literally serving shit to American children, or knowingly spinning a wheel where it is not unlikely that you will eventually serve shit—if that's your business model? Then I got no problems with a jury of your peers wiring your nuts to a car battery and feeding you the accumulated sweepings of the bottom of a monkey cage. In fact, I'll hold the spoon.

In this way, me and the PETA folks and the vegetarians have something in common, an area of overlapping interests. They don't want us to eat any meat. I'm beginning to think, in light of recent accounts, that we should, on balance, eat a little *less* meat.

PETA doesn't want stressed animals to be cruelly crowded into sheds, ankle-deep in their own crap, because they don't want any animals to die—ever—and basically think that chickens should, in time, gain the right to vote. *I* don't want animals stressed or crowded or treated cruelly or inhumanely because that makes them provably less delicious. And, often, less safe to eat.

Many people will tell you it is America's distorted relationship with what, in grammar school, we used to know as the "food triangle"—a hierarchy of food that always led up to meat—that's killing us slowly, clogging our airports and thoroughfares with the ever larger, ever slower-moving morbidly obese, huffing and puffing their way to an early grave. That our exploding health-care costs are increasingly attributable to what we eat (and how much) rather than, say, cigarettes—or even drugs. Which is fine, I guess, in a personal-choice kind of way if, as with heroin, you play and are then willing to pay.

I like to think of myself as leaning toward libertarianism—I am very uncomfortable when the government says that it has to step in and make that most fundamental of decisions *for* us: what we should or shouldn't put in our mouths. In a perfect world, individuals would be free to take all the heroin they wanted—and stuff their faces with trans fats as much as they like—until it becomes a problem for their neighbors. Which it clearly has.

Our insatiable lust for cheap meat is, in fact, fucking us up. Our distorted expectations of the daily meal are undermining the basic underpinnings of our society in ways large and small. That we're becoming a nation that (in the words of someone much smarter than I) is solely "in the business of selling cheeseburgers to each other" is pretty undeniable—if you add that we are, at even our most privileged end, in the business of lending money to people who sell cheeseburgers to each other.

The cruelty and ugliness of the factory farm—and the effects on our environment—are, of course, repellent to any reasonable person. But it's the general lowering of standards inherent in our continuing insistence on cheap burgers—wherever they might come from and however bad they taste; the collective, post-ironic shrug we've come to give each other as we knowingly dig into something that tastes, at best, like cardboard and soured onion—that's hurting us.

In the America *not* ruled by the imperative to buy and sell cheap ground meat, however, something has been happening to my beloved hamburger, something about which I have mixed emotions. The slow, creeping influence of the "boutique" burger, the "designer" burger.

Years ago—so many now that few of us even remember—there was a time when most Americans had similar expectations of coffee as they have traditionally had of the hamburger. That a decent, cheap—but not necessarily great—cup of coffee in a cardboard container or heavy Buffalo china receptacle was a birthright. Coffee, it was generally accepted, did, and should, cost about fifty cents to a dollar—often with unlimited refills. Then Starbucks came along, whose particular genius was not the dissemination of such concepts as "latte," "half-caf," and "mochaccino," or new terms for sizes, like "venti." Nor did their brilliance lie in the particularly good quality of their coffee.

Starbucks's truly beautiful idea was the simple realization that Americans *wanted* to spend more money for a cup of coffee, that they'd feel much better about themselves if they spent *five* dollars for a cup of joe rather than buy that cheap drip stuff that shows such as *Friends* suggested only fat white trash in housecoats (or people who actually worked for a living) drank anymore—in their trailer parks or meth labs or wherever such people huddled for comfort.

And America wanted to drink its coffee (or, more accurately, linger over it) in places that looked very much like . . . Starbucks, where young, attractive people (like the cast of *Friends*) sipped their coffees and spent their time and no doubt engaged in witty banter between cranberry muffins. To a faint soundtrack featuring the nonthreatening musical stylings of Natalie Merchant. For five bucks a pop.

A while ago, the guy behind the counter (and he sure as shit wasn't called a "barista") asked you for five bucks for a cup of coffee—*any* coffee—he'd better expect an argument, at least. Now? You wouldn't blink. The entire valuation of coffee has changed while we weren't looking.

This, I suspect, is what's already happened and will continue to happen with the hamburger. The fashion industry figured this out long ago. Relatively few people could afford a Gucci suit. But they could surely afford a T-shirt with GUCCI printed on it. What's happening is that five years from now, all those people who could never afford to eat at, say, Craft, will surely be able to buy a Tom Colicchio Burger. And I'm guessing, by the way, that—unlike a Chinese-made T-shirt with a logo on it—it'll be a pretty good burger.

Things keep going the way they're going, and the "good" burger, the designer burger, the one you'd entrust your child to, the one you want your friends to see you eating—that'll be $24, please.

You'd think the major meat-packers should have seen this coming—should have seen that saving 30 cents a pound is all fine and good—but not when, a few years down the line, they risk losing the market. A few more *E. coli* outbreaks in fast-food outlets or school systems, and you're likely to see a tail-off. Few parents are going to let their little Ambers or Tiffanys eat the stuff that they're talking about on CNN all the time—next to the pictures of dead children and diseased animals. It's really only a matter of time until—through a combination of successful demonization, genuine health concerns, and changing eating habits—America will actually start eating fewer of those gray disks of alleged "meat."

If recent history has taught us anything, though, it's that Big

Food is way ahead of us with their market research. In all likelihood, when and if America sours on the generic burger, they'll be waiting for us on the other end with open arms. As incisively pointed out in the documentary *Food Inc.*, an overwhelmingly large percentage of "new," "healthy," and "organic" alternative food products are actually owned by the same parent companies that scared us into the organic aisle in the first place. "They got you comin' and goin'" has never been truer. Like breaking a guy's leg—so you can be there to sell him a crutch. "We're here for you—when you get sick of, or too frightened of, our other product. Of course it'll cost a little more. But then you expected that."

Maybe an early warning sign, the beginning of a major shift in attitude came not from health concerns, or rising awareness, or the success of such excellent books as *Fast Food Nation* and *The Omnivore's Dilemma*, but from whatever devious and cynical chef first came up with the concept of the "Kobe burger."

He or she can hardly be blamed. The times when this seminal event occurred were surely ripe for it. New York City restaurants were clogged with loud, pin-striped, yet-to-be-indicted fuck-nuts hedge funders who relished the opportunity to showily throw a hundred dollars at a burger. Kobe, after all, was the "best" beef in the world, wasn't it? It came from, like, Japan, from, like, special cows who get . . . massaged in beer and shit, don't they? "I hear they even jack them off!!"

This was the story going around anyway, as high-fiving day traders from some by-now-defunct investment bank or brokerage house hurried, lemming-like, to order the "best burger ever." Of course, chances are, the "Kobe beef" in that Kobe beef burger had never been anywhere near Japan. It was a distant relative at best—and even if the sublimely fatty product of pampered Wagyu cattle *was* used in the burger, it would have been (and remains) an utterly pointless, supremely wasteful, and even unpleasant exercise.

What makes a Wagyu steak so desirable is the unbelievably prodigious marbling of fat that runs through it—often as much as 50 percent. Its resulting tenderness and richness, and the subtle—repeat—*subtle* flavor. When grinding a hamburger, you can put in as much fat as you like—just reach in the fat can and drop it in the machine—so there's no reason to pay a hundred bucks for a burger. A burger, presumably, already *is* about as tender as a piece of meat can be—and a taste as subtle as real Wagyu's would, in any case, be lost were you to do something so insensitive as bury it between two buns and slather it with ketchup.

A six-ounce *tataki* of real Wagyu steak, seared rare and sliced thinly, is about all you want or can eat in a sitting. It's that rich. It'll flood your head with so much fat you'll quickly reach a point of diminishing returns. Even an eight-ounce "Kobe burger" made from real Wagyu would be an exercise in futility—and pretty disgusting.

But no. The cream of big-city douchedom ordered these things in droves, bragging about it all the way. It quickly became clear to chefs and restaurateurs that there was a huge, previously untapped market out there for expensive hamburgers—that customers at a certain income level, clearly, were willing, even eager, to pay more. All you had to do was put a "brand" name next to the word "hamburger" and you could add value. That brand could be the name of a famous chef (many of whom wisely began to flock to the concept) or the name of a boutique producer (something that, like the word "Kobe," implied specially raised, artisanal, humanely treated, organic, or sexually satisfied cattle). Chefs added "extras" like foie gras, truffles, braised oxtail, the exotic cheeses of many lands.

Restaurateur Jeffrey Chodorow's New York restaurant Kobe Club— a name that implied an establishment where sophisticated gentlemen of the world could gather, mingle with others in the know, share meat-related experiences with like-minded movers and shakers—was meant to be the apotheosis of this concept.

But Chodorow was a little late to the party—New Yorkers had moved on.

Instinctively suspicious of designer labels—as potentially being something they might like in New Jersey—and uneasy with the crassness of the whole Kobe Club concept, New York foodies looked elsewhere for a prestige patty. Perhaps Kobe suffered from its association with Chodorow, a man whom food writers find an irresistible target. It's almost obligatory for food bloggers to mock his latest ventures—often before they are even open for business. Sneering at Chodorow is like making a mean crack about film director Brett Ratner if you're a budding film critic. It immediately asserts one's bona fides as a serious observer. (Chodorow, like Ratner, seems only too happy to oblige: see such absurd, bizarro pastiches of restaurants past as Rocco's, the reality show–driven abomination; Caviar and Banana, a vaguely Brazilian follow-up; English Is Italian [he isn't]; and his latest, a jumbo-size attempt to straddle the Asian fusion, sushi, and *izakaya* markets. Even veteran food critics can't resist giving him a kick whenever the opportunity presents itself. The jokes write themselves.)

In post-Kobe New York, a new way to pay more for a burger was needed. And smearing foie gras or house-made relish on it was not going to be enough. A return to purist notions of the hamburger began to take hold—even an orthodoxy—in such forums where these things are earnestly considered and discussed. A virtuous burger, it was argued by aficionados, was the "original" recipe, a "roots" burger, unsullied by "foreign" or modern flavors, one whose meaty charm spoke for itself. Said burger should come from the very best mix of the very best parts of the very best quality beef from animals of verifiably excellent breeding. And it should be cooked "right" (whatever that implied).

Enter New York's Minetta Tavern, where the Black Label Burger is of an exclusive blend prepared by Pat LaFrieda from grass-fed, free-range, organically raised Creekstone Farms beef. Seared simply and unapologetically on a griddle—where, we are assured, God intended us to cook our burgers—and served on a bun with a little onion confit, a slice of tomato, and a leaf of lettuce, everything new is old again. Only it's 26 dollars now.

This *is* indeed one king-hell, motherfucker of a burger—one that would be seriously difficult to top in a blind taste-off of "experts." Arguably, it's worth the bucks, if you have that kind of money—and, face it, if you're eating at the Minetta Tavern, you probably do.

But the speed with which accomplished and forward-thinking high-end chefs like Laurent Tourondel, Daniel Boulud, Tom Colicchio, Hubert Keller, Bobby Flay—and even Emeril—made their moves to exploit the new frontiers of the "hamburger concept" has been breathtaking. And all of them, let it be pointed out, indeed serve a damn good burger. It's already the Next Big Thing—and is likely to stay the big thing for the conceivable future. If anything, it's only the beginning—a trend that fits perfectly with the times, a relatively affordable (still) luxury item for a difficult economic environment, something that plays neatly into the national mood: the desire for comforting, reassuring food, the backlash against "fancy," "silly," or "hoity-toity"–sounding dishes, a growing sense of discomfort with the traditional food supply, and the reverse snobbery of foodie elites who enjoy nothing more than arguing over what might be the most "authentic" version of quotidian classics.

But what of the burger of lore? The adequate, presumably safe (we thought so, anyway) utility burger, draped and leaking clear grease across the bottom of an open bun, accompanied by an unripe tomato slice, a drying onion slice, and a leaf of iceberg that no one will ever eat . . . a limp wedge of obligatory dill pickle, a single slice of Kraft "cheese food," half-melted and congealing even now, kitty-corner across the top? Will it disappear like the vivid, brightly colored Americana on Howard Johnson's menus past? The ham steaks checkerboarded with grill marks and garnished with pineapple rings, and the thick-crusted chicken potpies of earlier decades?

Will more assurances be necessary to future customers before slightly more expensive patties can be sold?

"Now serving our Chaste Quaker Farms mélange of grain-fed Angus beef—minimally dosed with antibiotics and made only slightly uncomfortable during its final days in a dark, shit-smeared shed."

Or will the default-quality burger—the classic "mystery meat" patty—continue to survive and flourish indefinitely? Simply more expensive by two dollars or so?

Surely the message for the Greek couple at the luncheonette down the road, sizzling up the same frozen patties on a Mel Fry–smeared griddle, like they always have, is that for *some* reason or another, the ass-hats down the street are paying eighteen bucks for a burger. We can definitely get away with jacking up our price by a dollar or two.

Maybe this whole burger thing is part of a larger shift—where *all* the everyday foods of everyday Americans are being slowly, one after the other, co-opted, upgraded, reinvented, and finally marked up.

Look around.

In the hottest restaurants of New York, San Francisco, and Chicago, it's the rich who are lining up to eagerly pay top dollar for the hooves, snouts, shanks, and tripe the poor used to *have* to eat.

You'd have to go to Mario Batali and slap down twenty dollars to find an order of chitterlings these days. You can look far and wide in Harlem without finding pig's feet. But Daniel Boulud has them on the menu.

Regular pizza may be on the endangered list, "artisanal" pizza having already ghettoized the utility slice. Even the cupcake has become a boutique item . . . and the humble sausage is now the hottest single food item in New York City. Order a Heineken in Portland or San Francisco—or just about anywhere, these days—and be prepared to be sneered at by some locavore beer-nerd, all too happy to tell you about some hoppy, malty, microbrewed concoction, redolent of strawberries and patchouli, that they're making in a cellar nearby. Unless, of course, you opt for post-ironic retro—in which case, that "silo" of PBR will come with a cover charge and an asphyxiating miasma of hipness.

David Chang sells "cereal milk" in sixteen-ounce bottles for five bucks. An infusion, as I understand it, of the metabolized essence of cereal, the extracted flavors of Captain Crunch with Crunchberries perhaps, the sweet, vaguely pinkish milk left in the bottom of the bowl after you've drunkenly spooned and chawed your way through the solids. Maybe this is the high-water mark of the phenomenon. And then again, maybe not.

When and if the good guys win, will we—after terrifying consumers about our food supply, fetishizing expensive ingredients, exploiting the hopes, aspirations, and insecurities of the middle class—have simply made it more expensive to eat the same old crap? More to the point, have I?

Am I helping, once again, to kill the things I love?

10

Lower Education

My wife and I are speaking in hushed tones directly outside our daughter's bedroom door, where we're sure she's pretending to be asleep.

"Sssshhhh!! She can hear us," says my wife, with a theatricality intended to sound conspiratorial.

"No, she's asleep," I hiss—a little too loudly. A stage whisper.

We're talking about Ronald McDonald again. Bringing up the possibility of his being implicated in the disappearance of yet another small child.

"Not *another one*?!" gasps my wife with feigned incredulity.

"I'm afraid so," I say with concern. "Stepped inside to get some fries and a Happy Meal and hasn't been seen since . . ."

"Are they searching for her?"

"Oh yes . . . they're combing the woods . . . checked out the Hamburglar's place—but of course, they're focusing on Ronald again."

"Why Ronald?"

"Well . . . last time? When they finally found that other one? What was his name—Little . . . Timmy? The police found evidence. On the body . . . They found . . . cooties."

This is just one act in an ongoing dramatic production—one small part of a larger campaign of psychological warfare. The target? A two-and-a-half-year-old girl.

The stakes are high. As I see it, nothing less than the heart, mind, soul, and physical health of my adored only child. I am determined that the Evil Empire not have her, and to that end, I am prepared to use what Malcolm X called "any means necessary."

McDonald's have been very shrewd about kids. Say what you will about Ronald and friends, they know their market—and who drives it. They haven't shrunk from targeting young minds—in fact, their entire gazillion-dollar promotional budget seems aimed squarely at toddlers. They know that one small child, crying in the backseat of a car of two overworked, overstressed parents will, more often than not, determine the choice of restaurants. They know exactly when and how to start building brand identification and brand loyalty with brightly colored clowns and smoothly tied-in toys. They know that Little Timmy will, with care and patience and the right exposure to brightly colored objects, grow up to be a full-size consumer of multiple Big Macs. It's why Ronald McDonald is said to be more recognizable to children everywhere than Mickey Mouse or Jesus.

Personally, I don't care if my little girl ever recognizes those two other guys—but I do care about her relationship with Ronald. I want her to see American fast-food culture as I do. As the enemy.

From funding impoverished school districts to the shrewd install-ment of playgrounds, McDonald's has not shrunk from fucking with young minds in any way they can. They're smart. And I would not take that right to propagandize, advertise—whatever—from them. If it's okay for Disney to insinuate itself into young lives everywhere, it should be okay for Ronald. I see no comfortable rationale for attacking them in the courts. They are, in any case, too powerful.

Where you take on the Clown and the King and the Colonel is in the streets—or, more accurately, in the same impressionable young minds they have so successfully fucked with for so long.

My intention is to fuck with them right back.

It's shockingly easy.

Eric Schlosser's earnest call to arms, *Fast Food Nation*, may have had the facts on its side, but that's no way to wean a three-year-old off Happy Meals—much less hold her attention. The Clown, the King, the Colonel—and all their candy-colored high-fructose friends—are formidable foes. And if the history of conflict has taught us anything, it's that one seldom wins a battle by taking the high road. This is not a debate that will be won on the facts. Kids don't give a shit about calorie count—or factory farming, or the impact that America's insatiable desire for cheap ground meat may have on the environment or our society's health.

But cooties they understand.

What's the most frightening thing to a child? The pain of being the outsider, of looking ridiculous to others, of being teased or picked on in school. Every child burns with fear at the prospect. It's a primal instinct: to belong. McDonald's has surely figured this out—along with what specific colors appeal to small children, what textures, and what movies or TV shows are likely to attract them to the gray disks of meat. They feel no compunction harnessing the fears and unarticulated yearnings of small children, and nor shall I.

"Ronald has cooties," I say—every time he shows up on television or out the window of the car. "And you know," I add, lowering my voice, "he *smells* bad, too. Kind of like . . . *poo!*" (I am, I should say, careful to use the word "alleged" each and every time I make such an assertion, mindful that my urgent whisperings to a two-year-old might be wrongfully construed as libelous.)

"If you hug Ronald . . . can you get cooties?" asks my girl, a look of wide-eyed horror on her face.

"Some say . . . yes," I reply—not wanting to lie—just in case she should encounter the man at a child's birthday party someday. It's a lawyerly answer—but effective. "Some people talk about the smell, too . . . I'm not saying it rubs off on you or anything—if you get too close to him—but . . ." I let that hang in the air for a while.

"Ewwww!!!" says my daughter.

We sit in silence as she considers this, then she asks, "Is it true that if you eat a hamburger at McDonald's it can make you a *ree-tard*?"

I laugh wholeheartedly at this one and give her a hug. I kiss her on the forehead reassuringly. "Ha. Ha. Ha. I don't know *where* you get these ideas!"

I may or may not have planted that little nugget a few weeks ago, allowing her little friend Tiffany at ballet class to "overhear" it as I pretended to talk on my cell phone. I've been tracking this bit of misinformation like a barium meal as it worked its way through the kiddie underground—waiting, waiting for it to come out the other side—and it's finally popping up now. Bingo.

The CIA calls this kind of thing "Black Propaganda," and it's a sensible, cost-effective countermeasure, I believe, to the overwhelming superiority of the forces aligned against us.

I vividly recall a rumor about rat hairs in Chunky candies when I was a kid. It swept across schoolyards nationwide—this in pre-Internet days—and had, as I remember it, a terrible effect on the company's sales. I don't know where the rumor started. And it was proven to be untrue.

I'm not suggesting anybody do anything so morally wrong and unquestionably illegal.

I'm just sayin'.

Posting calorie information is, according to a recent *New York Times* article, not working. America's thighs get ever wider. Type-2 diabetes is becoming alarmingly common among children.

It is repugnant, in principle, to me—the suggestion that we legislate against fast food. We will surely have crossed some kind of terrible line if we, as a nation, are infantilized to the extent that the government has to step in and take the Whoppers right out of our hands. It is dismaying—and probably inevitable. When we reach the point that we are unable to raise a military force of physically fit specimens—or public safety becomes an issue after some lurid example of large person blocking a fire exit—they surely shall.

A "fat tax" is probably on the horizon as well—an idea that worked with cigarettes.

First they taxed cigarettes to the point of cruelty. Then they pushed smokers out of their work spaces, restaurants, bars—even, in some cases, their homes. After being penalized, demonized, marginalized, herded like animals into the cold, many—like me—finally quit.

I don't want my daughter treated like that.

I say, why wait?

I don't think it's right or appropriate that we raise little girls in a world where freakishly tiny, anorexic actresses and bizarrely lanky, unhealthily thin models are presented as ideals of feminine beauty. No one should ever feel pressured to conform to that image.

But neither do I think it's "okay" to be unhealthily overweight. It is not an "alternative lifestyle choice" or "choice of body image" if you need help to get out of your car.

I think constantly about ways to "help" my daughter in her food choices—without bringing the usual pressures to bear. "Look how nice and *thin* that Miley Cyrus is" are not words that shall leave my lips, as such notions might drive a young girl to bulimia, bad boyfriends, and, eventually, crystal meth.

So, when I read of a recent study that found that children are significantly more inclined to eat "difficult" foods like liver, spinach, broccoli—and other such hard-to-sell "but-it's-good-for-you" classics—when they are wrapped in comfortingly bright packages from McDonald's, I was at first appalled, and then . . . inspired.

Rather than trying to co-opt Ronald's all-too-effective credibility among children to short-term positive ends, like getting my daughter to eat the occasional serving of spinach, I could reverse-engineer this! Use the strange and terrible powers of the Golden Arches for good—not evil!

I plan to dip something decidedly unpleasant in an enticing chocolate coating and then wrap it carefully in McDonald's wrapping paper. Nothing dangerous, mind you, but something that a two-and-a-half-year-old will find "yucky!"—even upsetting—in the extreme. Maybe a sponge soaked with vinegar. A tuft of hair. A Barbie head. I will then place it inside the familiar cardboard box and leave it—as if forgotten—somewhere for my daughter to find. I might even warn her, "If you see any of that nasty McDonald's . . . make sure you don't eat it!" I'll say, before leaving her to it. "Daddy was stupid and got some chocolate . . . and now he's lost it . . ." I might mutter audibly to myself before taking a long stroll to the laundry room.

An early, traumatic, Ronald-related experience can only be good for her.

11

I'm Dancing

Well I don't want some cocaine sniffing triumph in the bar
Well I don't want a triumph in the car
I don't want to make a rich girl crawl
What I want is a girl that I care about
Or I want no one at all . . .
   —JONATHAN RICHMAN, *"Someone I Care About"*

I'm dancing.

The twist, actually—or something very much like it. And though I am mortified by the very thought of dancing in front of witnesses, I am not alone in this room. Around me, nine or ten Filipina nannies and their charges are also swiveling their hips and moving to the music in their stocking feet. My dance partner is a two-year-old girl in pink tights and a tutu. The red stuff beneath my fingernails is, I suspect, vestigial Play-Doh.

This, I am fully aware, is not cool. This is as far away from cool as a man can get. But I am in no way troubled by such thoughts. I crossed that line a long time ago. If anything, I'm feeling pretty good about myself—in the smug, Upper East Side, Bugaboo-owning, sidewalk-hogging, self-righteous kind of a way indigenous to my new tribe. I am, after all, the only parent here on this fine Tuesday afternoon, alone among the gyrating nannies, the little Sophias, Vanessas, Julias, Emmas, and Isabellas. My daughter, grinning maniacally as she jumps and twists about three feet below me, is very pleased that I am here. "That's right, I *do* love you *more* than the mothers of all these other children love *them*. That's why Daddy's here—and they're *not*. *They're* getting their fucking nails done, having affairs, going to Pilates class, or whatever *bad* parents do . . . I'm here for you, *Boo* . . . twistin' my heart out—something I would never ever have done for any other person in my whole life. Only for you. I'm a good daddy. *Goooood* Daddy!"

Later, if she's good, there will be ice cream. I will seat her prominently next to me, facing the street in her Petit Bateau jumper, secretly hoping that passersby will notice how beautiful she is, how cute we are together, what a *great* dad I am. Holding her little hand, or carrying her on my shoulders, I will float home on a cloud of self-congratulation.

I'm through being cool. Or, more accurately, I'm through entertaining the notion that anybody could even consider the possibility of coolness emanating from or residing anywhere near me. As any conscientious father knows in his bones, any remaining trace elements of coolness go right out the window from the second you lay eyes on your firstborn. The second you lean in for the action, see your baby's head make that first quarter-corkscrew turn toward you, well . . . you know you can and should throw your cherished black leather motorcycle jacket right in the nearest trash bin. Clock's ticking on the earring, too. It's somehow . . . undignified now.

Norman Mailer described the desire to be cool as a "decision to encourage the psychopath in oneself, to explore that domain of experience where security is boredom and therefore sickness and one exists in the present, in that enormous present which is without past or future, memory or planned intention."

I encouraged the psychopath in myself for most of my life. In fact, that's a rather elegant description of whatever it was I was doing. But I figure I put in my time.

The essence of cool, after all, is not giving a fuck.

And let's face it: I most definitely give a fuck now. I give a huge fuck. The hugest. Everything else—*everything*—pales. To pretend otherwise, by word or deed, would be a monstrous lie. There will be no more Dead Boys T-shirts. Whom would I be kidding? Their charmingly nihilistic worldview in no way mirrors my own. If Stiv Bators were still alive and put his filthy hands anywhere near my baby, I'd snap his neck—then thoroughly cleanse the area with baby wipes.

There is no hope of hipness.

As my friend A. A. Gill points out, after your daughter reaches a certain age—like five—the most excruciating and embarrassing thing she could possibly imagine is seeing her dad in any way threatening to *rock*. Your record collection may indeed be cooler than your daughter's will ever be, but this is a meaningless distinction now. She doesn't care. And nobody else will. If you're lucky, long after you're gone, a grandchild will rediscover your old copy of *Fun House*. But it will be way too late for you to bask in the glory of past coolness.

There is nothing cool about "used to be cool."

All of this, I think, is only right and appropriate. Too much respect for your elders is, historically, almost always a bad thing. I want my daughter to love me. I don't necessarily want her to share my taste for Irish ale or Hawaiian bud.

When you see the children of the perennially cool—on shows like *Behind the Music*—they look sheepish and slightly doomed, talking about their still-working rock-'n'-roller dads, as if they are the reluctant warders of some strange breed of extravagantly wrinkly and badly behaved children. Kids may not be old enough to know what cool *is*, but they are unerring in their ability to sense what *isn't*.

No kid really wants a cool parent. "Cool" parents, when I was a kid, meant parents who let you smoke weed in the house—or allowed boyfriends to sleep over with their daughters. That would make Sarah Palin "cool." But, as I remember, we thought those parents were kind of creepy. They were useful, sure, but what was wrong with them that they found us so entertaining? Didn't they have their own friends? Secretly, we hated them.

Turning thirty came as a cruel surprise for me. I hadn't really planned on making it that far. I'd taken seriously the maxims of my time—"Never trust anyone over thirty" and "Live fast, die young"—and been frankly shocked when I found that I'd lived that long. I'd done everything I could think of to ensure the opposite result, but there I was—and without a Plan B. The restaurant business provided a degree of stability in that there were usually people who expected me to get up in the morning and go somewhere—and heroin, if nothing else, was useful in giving me a sense of *purpose* in my daily movements. I *knew* what I had to do every day for most of my early thirties: get heroin.

Of my first marriage, I'll say only that watching Gus Van Sant's *Drugstore Cowboy*—particularly the relationship between Matt Dillon's Bob and Kelly Lynch's Dianne—inspires feelings of great softness and sentiment in me. It's a reminder that even the worst times can be happy ones—until they aren't.

By my late thirties, I found that I was still lingering, and I admit to a sense of disappointment, confusion—even defeat. "What do I do *now*?" I remember thinking. Detoxed from heroin and methadone, and having finally—*finally*—ended a lifelong love affair with cocaine. Where was my reward for all this self-denial? Shouldn't I have been feeling good? If anything, all that relative sobriety pointed up a basic emptiness and dissatisfaction in my life, a hole I'd managed to fill with various chemicals for the better part of twenty-five years.

At forty-four, shortly after writing *Kitchen Confidential*, I found myself suddenly with a whole new life. One minute, I was standing next to a deep fryer, pan-searing pepper steaks—and the next, I was sitting on top of a dune, watching the sun set over the Sahara. I was running road blocks in Battambang; tiny feet were walking on my back in Siem Reap; I was eating at El Bulli.

Shortly before the breakup of my first marriage, I embarked on the equivalent of a massive public works project in my apartment: new shelves, furniture, carpets, appliances—all the trappings, I thought, of a "normal" and "happy" life—the kind of things I'd never really had or lived around since childhood. I wrote a crime novel around that time, in which the characters' yearnings for a white-picket-fence kind of a life reflect my own far more truthfully than any nonfiction I've ever written. Shortly after that, I cruelly burned down my previous life in its entirety.

There was a period of . . . readjustment.

I recall the precise second when I decided that I wanted to—that I was going to be—a father.

Wanting a child is easy enough. I'd always—even in the bad old days—thought fondly of the times my father would carry me aloft on his shoulders into the waves off the Jersey Shore, saying, "Here comes a *big* one!" I'd remembered my own five-year-old squeals of terror and delight and thought I'd like to do that with a child someday, see that look on my own child's face. But I knew well that I was the sort of person who shouldn't and couldn't be a daddy. Kids liked me fine—my niece and nephew, for instance—but it's easy to make kids like you, especially when you're the indulgent "evil uncle."

I'd never lived in an environment where a child would have been a healthy fit—and I'd never felt like I was a suitably healthy person. I'd think of fatherhood from time to time, look at myself in the mirror, and think, "That guy may *want* a child; he's simply not up to the job." And, well, for most of my life I'd been way too far up my own ass to be of any use to anyone—something that only got worse after *Kitchen Confidential.*

I don't know exactly when the possibility of that changing presented itself—but sometime, I guess, after having made every mistake, having already fucked up in every way a man can fuck up, having realized that I'd had *enough* cocaine, that no amount in the world was going to make me any happier. That a naked, oiled supermodel was not going to make everything better in my life—nor any sports car known to man. It was sometime after that.

The precise moment of realization came in my tiny fourth-floor walk-up apartment on Ninth Avenue. Above Manganaro's Heroboy restaurant—next building over from Esposito Pork Shop. I was lying in bed with my then-girlfriend—I guess you could diplomatically call it "spooning"—and I caught myself thinking, "I could make a baby with this woman. I'd *like* to make a baby with this woman. *Fuck*, I'd not only be *happy* to make a baby with this woman, I think . . . I'm pretty sure . . . I'd actually be *good* at it."

We discussed this. And Ottavia—that was (is) her name—also thought this was a fine idea, though of my prospects for a quick insemination she was less optimistic.

"Baby," she said (insert a very charming Italian accent—with the tone and delivery of a busy restaurant manager), "you're old. Your sperm. Eez—a dead."

Assuming a long campaign, we planned to get at it as soon as I returned from shooting my next show. In Beirut.

Of that episode I've written elsewhere. Long and short of it: my camera crew and I were caught in a war. For about a week, we holed up in a hotel, watching and listening to the bombs, feeling their impact rolling through the floors. After some drama, we were evacuated from a beach onto Landing Craft Units by American Navy and Marine personnel and taken first to a cargo vessel in the Med and then on to Cyprus.

My network had very generously provided a private jet to take me and the crew back home. None of my crew had ever been on a private jet before, and we slept and played cards and ate omelets prepared by the flight attendant, finally landing on a rainy, gray morning in Teterboro, New Jersey. We walked across the tarmac to a small private terminal, where Pat Younge—the president of the network—and Ottavia, as well as the crew's wives and family, were there to meet us. It was, to say the least, an emotional homecoming with much hugging and crying.

I took Ottavia back to my crummy apartment and we made a baby. Nothing like eight days of fear and desperation to concentrate the mind, I guess. A few weeks later, we were in a car on the way from LAX into Los Angeles, where I was about to appear as judge on *Top Chef*, when we got the news from Ottavia's doctor over the phone. There are photos of me, sitting on a bed in the Chateau Marmont, holding five different brands of drugstore pregnancy tests—all of them positive—a giddily idiotic grin on my face. Strangely, perhaps, I had no fear. At no time then—or since—did I have second thoughts. "What am I getting into?" never flashed across my brain.

I was the star pupil at Lamaze class. If your water ever breaks at the supermarket and I'm nearby? I'm your boy. I know just what to do.

I look back on my less well-behaved days with few regrets. True, the responsibilities of marriage and fatherhood demand certain behavioral adjustments. But my timing couldn't have been better. I find myself morphing—however awkwardly—into respectability just as things are getting really hot on the streets for any of my peers who are even semi-recognizable. The iniquitousness of Twitter and food- and chef-related Web sites and blogs has totally changed the game for anyone with a television show—even me. You don't have to be very famous at all these days to end up with a blurry photograph on DumbAssCelebrities.com. You don't want your daughter's little schoolmates reading about her daddy, stuttering drunk, two o'clock in the morning, at a chef-friendly bar, doing belly shots from a chunky and underdressed cocktail waitress—something that could well have happened a few years ago. In a day when a passing cell-phone user can easily get a surreptitious photo of you, slinking out of the porn shop with copies of *Anal Rampage 2* and *MILFBusters* under your arm, and post it in real time, maybe that's a particularly good time to trade in the leather jacket for some cotton Dockers.

I love the saying "Nobody likes a dirty old man or a clean little boy." I was, unfortunately, overly clean as a child—the fruit of a fastidious household. I shall try and make up for those years by doing my best to avoid becoming the former. Like I said, my timing—even without the daddyhood thing—was good.

It's all about the little girl. Because I am acutely aware of both her littleness (how could I be otherwise) and the fact that she's a blank page, her brain a soft surface waiting for the irreversible impressions of every raised voice, every gaffe and unguarded moment. The fact that she's a girl requires, I believe, extra effort. Dada may have, at various times in his life, *been* a pig, but Dada surely does not want to ever *look* like a pig again. This can't possibly be overstated. As the first of two boys, I can't even imagine what it must be like for a little girl to see her dad leering at another of her sex. This creature will soon grow up to be a young *woman* and that's something I consider every day.

I figure, I'm going to spoil the shit out of this kid for a while, then pack her off to tae kwon do as soon as she's four years old. Her first day of second grade and Little Timmy at the desk behind her tries to pull her hair? He's getting an elbow to the thorax. My little girl may grow up with lots of problems: spoiled; with unrealistic expectations of the world; cultural identification confusion, perhaps (a product of much traveling in her early years); considering the food she's exposed to, she shall surely have a jaded palate; and an aged and possibly infirm dad by the time she's sixteen. But she ain't gonna have any problems with self-esteem.

Whatever else, she's never going to look for validation from some predatory asshole. She can—and surely will—hang out with tons of assholes. Dads, I'm assured, can never hope to control that. All I can hope for is that she hangs out with assholes for her own reasons—that she is genuinely amused by assholes rather than needing them to make her feel better about herself.

I wish.

John F. Kennedy said something truly terrifying—guaranteed to make every parent's blood run cold: "To have a child is to give fate a hostage."

Something I wish I'd never read. I can only hope she's happy—even weird and happy will suit me just fine. She will feel loved. She'll have food. And shelter. A large Italian and Sardinian family—and a smaller American one. She'll have seen, by the time she's six years old, much of the world, and she'll have seen, as well, that not everybody on this planet lives—or can live—anything like the way she lives. She will, hopefully, have spent time playing and running barefoot with the children of fishermen and farmers in rural Vietnam. She will have swum in every ocean. She will know how to use chopsticks—and what real cheese is. She already speaks more Italian than I do.

Beyond this, I don't know what else I can do.

12

"Go Ask Alice"

*To him the markets were like the stomach of the
shopkeeping classes, the stomach of all the folks of average
rectitude puffing itself out, rejoicing, glistening in the
sunshine, and declaring that everything was for the best.*
—ÉMILE ZOLA, *LE VENTRE DE PARIS*

Alice Waters wants to help. Shortly after Barack Obama's election victory, the "Mother of Slow Food" wrote the new president a letter, advising him of his first order of business: that "the purity and wholesomeness of the Obama movement must be accompanied by a parallel effort in food at the most visible and symbolic place in America—the White House."

Reminding the president that they had helped raise money for him, she proposed that she and her friends, then–*Gourmet* editor Ruth Reichl and restaurateur Danny Meyer, be brought aboard immediately, "as a small advisory group—a 'Kitchen Cabinet' if you will—to help with your selection of a White House chef. A person with integrity and devotion to the ideals of environmentalism, health and conservation . . ."

That there already *was* a chef at the White House, a person of "integrity and devotion," seems not to have occurred to Ms. Waters. Nor did it seem to matter that this chef had been sourcing and serving largely organic, local, and sustainable food for years—or that there already *was* a kitchen garden. Making the mistake of judging a kitchen staff solely by its customers, Waters, observing—or at least hearing of—the previous tenant, no doubt assumed the worst. But I doubt she considered the matter long enough for even a cursory Google search.

It was, as it so often is, ultimately, all about Alice.

"I cannot forget the vision I have had since 1993," she gushed beatifically, "of a beautiful vegetable garden on the White House lawn. It would demonstrate to the nation and to the world our priority of stewardship of the land—a true *victory* garden!"

She got her garden in the end, as things turned out. Though the new president managed to resist the temptation to appoint Ms. Waters to government office.

As ham-fisted and clumsy as this approach was, a crude and obvious blend of self-aggrandizement and genuine good intentions, it would probably have gone down a lot better had Waters bothered to vote in the previous *forty-four years*. Whatever your politics, you have to admit that the differences both philosophical and practical between Bush and Gore and Bush and Kerry were . . . striking, to say the least. Those were close contests. Whichever way you went—your vote inarguably *counted* for something. One need only read the front page of the newspaper to see how that decision played out and will continue to play out for some years. So there's simply no way Alice or anybody else can realistically make the argument that "there's no difference, man, it's all the same military-industrial complex." I am, admittedly, bitter about this. It sticks in my craw. It's something about Waters that I just can't get past.

After she had boasted of *not* voting since 1966, it seemed a little . . . crass of Waters to presume to now tell the president what to do. Particularly as he'd arrived in the White House facing a newly collapsed worldwide financial system, spiraling unemployment, and two wars—both of which were going badly. Americans were being thrown out of work in unheard-of numbers, and here was Alice, leaping on board to promote, among other things, the idea that we should be spending *more* on food. But then, tone and timing have never been a strong point with Waters.

Let it be said that, on balance, I would like the world to look, someday, much like Alice probably wants it to look. A city on a hill—or many cities on hills—surrounded by unbroken vistas of beautiful countryside; small, thriving, family-run farms growing organic, seasonal, and sustainable fruits and vegetables specific to the region. Healthy, happy, antibiotic-free animals would graze freely over the land, depositing their perfectly odorless, organic shit back into the food chain so other wonderful things might grow . . . The schoolchildren of the inner cities would sit down each day to healthy, balanced, and entirely organic meals cooked—by happy, self-actualized, and enlightened workers—to crispy perfection. Evil lawyers and stockbrokers and vice presidents of development for Bruckheimer Productions would leave their professions and return in great numbers to work the fields of this new agrarian wonderland, becoming better people in the process. In this New Age of Enlightenment, the Dark Forces of Fast Food would wither and die—as the working poor abandoned them to rush home between jobs and cook wild-nettle risotto for their kids. It would all be clean and safe and nobody would get hurt. And it would all look . . . kind of like Berkeley.

Or Italy. Not the real Italy, mind you. But the Italy of wine labels. The Italy of romantic-weekend comedies, where lonely, wistful divorcees end up getting joyously boned by lusty young handymen who wear bandannas around their necks and speak with charming accents. The Italy of *I Love Lucy*, where Italian peasants pick and stomp grapes themselves.

Spend any time in the real Italy, however, and you quickly realize that Italians don't really pick grapes much anymore, and they certainly don't stomp them either. They don't pick tomatoes—or olives—and they don't shear their sheep. Their tomatoes and olives are picked largely by underpaid Africans and Eastern Europeans, seasonal hires, brought in for that purpose—who are then demonized and complained about for the rest of the year. (Except when blowing motorists in the off-season—as can be readily observed on the outskirts of even the smallest Italian communities these days.) The vaunted soil of Italy is as advertised, depending on who you are and where you live. If you live near Naples, though, the chances are good that your farmland is a not-so-secret dumping ground for toxic industrial waste from the north. Here, the true stewards of the earth are neither chefs nor grandmothers nor slow-food devotees. They're the Naples-based fraternal organization, the Camorra. And the old man growing olives in his backyard in Chianti probably doesn't make a living selling olive oil. He gets by renting his house to Germans.

So, who will work the Elysian Fields of Alice's imaginary future?

Certainly not her neighbors—whose average household income is currently about $85,000 a year. Unless, perhaps, at the point of a gun. And with Waters's fondness for buzzwords like "purity" and "wholesomeness," there is a whiff of the jackboot, isn't there? A *certainty*, a potentially dangerous lack of self-doubt, the kind of talk that, so often in history, leads to actions undertaken for the "common good." While it was excessive and bombastic of me to compare Alice to "Pol Pot in a muumuu," it is useful to remember that he was once a practicing Buddhist and, later, attended the Sorbonne. And that even in his twisted and genocidal "back to earth" movement, he might once have meant well, too.

Who will work these fields?

No. Really. Somebody's going to have to answer that question soon.

If, somehow, we manage to bring monstrously evil agribusinesses like Monsanto to their knees, free up vast tracts of arable land for small, seasonal, sustainable farming, where's all the new help coming from? Seems to me, we're facing one of two scenarios. Either enormous numbers of people who've never farmed before are suddenly convinced that waking up at five a.m. and feeding chickens and then working the soil all day is a desirable thing. Or, in the far more likely case, we'll revert to the traditional method: importing huge numbers of desperately poor brown people from elsewhere—to grow those tasty, crunchy vegetables for more comfortable white masters. So, while animals of the future might be cruelty-free, which would allow those who can afford to eat them to do so with a clean conscience, what about life for those who will have to shovel the shit from their stalls?

Okay. Let's say the entire American economy upends itself in fabulous and unpredictable ways, that America suddenly craves fresh vegetables with the ferocity it now has for chicken parts (or anything else) fried in batter—that the boards of directors and top management at Monsanto and Cargill and Con-Agra and Tyson and Smithfield are all indicted, convicted, and packed off to jail (something I'd very much like to see, by the way) for . . . I don't know . . . criminal mediocrity. That farming suddenly becomes the profession of choice for a whole new generation of idealistic Americans. Groovy. I know I'm for it.

I am a proud hypocrite. I feed *my* two-and-a-half-year-old daughter exclusively organic food. My wife is Italian. Around my house, we're more than willing to wait until next year for fresh tomatoes. We enjoy the changing of the seasons and the bounty of the surrounding Hudson Valley—and, of course, the bounty of Spain and Italy as well, readily available at Agata and Valentina, the fantastic but nosebleed-expensive Italian market in our neighborhood, New York's Upper East Side. This celebrity-chef thing is a pretty-good-paying gig.

But what about the Upper Peninsula of Michigan? Or somewhere on the margins of Detroit? What if I were an out-of-work auto worker, living on public assistance or a part-time job? At least I have time to dig a "victory" garden, right? What does Alice suggest I do if I don't live in the Bay Area, my fields turgid with the diverted waters of the Colorado River?

Not a problem!

"You have to think of a different kind of menu," says Alice. "You eat dried fruit and nuts. You make pasta sauces out of canned tomatoes . . . you're eating different kinds of grains—farro with root vegetables. All the root vegetables are there, and now, because of the heirloom varieties, you can have a beautiful winter palette . . . Turnips of every color and shape! Carrots that are white and red and orange and pink! You have different preparations of long-cooking meat . . . Cabbages! . . ."

Basically, you can eat like a fucking Russian peasant, is what she's saying. I don't know if that's what they want to hear in the Upper Peninsula of Michigan or Buffalo.

And . . . what about the healthy, pure, wholesome, and organic foods that Alice says I should be buying—particularly if I have children? If I'm making an even average wage as, say, a sole-providing police officer or middle manager? Regular milk is about four bucks a gallon. Organic is about twice that. Supermarket grapes are about four bucks a bunch. Organic are six. More to the point, what if I'm one of the vast numbers of working poor, getting by in the service sector? *What should I do? How can I afford that?*

Asked this very question directly, Alice advises blithely that one should "Make a sacrifice on the cell phone or a third pair of Nike shoes."

It's an unfortunate choice of words. And a telling one, I think. You know, those *poor people*—always with their Nikes and their cell phones. If only they'd listen to Alice. *She'd* lead them to the promised land for sure.

What else should we be doing? Alice says we should immediately spend 27 billion dollars to ensure every schoolchild in America gets a healthy, organic lunch. More recently, she added to this number with the suggestion that fresh flowers on every lunchroom table might also be a worthwhile idea.

This is, after all, "more important than crime in the streets. This is not like homeland security—this actually is the ultimate homeland security. This is more important than anything else."

Which is where Alice really loses me—because, well, for me, as a New Yorker, however quaint the concept, homeland security is still about keeping suicidal mass murderers from flying planes into our fucking buildings. And organic school lunches might be more important to you than crime in the streets in Berkeley—but in the underfunded school systems of West Baltimore, I suspect, they feel differently. A healthy lunch is all fine and good—but no use at all to Little Timmy if he gets shot to death on the way to school. In fact, 27 billion for organic food for Timmy seems a back-assward priority right now—as, so far, we've failed miserably to even teach him to read. What kind of dreams can a well-fed boy have if he doesn't even have the tools to articulate them? How can he build a world for himself if he doesn't know how to ask for—much less how to get—the things he wants and needs? I, for one, would be very satisfied if Timmy gets a relatively balanced slab of fresh but nonorganic meatloaf with a side of competently frozen broccoli—along with reading skills and a chance at a future. Once literate, well read, and equipped with the tools to actually make his way in this world, he'll be far better prepared to afford Chez Panisse.

As of this writing, not too far from Berkeley, just across the bridge, in San Francisco's Mission District, they line up every Tuesday for the $1.99 special at Popeye's Fried Chicken. They don't stand in the street waiting for forty-five minutes to an hour because it's particularly healthy chicken, or organic chicken, or conscientiously raised chicken—or even good chicken. They do it because it's three fucking pieces for a dollar ninety-nine. Unless we respect that reality, Alice? We're lost.

I remember well, when I was eleven and twelve years old, demonstrating against the war in Vietnam. My dad and I would travel to Washington. Later, my friends and I would march in New York. And what left a powerful impression in my mind, a lesson worth remembering, was how deeply and instinctively the construction workers, the cops and firemen—the very people whose families were most likely to be affected by the war—how they hated us. The message was lost—coming as it did from what they saw (rightly) as a bunch of overprivileged college kids, whose mommies and daddies were footing the bill for educations these folks would unlikely to ever be able to afford for their own kids. Here were these loud, self-absorbed ideologues who looked unlike anyone from their world and who lived nothing like them—but who had no problem talking down to them at every opportunity about the problems of the "working classes"—usually from the steps of Columbia University. The actual "working classes" we were shouting at knew what work was—every time they rolled into bed at night and woke up the next day. Who were these seemingly unemployed, hairy, pot-smoking freaks with their compliant girlfriends and their big talk about the Means of Production? What production? These cocksuckers didn't produce anything!

Thus, a perfectly good message got lost with the messenger.

In the same way, having Alice Waters on your side of the argument is like having Alec Baldwin or Barbra Streisand endorse your candidate (a feeling I know all too well). You may agree with everything they say, but you wish they'd just shut the fuck up. No independent voter, disenchanted with the Republicans but struggling to pay his bills, wants to hear about what he *should* be doing or whom he *should* be voting for from some spectacularly wealthy "artiste" who lives in a compound in Hollywood—far from the pain and daily toil of ordinary Americans.

There is no better example of a counterproductive exercise in advocacy than Alice's recent appearance on *60 Minutes*. Introduced by a shockingly lazy and credulous Leslie Stahl as the "Mother of Slow Food" (a provably false assertion that thirty seconds of Googling would have put to rest), St. Alice of Berkeley was depicted floating ethereally above the fray as she grazed through an expensive greenmarket, pontificating dreamily about the joys of local produce and sustainable, socially conscientious eating.

Then she chose to cook Leslie a single egg over a roaring wood fire in her Berkeley home. I don't know about you, but burning up a couple of cords of firewood for a single fucking egg doesn't exactly send a message of sustainability to me. I believe the restrictions on wood fires are, in fact, particularly restrictive in Berkeley. I know I can't have one in Manhattan without a spectacularly expensive combination of bafflers, catalytic converters, filters, and exhaust system, as well as the permits and legal work that one would need before installing them. They're sensitive about such things in Berkeley—what with half the world's carbon emissions said to come from wood fires and all. If Alice is cooking eggs like that every morning with her oatmeal and fresh-squeezed orange juice, her neighbors are enjoying the secondhand equivalent of a pack of Pall Malls.

Later in the program, when the action moved over to Chez Panisse, Alice, continuing to fetishize "local" produce, proudly commented on a delivery of brightly colored vegetables from "Chino Farms." Here, her argument was undercut somewhat by the fact that Chino Farms—last time I looked, anyway, is *in San Diego*. That's a nearly *twelve-hour* drive by truck to Chez Panisse—or an hour or so on a jet plane. Exactly how "local" or "sustainable" is that?

But then, this is kind of par for the course. What's okay for Alice is . . . well . . . different . . . than what's okay for you. That was certainly the unmissable (by anyone but Stahl) message of the *60 Minutes* segment.

Examine the case of the series of dinners Alice threw in Washington, DC, to celebrate the Obama inauguration. Promoted in the press as an exemplary series of "small" affairs celebrating her sustainable, locavorian values, the thing mushroomed into a five-hundred-dollar-a-plate clusterfuck. In spite of the fact that Washington, DC, has plenty of excellent chefs and cooks of its own, Alice flew in well-known chefs, their crews, and (presumably) many of the ingredients they'd need from all over the country. How much hydrocarbon was released into the atmosphere bringing in these outsiders (clearly better than the local yokels, it was implied) will never be known. But one imagines that the cooks could have been sourced locally with little difficulty.

It's unfair and nitpicking, but it's irresistible for me not to point out one particular magic moment at a meal Alice threw with chef Tom Colicchio and cookbook author Joan Nathan. At one point, after taking a bite of food, Nathan started to choke. Waters's reaction was to charge out into the dining room and inquire if "anyone knew the Heimlich maneuver." Now, Chez Panisse has been open since 1971, one of the longest-running restaurant successes in America. Alice, it was my understanding, was the "executive chef," a title that, if nothing else, implies spending a fair amount of your adult life in proximity to the "choking victim" sign ubiquitous (and mandated by law) in every professional kitchen. There's not an American chef alive who doesn't have that diagram imprinted on his or her brain. 'Cept'n Alice.

Tom Colicchio, who also has seen more than his share of television studios, certainly knew what to do. He stepped right up, placed his fist in the appropriate area, and dislodged the obstruction, thus saving Ms. Nathan's life.

Which leads one to the question: Is Alice even a chef? *Was* she ever a chef—in any conventional sense of that word? I, for one, after reading all the accounts, official and unofficial, of Alice's career and the history of Chez Panisse, can't find a single supporting source to verify that she was ever a chef. And yet, year after year, she is described adoringly as such by people who know better.

And if she's not a chef . . . well then, who *is* she? And why is she allowed to annoy me? Why do I listen to her? Why do I care?

There it is again. That faint, mellifluous voice in my head, telling me, "Alice is right."

Alice . . . is riiiiight . . . about . . . everything . . .

Granted, this is the same voice that once compelled me to sit repeatedly, for hours at a time, in crowded halls that reeked of poor-quality Mexican weed, watching Hot Tuna. Actually, if the voice sounds like anybody, it's David Crosby singing "Almost Cut My Hair" (a song about which I am still, in some secret place, uncontrollably sentimental). The voice persists. It tells me, "Fuck *reality*, man— embrace the Dream. Let your freak flag fly . . ."

Just because the counterculture, the "revolution," all those '60s hopes and dreams were corrupted, co-opted, and eventually crushed by the overpowering weight and impermeability of "the system"—as we should have known they always would be—that doesn't mean it wasn't, at least for a while, sometimes, a beautiful thing, right? *Something* got better for all that, right? I can't think now what, exactly, but I'm sure the world improved in some way in spite of all the nonsense and self-indulgence. In spite of the way things turned out.

LSD sure raised *my* consciousness a bit. There's no doubt that it made me think about the world from perspectives I might otherwise never have visited. From that first barrel of "Purple Haze," the opening bars of "Court of the Crimson King," I'm pretty sure I achieved enlightenment of a sort. That and a few records are what I got out of the '60s. So, maybe LSD is a good metaphor for Alice. I may not want any now—but I'm glad she was around. And I may even be slightly better for the experience.

I'm constantly having an argument with Alice in my head, an ongoing conversation/disagreement—and she always wins. Just as in life. When I met her for a panel discussion a while back, I was loaded for bear. I'd reread her biographies, consulted contemporaneous accounts, tracked down every silly thing she's ever said, briefed myself for a showdown.

But then, there she was, a nice old lady with (literally) an armload of produce and an expression that could only be described as serene . . . She floated across the room, clasped my hand between both of hers, smiled warmly, and I knew then that I could never pull the trigger.

Maybe Alice's dream is what's important. Maybe it doesn't matter whether that dream leads anywhere beyond where we already are—or even if it leads, eventually, to a bad place. That can hardly negate the beauty of the original idea.

So, maybe the big winner, who gets to scoop up the gold at the end of Alice's rainbow, turns out to be Whole Foods, with their fifty-odd checkout counters and their sanctimony at any price. The bad guys always win in the end, right? She can't have seen that coming.

If I think about Alice Waters in this fashion, it becomes much less painful.

Who cares how "great" Chez Panisse is now? Or whether or not Alice Waters was ever a "chef" in the conventional sense of that word? Looking back at that Golden Time in Berkeley, it matters not at all *who* was responsible for the Revolution or in what measure. If the true genius who created what we came to know as California and then New American, or Seasonal Regional, who changed menus and dining as we know it forever, was Alice or Jeremiah Tower—or Joe Baum, years earlier. Does. Not. Matter.

What we *do* know is that whatever happened, it "happened," undeniably caught on, and finally exploded out of Alice's restaurant. She created a space where something really really important came together, involving some very talented, very creative people—who in any other setting or combination would probably not have flown so far and so high. Hers was a virtual cradle of revolution. As far as map coordinates go, there's little doubt of that.

What is also certain is that Alice appreciated the food of France—and what it might mean to us—in a way that few others did at the time. And she applied that passion in ways that no one in America had previously considered. In those days, when the Dream was new and Chez Panisse was just starting up, it was democratic, inclusive, dysfunctional, and ludicrously, admirably, unprofitable. Had someone with any business sense at all attempted to do what Alice was trying to do, it never would have happened. Surely, this was a very fine and good thing.

Alice thinks what we eat is important. So do I. She thinks it's *the* most important thing in the world. I do not. But I'm quite sure that we both have made major decisions in our lives, gained and lost friends, based on what's to eat.

Alice thinks farmers should make more money—growing stuff that's both good-tasting and good for us. Who could be against that? I like farms. So I don't want to work on one. I doubt very much that Alice does either. So we have that in common, too.

She thinks, as I do, that we should be aware of what's good in our own backyards and support those things—by eating them, and growing more of them. I'm with her, to a point. But then I don't *have* a backyard.

Strikingly, she is, and always has been, a carnivore. There is no question as to her position on foie gras. For decades, in the middle of Berkeley, she has unapologetically championed the use of animal flesh as food rather than as something that should someday win the right to vote. In this respect, being blissfully out of touch with what's going on around her has served her well.

In fact, it's Alice's very hypocrisy that belies her true virtues. Because what's truly wonderful about Alice is that she is, first and foremost, a sensualist. When you see Alice preaching about how you should be eating local—while nibbling on sea urchin roe from Hokkaido or foie gras from Gascony—at least you know she *really* appreciates the good stuff. It may be strategically foolish and inappropriate and bad for her argument to be seen cooking a fresh-laid organic egg over an open fire for Leslie Stahl—but I'll bet it tasted fucking delicious.

What makes Alice Waters such a compelling character is her infectious enthusiasm for pleasure. She's made lust, greed, hunger, self-gratification, and fetishism look *good*. When Alice shows you a bunch of radishes, you fucking *want* them. Where have those radishes *been* all my life? I *need* them!

Who cares if she knows the Heimlich maneuver? Did Gandhi know the Heimlich maneuver? Does Bono?

And skimming over the pages of a recent biography, I see there is the oft-cited charge that Alice has made a career of taking credit for the work of others.

To which I'd reluctantly have to ask: Exactly which chefs—to one extent or another—*haven't* done that? How could the batty hippie chick have *really* been responsible for such an important era in gastronomy, is the implied question. Yet, so many male chefs have climbed or leaped to the top over the smashed bodies of subordinates and peers—without accruing fault or foul. The question lingers—and, along with it, I gather, some animus—because Alice survived and prospered where many of her original hippie contemporaries did not. She had the temerity to make money eventually. To figure out, or at least accept, that the Dream could not grow, much less survive, in a commune.

If you're still looking to find "the True Genius behind the Whole Thing"—examining old menus at Chez Panisse, pre-Tower and post-Tower, for instance—you may as well be scrutinizing blurry photographs of the grassy knoll. There is, as with the Kennedy assassination, a case to be made for a second shooter. But spend too long looking and, in the end, you miss the point entirely.

Alice Waters is still here. Jeremiah Tower is not.

Alice is widely known—and will probably always be known—as the "Mother of Slow Food." Jeremiah Tower allowed himself to become a footnote to history.

And history, as they say, will always be written by the victors.

13

Heroes and Villains

Fergus Henderson is a hero.

In the best heroic tradition, he'd be mortified to hear this. He's English, for one—and painfully modest about all the adulation. His restaurant, St. John, was intended as an equally modest venture: a plain white room in a former smokehouse, where a few like-minded Englishmen could eat traditional English food and drink French claret. I am quite sure that his aspirations for the book *Nose to Tail Eating* (aka *The Whole Beast* in the United States), a collection of recipes and related musings, were even more limited.

Yet *Nose to Tail* is now considered one of the classic cookbooks of All Time, a collector's item, a must-have for any chef anywhere in the world wanting cred from his peers, the Bible for the ever-growing "guts mafia," the opening shot in an ongoing (if slow-motion) battle that's still, even today, changing the whole world of food. St. John the restaurant, an undecorated white room serving barely garnished English country fare, continues to be lavishly (and, at times, ludicrously) over-

praised: frequently named "one of the best restaurants in the world"—
ahead of temples of haute gastronomy that are (technically) far more
deserving of those kinds of official honors. I believe Fergus has even
been honored by the Queen—for his service to the Crown—which is
also crazy, if you think about it, for a one-time architect who dropped
out and started cooking bistro grub, soon after to specialize in the kind
of country-ass stuff his grandmother used to cook.

But he *is* a hero. That he's *my* hero is well documented. Since my
first meal at St. John, when I flopped onto my knees in the kitchen,
babbling something spectacularly idiotic but heartfelt, like "You
RAWK!!!" (Fergus wasn't even there that evening), I've shamelessly
basked in his reflected glory at every opportunity. I am a supporter, an
acolyte, a devotee, an advocate for all things Henderson. I am a True
Believer.

I believe that Fergus Henderson, in a way that very few chefs have
ever been, is good for society as a whole. Because, unlike any chef I've
ever heard of, he has influenced people who've never been to St. John,
never eaten his food, certainly *never* read his book, and don't have
any idea who the fuck this Fergus Henderson guy might be. He has,
however unwittingly, given permission to generations of chefs and
cooks to follow their hearts in ways that were unthinkable only a few
years ago. Simply by doing what he's doing, he's inspired others to put
things on their menus and look at ingredients they might never have
thought of had he not done it first—and, as the word spreads, minds
and menus change, and no one even knows where it all might have
started.

Mario Batali, Chris Cosentino, Martin Picard, April Bloomfield,
Gabrielle Hamilton are obvious examples of chefs who felt liberated
by Fergus's early example. I say "obvious," because they'd be the first to
tell you. But it's all the others . . . the lone chefs and cooks out there,
in the Heartland of America, England, and Australia, who yearned

for a Fergus to come along and inspire them, give them courage, long before he actually appeared.

I will never forget the smell of the rooms, years ago, tiny venues in rural England, in working-class cities where Fergus was on book tour. All the kids came out, still stinking of the deep fryer, the chip shop, whatever crappy pub, depressing and wrongheaded "lounge/restaurant" they might have been working at at the time. Many of them had never even been to London. But they knew who Fergus was alright—and what he was all about. And the look on their faces—of ambition and hope—was inspiring.

My most treasured Fergus-related memory—and one of the most moving goddamn things I've ever seen—was when he accompanied me to my old alma mater, the CIA.

I was concerned. I *knew* that the three-hundred-seat auditorium would fill with my fans. It had been my school, after all, the home team—and twenty-year-old slacker male culinary students, freshly tattooed with "Cook Free or Die," are usually not a tough crowd for me. But I was worried about the reception Fergus might get. He was English—with the kind of upper-class speech patterns filled with Britishisms one would expect of an eccentric country squire. He spoke faintly—and with a pronounced stammer. He was sick. Very sick. He had not yet had the experimental surgery that would help mitigate the symptoms of his Parkinson's, and his body jerked around at times, robotically, sending an arm straight out into space. He was funny-looking in the best of circumstances; often described as "owlish" behind round glasses.

Would any of these young louts know who he was, I wondered? More important, would they *listen*, would they pay attention during his talk—would they give this man the *respect* he was due—or would they, after a few minutes, start staring off into space, or dribbling off to the exits?

I ended my litany of war stories and dick jokes and handed the floor over to Fergus.

He began to speak, faintly, worryingly flushed, arm wonky . . .

And every fucking kid in that room leaned forward in their seat and held their breath.

For forty-five minutes, no one made a sound. They listened— absolutely rapt—to the master. They knew who he was, alright. *Fuckin'- A* they did. And at the end of the talk, they asked questions—bright, incisive, enthusiastic ones, too. I stood silently in the rear, trying not to start blubbering like a fucking baby. It was like the end of *Pride of the Yankees* (and I *do* start weeping when I see that shit).

I'd never seen anything so . . . encouraging . . . in my life.

Which is why I'm putting Gael Greene on my list of villains. Not be- cause she deserves to be vilified for her writing, which was once very important, and is still, more often than not—when she's not talking about boning Elvis—quite good. I probably couldn't be doing what I'm doing if she hadn't done it first. Or for any of the obvious reasons why one would want to make fun of the woman referred to by chefs as Sgt. Pepper for her bizarre, look-at-me, Peter Frampton/Michael Jackson/ Gopher-from-*Love Boat* outfits. Hell—in another context, she'd prob- ably be a hero.

But no. Gael joins the ranks of the damned because she moder- ated a panel discussion at the 92nd Street Y in New York City a while back—and she was lucky enough to have Fergus Henderson on her panel and she barely acknowledged him. She kept getting his name wrong. She blathered on and on about her favorite subject (herself) while ignoring the most influential chef of the last ten years sitting a few feet away. For abusing this opportunity, for paying insufficient respect to my friend, for treating the Great Man as any less than the titan he is—for this alone—let her join the ranks of the damned.

. . .

Jonathan Gold, the food writer for *LA Weekly*, is a hero.

I'm hardly the first to notice. He won a Pulitzer Prize for his dedicated and pioneering coverage of all those places in the LA area that nobody had ever covered before. (His award was the first for a food writer.) He gave them respect, treating little mom-and-pop noodle shops in strip malls with a degree of importance they hadn't enjoyed before. He helped give a "legitimacy" to serious critical analyses of Thai, Vietnamese, inexpensive Mexican, and less appreciated regional cuisines, which hadn't really existed before. He put them on a par with fine dining and wrote about them with as much—if not more—enthusiasm, helping to usher in a (very useful) kind of reverse snobbism, a skepticism about fine dining that has only been helpful and a good thing in the long run.

And the motherfucker can write. Oh, can he write. Good, original sentences on the subject of food are an all-too-rare thing—and Gold pretty much owns his territory. As a writer, as a force for good, as a guy who upped the ante for anyone daring to write about food or simply looking for food to eat, he's a hero. By writing about food, he's helped change how and where people eat it. In a near unbroken field of mediocrity, here is a man who makes just about anything or any place he cares to talk about seem like someplace *you* should care about.

Since we're in LA, allow me to take the opportunity to put Wolfgang Puck on the villains list. Puck goes on the list precisely *because* he's one of the biggest, best, and most important chefs of the last few decades. What you think of his airport pizza is completely beside the point. Puck long ago *did* enough important, world-changing work to ensure his status as one of the Greats. He was a vital part of the American food revolution. He made serious contributions to changing the whole popular notion of who and what a chef even *was*—part of the whole tectonic shift away from the idea of the maître d' being the star—to the new idea: that it was the *chef* who was important. The chefs and cooks who came up with and graduated from Puck's kitchens (so many of them) make for a breathtaking lineup. His is a major tree trunk in the genealogy of American cooking.

With God knows how many restaurants and the merch line and everything else going on in PuckLand, presumably, Wolfgang has plenty of money. He is, inarguably, BIG. Maybe *the* Big Tuna—in a town of big fishes. He is a powerful, influential, and deservedly respected chef and one of the most recognizable names in the business.

So, I was really disappointed, felt . . . betrayed, when he knuckled under to the anti–foie gras people and announced he'd take it off all his menus in all his businesses.

When more vulnerable, less well-capitalized, less famous peers were standing up—when some chefs were being threatened, their families *terrorized*, why did Puck go over to the other side? It seemed that of all the chefs in the country, he was best situated to simply say "Fuck you!" to the Forces of Darkness, and tough it through.

Here, I assumed, was a wealthy, powerful, influential man with— one would imagine—many powerful friends.

I figured he looked at the situation and calculated that it would be easier to just give the assholes what they wanted. At the time, I believe, I called it treason. But I'm told the story was a little more complicated than that—and the pressures on Puck more severe than a few protesters out front. He was getting it from all sides, from within and without his organization, it is said. His partners and allies, squeezed themselves, in turn squeezed Puck. Wolfgang is not the only shareholder of Wolfgang Puck Worldwide, Inc., and, apparently, his partners made things very, very hot for him.

So maybe "victim" *and* "villain" would be more appropriate. I'm not as pissed off as I was. Just really disappointed. Because if not Puck—then who?

. . .

Jamie Oliver is a hero.

Before you spit up your gnocchi, turn back to the cover of this book, and make sure you're reading the right author, let me explain. I hated *The Naked Chef,* too. And all that matey, mockney bullshit. And the Sainsbury's business . . . and the band . . . and the scooter—all that shit that made Jamie a star.

But I don't know what I would do if I Googled "I Hate Anthony Bourdain" and saw a million or so hits, like Jamie would find if he Googled the same phrase but with his name. I don't know what I would do if I woke up one morning, and, like Jamie, found a Web site dedicated to me named FatTonguedCunt.com, where hundreds, if not thousands, of people appeared to be spending half their working hours—and maybe all their leisure time—Photoshopping movie posters and twisting titles to refer, as disparagingly as possible, to me. I'd be afraid to leave the house—seeing that kind of ferocity and loathing.

I *do* have a pretty good idea what I'd do, however, if I had the kind of big money Jamie's got. And it would *not* be the same as what he's doing with it.

Say what you will about how well, how attractively or advisably, but Jamie Oliver puts his money where his mouth is. The sincerity with which he's focused on school lunches, educating kids on how to cook—and even how to eat—is largely, I gather, unwelcomed, and, relative to potentially more purely profit-oriented exercises, maybe not the best of options.

Jamie would clearly prefer to be an annoying nag, reminding us that we're fat and unhealthy, than make more money. You have to admire that. Sure, he's still bringing down plenty of dough—but you gotta respect a guy who manages to embarrass the whole British government with a show about what their schoolkids are actually eating.

That kind of talk will eventually make you unpopular. It's very rarely a good career move to have a conscience.

If experience teaches us anything, it's that the very last thing a television audience wants to hear or be reminded of is how *bad* things are, how unhealthy or how doomed—that we're heading off a cliff and dragging our kids after us. (Unless it's accompanied by bombastic accusations of conspiracy—and a suitable candidate to blame for the problem.) It's bad business to be saying all sorts of awful, alarmist shit like that—particularly when it's true. It is much better business, always, to tell people, over and over again, in a reassuring voice (or, better yet, a loud, annoying one) that everything is just *fine*. It'll all work out. The kids can *keep* jamming soda and chips into their neckless maws. They'll be okay. No need to worry. You're *great*! You're *awesome*! And here's a recipe for deep-fried potato pizza!

Jamie Oliver is a hero for doing the harder thing—when he surely doesn't *have* to do anything at all. Most chefs I know, were they where Jamie is on the Success-O-Meter? They'd be holed up at a Four Seasons somewhere, shades drawn, watching four tranny hookers snort cocaine off each other.

Brooke Johnson, the head honcho at Food Network, is a villain. That's an easy one.

But she's a villain for being right—not for the cynical, fake-ass, soul-destroying, lowest-common-denominator shit-shows she's nurtured and supported since taking the helm. She's a villain for being, clearly and demonstrably, right about *everything*.

On her watch, the network's audience share has exploded. The number of male viewers most treasured by advertisers expands exponentially every year, demographics of viewers watching Food Network tilting to the good in ways that are the envy of every other network—that prime-quality cut of big-spending, ever-younger male viewers getting larger and larger with each financial quarter. Every clunky, bogus, critically vilified clusterfuck that drops from FN's hindquarters, still steaming and seemingly dead on arrival, turns out to be an unprecedented ratings success.

Even the FN-branded *magazines* are doing monster business: nearly alone in an otherwise bleak field littered with the dead, they have thrived, becoming plump and then plumper with ad pages.

There is an unimpeachable logic to your argument when no matter what one may say about what you do—or even how true their observations might be—you can respond with two words: "It works."

Whatever Brooke Johnson has done, it is working. That success ensures that whoever complains about "quality" sounds quaint—even deranged—like some sad Old Hollywood shrunken head, talking about Ford and Lubitsch, Selznick and Thalberg—to an interviewer who has no idea who or what they're talking about.

And for that, and the fact that she couldn't and probably shouldn't give a shit whether she's a villain or not—she's a villain.

Wylie Dufresne is a hero.

Because he's made a life's work of doing exactly the opposite of what Brooke Johnson does. At his restaurant, WD-50, where you're likely to actually find him most nights, he doesn't care if you don't understand the food. He will not be moved from his plan if people hate an occasional dish. It doesn't matter to Wylie if, on balance, most of you would rather have a steak—that he would surely struggle less, and make a lot more money, please more of the dining public, if he only made some compromises. He knows that even if you *love* everything on his menu, his is not the kind of meal that people come back for every week.

Wylie Dufresne is a fucking hero because he's got amazing skills, a restless mind—and balls the size of pontoons. He's decided to do the hard thing—whatever the cost—rather than following the much easier path that has always been readily available to a chef of his considerable advantages. He could have been anybody he wanted—had whatever kind of restaurant, whatever kind of career. And he chose . . . this. To his constant peril, he experiments, pushes boundaries, explores what is possible, what might be possible. In doing so, he develops techniques and ideas that, after he's done all the work and taken the time and risk, are promptly ripped off by chefs all over the world—usually without any acknowledgment.

For exactly the same reasons, Grant Achatz is a hero. Only more so—because he not only put what is perhaps the most impressive résumé a chef could have at the service of innovation, experimentation, and the investigation of those things about which he is curious, but he also risked his *life* in order to continue doing so. When you're talking about commitment to one's craft—about rigorously and inflexibly sticking with one's goals and the highest possible standards—there's really no one who's demonstrated that so consistently, or been willing to sacrifice so much.

Alain Ducasse, on the other hand, is a villain. Because he almost sin-glehandedly brought down fine dining in America with his absurdly pretentious restaurant Alain Ducasse New York (or ADNY, as it was known). While total destruction might narrowly have been avoided, public perception—even among friendlies—of the kind of European-style, Michelin-star place that he aspired to took a serious hit, causing the beginnings of a slow bleed that continues to this day.

Walking into ADNY, I loved the idea of haute cuisine uncon-ditionally. I left, a heretic, the seeds of doubt planted in my heart—like the first toxic pangs of jealousy in a lover. And it wasn't just me.

ADNY damaged, in many minds, the whole idea of luxurious dining rooms and service, made those things dangerously uncool, features you almost have to explain or apologize for these days, something to be overcome by the food.

To use an egregiously overused expression, ADNY was where fine dining jumped the shark. Ducasse revved up the engine of his bike, released his hand from the brake, and took the whole concept hurtling heedlessly across the shark tank, where, unlike in Fonzi's case, it was doubtful in the extreme that Pinky Tuscadero would be waiting for him.

When he rolled into New York with his bad attitude, ungracious proclamations of how exclusive his new place would be, how unwelcome New Yorkers might be—if they were not already acquainted with Himself via Monaco or Paris—Ducasse did nothing so much as drop a gigantic Cleveland Steamer into a small pond previously occupied by his much smarter and savvier compatriots. And you can bet they saw it for what it was.

Previously, you'd *never* heard members of the old French guard talking shit about one of their own—not publicly, anyway—but this was different. This guy was fucking it up for everybody.

The little tuffets for ladies' bags, the selection of steak knives to choose from, the waiters who put on white gloves to trim fresh herbs tableside. The fucking *water* cart. The even more painful array of Montblanc pens to choose from so that one might more elegantly sign one's check. The dark, hideous, and pretentious dining room. All of it conspired to smother any possibility of a good time stone-dead in a long, dreary dirge. Nothing could live in this temple of hubris. The generally excellent food was no match for the forces aligned against it. And it just wasn't, in the end, excellent enough to prevail against the ludicrousness of what surrounded it.

Like watching *Bonfire of the Vanities* or *Heaven's Gate*—or one of the other great examples of ego gone wild in the movie business—there were so many miscalculations, large and small, that the whole wrong-headed mess added up to something that wasn't just bad but insulting. You left ADNY angry and offended—that anyone, much less this out-of-touch French guy, would think you were so stupid.

New Yorkers don't like to be treated like rubes. Tends to leave a bad taste. And the bad taste one left with after ADNY metastasized into something larger—feelings of doubt about the desirability—and even the morality—of that kind of luxury. Few in the hermetic world of Francophile New York foodies had ever really asked those questions before. Now, they were asking.

There's been no sign since, by the way, that Ducasse has gotten much smarter. Other than having the wisdom to close ADNY. After initial reviews of a new "brasserie" concept were negative, he suggested publicly that New Yorkers were unfamiliar with this kind of food and that it was up to critics to educate them to the complexities of exotica like *blanquette de veau* and *choucroute*. Which came as news, I'm sure, to the many, many distinguished French chefs who'd been doing exactly that—to great acclaim—for decades.

For being an arrogant fuckwit who nearly ruined it for all of us, Alain Ducasse is a villain.

Terrance Brennan is a hero because, back in the Stone Age, he was the only guy around who loved cheese enough to lose money on it. For years. Brennan, the chef/owner of Picholine and Artisanal in New York City, was the first American chef to get really serious about the French-style cheese course. It's not like anybody was asking. It wasn't like there'd been a popular outcry for soft, runny, prohibitively expensive cheeses with which few Americans were familiar—and even fewer inclined to ever like. Even today, mention "stinky cheese" and relatively few are they who will respond positively.

Sure, heroic cheesemongers like Robert Kaufelt at Murray's Cheese

Shop had been making a good living selling an impressive variety of the world's great cheeses for ages. But making a go of cheese in a restaurant situation was a very different matter.

Back in the day, the cheese board was, at restaurants of a certain type, an obligatory exercise at best. At the kind of fine-dining Frog ponds where the waiters spoke with French or Italian accents, and the crystal and linens were of good quality, the flowers freshly cut, the menu French or "continental," cheese was something you offered because that was the sort of thing your customers expected. They'd been to Europe—many times. They knew that after the main courses, cheese is offered. Nobody actually ordered the shit. And had they tried, they would often find a perfunctory display of usual suspects: unripe (or too ripe) Brie, maybe a Camembert (usually in even worse shape), a sad disk of undistinguished chèvre, something hard and vaguely Swiss— and a lonely and unloved wedge of something blue. Probably the same Roquefort used elsewhere on the menu. In fact, the key to offering a cheese course and getting away with it was to make sure that *everything* on the cheeseboard was used elsewhere on the menu.

Cheese is expensive. Very expensive. And perishable. And delicate. Properly aged, stored, served, and handled cheese is even *more* expensive. Every time you cut into an intact cheese, its time on this earth becomes limited. Every time you pull one out of the special refrigerated cave it lives in, you are killing it slowly. Every time you return it, partially served, *back* to the refrigerator, you are also killing it. Whichever employee is serving your cheese? Every uneven cut, every pilfered slice or smear can pretty much end any possibility of a return on your investment. In fact, to properly serve a reasonably excellent selection of cheeses—always at their peak ripenesses and at proper temperatures—one almost *must* accept the imperative of throwing a lot of it out sooner or later, or find a way to use it elsewhere. And the more varieties of cheese you offer, the less likely you will be able to merchandise all of the remnants as ingenious appetizers.

It is very rare, even in the best of circumstances, that a customer will order a separate cheese course—prior to and distinct from—dessert. The arrival of cheeses on a cart tableside presents a potentially awkward situation for a large party: should we wait for the asshole here—who insisted on ordering a few reeking blues and some port—or should we just go ahead and order desserts?

So, cheese is not exactly a "loss leader"—meaning, an expensive or cumbersome item that does not in itself make money but which somehow inspires others to order things that *will* make money. If people *do* decide to have cheese as a dessert course, there's no way you're making more money on a nicely aged Stilton than you would be had everybody simply ordered crème brûlée or ice cream, which cost much less to produce.

You have to be a romantic to invest yourself, your money, and your time in cheese. And that's a very dangerous thing to be in the restaurant business. One of the great suicidal expressions has always been "educate the customer." You hear that kind of talk from your business partner, it's usually way too late to roll your eyes at the ceiling and plead for sanity.

But Terrance Brennan actually *did*—and continues to—"educate" his customers. And somehow to get away with it—even succeed and expand. After introducing the cheese concept at Picholine, he built a whole additional business around it at Artisanal—so far in front of everybody else he's *still* out front, years later. He not only heroically defied the conventional wisdom of the times, he helped *change* the conventional wisdom. Where there was no market at all, he created one.

The dining public may not have known that it needed a selection of over a hundred cheeses. They certainly didn't know they needed to know about small-production American cheeses from previously unknown cheese-makers in Maine, Oregon, and even New Jersey. Brennan, by taking a chance on cheese, helped create not just a market to sell cheese—but an emerging sector dedicated to *making* cheese. Finally, for all those lonely would-be cheese-makers pondering the possibilities of great, homegrown American cheese, there was a chef/ restaurateur out there who might buy them, promote them, dedicate himself and his business to hand-selling them to the public.

Terrance Brennan is a hero. By taking a series of mad risks, he's raised all boats—made things better for all of us.

Jim Harrison is a hero.

Because there's nobody, *nobody* left like him. The last of the true gourmands—the last connection to the kind of writing about food that A. J. Liebling used to do. Passionate, knowledgeable, but utterly without snobbery—as likely to gush over an ugly but delicious tripe à la mode or order of roasted kidneys as a once-in-a-lifetime meal at a triple-starred Michelin. Harrison, author of many fine books and even more fine poems, has done everything cool with *everybody* who's ever been cool dating back to when they invented the fucking word. He knows how to cook. He has impeccable taste in wine. He knows how to eat.

At his own book party in New York City a while back, Harrison, whom I'd met previously only once, spent the entire evening standing outside with me, whom he hardly knew, chain-smoking and talking about food, ignoring the rich, the powerful, the famous, and the smart who waited for him inside. At the grizzled age of seventy-two, suffering variously from gout and many other complaints, he is a rock star in France—barely able to walk down the street without being mobbed—and he lives like one. The French understand the greatness of such men immediately.

The lazy and the foolish compare him to Hemingway—which is a terrible injustice, as Jim is both a better writer and a better man.

I don't know many people who could be called "great." But Jim would be one of them. He smokes, he drinks—and regularly attempts frottage with an impunity and a style that will disappear after him.

Speaking of Old Fuckers: the James Beard House goes on the villain list—because it harbors and gives safe haven to villains. It gives them somewhere to go. It provides comfort and succor and the illusion of importance to a bunch of supremely irrelevant old fucks who have nothing to do and nothing to say of any significance to the restaurant business they claim to support and love. It's a private dining society for the soon-to-be-incontinent—like the Friars Club for old mummies who never themselves told a joke but like to hang around comedians.

When the president of the Beard Foundation got pinched for embezzlement a while back, it should have come as a surprise to no one. For years, even the casual observer could watch as "money goes in—nothing comes out," but nobody gave a shit. After the news went public that this nobody, this nebbish from nowhere, had been feathering his nest, everybody was shocked! shocked! and rushed to separate themselves from the wreckage with unseemly speed and appropriate expressions of outrage. But that was the purpose of the whole enterprise. To give jobs and power to the otherwise powerless and unemployable.

I'll never forget my friend, chef Matt Moran's experience. Matt is a Big Cheese in Sydney; his restaurant, ARIA, one of the best in the country. Invited to cook a meal at the Beard House, he packed the best of his kitchen staff, all his ingredients and his bags, and flew them all, at great expense, to New York. Having heard of the notoriously impossible-to-work-in kitchen at the House (why would an institution honoring the work of *chefs* actually have a kitchen they could cook in?), he managed to arm-twist every chef friend he had in New York to make use of their busy restaurants' kitchens to prepare. I agreed to help finish and serve the meal.

We managed to crank out the meal—a very ambitious, very modern menu featuring the best of Australian seafood, meat, cheese, and wines—and afterward, when the chef was summoned to the dining room to take a bow, receive much deserved kudos, and answer a few questions, I watched.

He walked into the room expecting the "cream" or at least "some" of New York's food media. There was none. There rarely is. He would surely have settled, I'm guessing, for what could optimistically be called a complement of the town's "influential" diners—or "foodie elite." No. Not at all.

One look at the clueless duffers blinking up at him uncomprehendingly from their tables, and it was clear he'd been snookered. How much had he spent on this exercise in futility? To fly all that food, all those cooks, all those miles from the other side of the world? Put them up in hotels? Ten, fifteen, twenty thousand dollars? All that work? And here comes the first question from the floor—yes, the gentleman over there, who looks like he just limped away from the shrimp buffet at a suburban golf club.

The man fixes Moran in his blurry gaze, leans back in his chair, pats his belly for effect, and asks, "So, chef. You're from Australia, right? How come we didn't have any kangaroo—or like . . . *koala* on the menu?"

Somewhere inside Moran, I saw something die. He knew now. He had the information.

Beard House. Evil.

Ariane Daguin is a hero.

Twenty-five or twenty-six years ago, Ariane, who had been working for a purveyor/manufacturer of French-style charcuterie, started up a small business dedicated to producing and providing to local chefs New York State foie gras, as well as other products and preparations that French chefs of the time wanted, needed, and had not previously been able to get. She started out with one truck and a dream.

A quarter century later, her business, D'Artagnan, has become very successful. But at great personal and financial cost. She's had to wage a constant and very expensive war—both legal and for the hearts and minds of the public—to protect her right to sell this traditional product. Yet she has gone way, way beyond protecting her own interests and her own business. Almost alone, she has been there for chefs and purveyors across the country who have run afoul of the at-times dangerous anti-foie activists. She was a prime mover in the counterattack after foie gras was banned in Chicago. She is there to offer support when individual chefs are terrorized or their businesses targeted for vandalism or disruption. She has put her money at the service of people who will never buy her products or know her name. Nearly alone, she defends a culinary tradition dating back to Roman times: the right to hand-feed ducks and geese, who live in far better conditions than any chicken ever sold at the Colonel's, until their livers become plump and delicious.

She has shown far, far more courage on this issue than any chef I know.

Mario Batali and Eric Ripert and José Andrés are heroes because they raise more money for charity—and put in more time doing it—than movie stars and CEOs fifty times wealthier than they are.

José Andrés is also a hero because (I strongly suspect) he's secretly an agent for some ultra-classified and very cool department of the Spanish Foreign Ministry. He's the unofficial food ambassador for Spain, Spanish products, and Spanish chefs. You can't talk to the motherfucker for five minutes without him gently slipping mention of Spanish ham or Spanish cheese or Spanish olive oil into the conversation. When José's lips move, you never know who's actually talking: Ferran Adrià? Juan Mari Arzak? Andoni Aduriz? Or the nation itself? Somebody is sending you a message—you can just never be sure who. At the end of the day, all you can be sure of is that the message will be delicious.

Regina Schrambling is both hero and villain. My favorite villain, actually.

The former *New York Times* and *LA Times* food writer and blogger is easily the Angriest Person Writing About Food. Her weekly blog entries at gastropoda.com are a deeply felt, episodic unburdening, a venting of all her bitterness, rage, contempt, and disappointment with a world that never seems to live up to her expectations. She hates nearly everything—and everybody—and when she doesn't, she hates herself for allowing such a thing to happen. She never lets an old injury, a long-ago slight, go. She proofreads her former employer, the *New York Times*, with an eye for detail—every typo, any evidence of further diminution of quality—and when she can latch on to something (as, let's face it, she always can), she unleashes a withering torrent of ridicule and contempt.

She hates Alice Waters. She hates George Bush. (She'll still be writing about him with the same blind rage long after he's dead of old age.) She hates Ruth Reichl, Mario Batali, Frank Bruni, Mark Bittman . . . me. She hates the whole rotten, corrupt, self-interested sea in which she must swim: a daily ordeal, which, at the same time, she feels compelled to chronicle. She hates hypocrisy, silliness, mendacity. She is immaculate in the consistency and regularity of her loathing.

She is also very funny—and, frequently, right about things. And always, even when I strongly disagree with her, worth reading. She rarely if ever commits the first and most common sin of food writing—being boring.

For inventing cute names for her targets, though, and not having the stones to simply say what everybody knows she *is* saying, she's a villain. If you're going to piss on Mario every other week, say "Mario Batali." Not "Molto Ego." Stand up fucking proud and tell us why you hate Mario Batali and everything he touches. Which also makes her a villain in my book: because it's all fine and good to loathe Mario in person and in principle, but to deny any value at all in any of his enterprises is criminally disingenuous—particularly for a food writer.

His name is "Frank Bruni," not the funny name "Panchito" she refers to him by. And for the unpardonable act of being insufficiently critical of George W. Bush in the run-up to the election (a transgression Bruni was hardly alone in committing), his every word as the eventual *Times* dining critic was (for Ms. Schrambling, anyway) utterly worthless—or worse.

I think Alan Richman is a douchebag. Writing the chapter about him in this book felt really good. Regina should try to be as specific as possible and clearly identify the targets of her derision.

Hero/villain, with Regina Schrambling it doesn't matter. She is—even at her crankiest, most unfair, and most vindictive—good for the world of food and dining: a useful emetic, a periodic scourging, the person shouting "Fire!" repeatedly in a too-crowded room. You have to respect the depth and duration of her scorn. I do.

She is, unfortunately, a return to that vanishing breed of food writer and "gourmet" who claims to love food yet secretly loathes the people who actually *cook* it.

While this might, if you think about it, be an indicator of good instincts on her part, it is unlovely, to be sure. But *somebody* has to call "bullshit"—regularly—on those of us who cook or write about food or talk about it. Even when wrong. There needs to be someone out there, constantly watching. It may as well be Regina.

I can't wait to read her next blog entry.

14

Alan Richman Is a Douchebag

The intersection where chefs, writers, restaurant reviewers, publicists, and journalists meet has always been a swamp, an ethical quagmire where the lines between right and wrong are, by unarticulated consensus, kept deliberately permeable. It's like a neverending hillbilly joke: we've all fucked each other's sisters. Everybody in the family is aware of it—but we delicately avoid the subject.

The *New York Times* struggles mightily to remain above the orgy of pride, vanity, greed, gluttony, and other sinful behaviors around it—traditionally by keeping its critic as anonymous as possible. False identities, wigs, and other disguises are employed in an effort to keep their writer from being recognized. It doesn't always work, of course. Any restaurant with serious four-star aspirations always has someone on staff who can pick out Frank Bruni or Sam Sifton from across a crowded room. To what degree that helps, however, is debatable. To the *Times'* credit, I've never heard of anyone "reaching" a full-time reviewer, influencing the review through favors, special access, or things of value. From what I've heard, lavishing extra attention on them is risky—and not necessarily rewarding. Knowing the *Times* guy by sight is useful mostly for making extra-sure you don't fuck up—rather than providing you with a real edge. Those chef-players who *do* dare to send extras are very careful to do the same for all the surrounding tables as well. Anonymity does not provide 100 percent protection from special treatment. But it's an extra layer, an added degree of difficulty—the ethical version of a wet suit or hazmat garment, keeping the *Times* man (or woman) safe from contamination in the primordial soup of free food, bodily fluids, and slow-festering morals they must swim in.

Journalists who write about food and chefs are in the business of providing punchy, entertaining prose—hopefully with a good human-interest story attached, and some good quotes. More important, they want and need an angle or perspective different from what every other food or dining writer is doing. They would greatly prefer it if a Web site or food blogger has not already comprehensively covered the same subject. This is, to be fair, extraordinarily difficult. People who write professionally about food—to the exclusion of all other topics—are painfully aware of the limitations of the form. There are only so many ways to describe a slow-roasted pork belly before you run into the word "unctuous"—again. Trying to conjure a descriptive for salad must be like one's tenth year writing "Penthouse Letters": the words "crunchy," "zing," "tart," and "rich" are as bad as "poon," "cooter," "cooz," and "snatch" when scrolling across the brain in predictable, dreary procession. Worse, while your editor has just asked for an overview of "Queens ethnic" in a week, some lonely food nerd has been methodically eating his way, block by block, across the entire borough and blogging about it for years.

Pity, too, the poor chefs. One of their new jobs in this brave new world of dining is co-opting, corrupting, and otherwise compromising food writers whenever possible. The care and feeding of the Fourth Estate—and their bastard offspring, food bloggers—has become an important skill set for any chef looking to hit the Big Time. It's no longer enough to cook well, to be able to run a kitchen. You have to be able to identify and evaluate all the people who might hurt you—and (as best as possible) neutralize them ahead of time. One memorably bad review can punch a hole in a restaurant's painstakingly acquired reputation, letting the air out of one's public profile in a way that's often hard to put back. One snarky Web site, early in a restaurant's life, can hobble it in ways that might well prove fatal in the long run.

When you are repeatedly made to look ridiculous, lowbrow, or déclassé, on Grub Street or Eater, it's very hard to get your mojo back—as operators like Jeffrey Chodorow have found, to their displeasure. Nowadays, the professional snarkologist will confidently imply that a Chodorow place will surely suck even *before* it opens. In a business where something as nebulous and unmeasurable as "buzz" is seen as a vital factor for the bottom line, everybody with a keyboard is a potential enemy.

But, traditionally at least, "turning" a journo is usually a pretty simple matter. Just feed them for free. You'll never have to remind them about it later. Believe me. They'll remember. It's like giving a bent cop a Christmas turkey. They may not be able to help you directly—but they'll at least make an effort to not hurt you. And if you can make a journalist or a Webmaster your "special friend," you have a powerful ally. In addition to singing your praise early and often from the rooftops, they can act as your proxy, shouting down those who might question your magnificence.

Every time a restaurant opens, the joint's PR firm sits down with the chef and the owner and starts running down the list of usual suspects, wanting to know who are the "friendlies" and who are not. Most restaurants have one version or another of the same list. They are all, presumably, the sort of people who want to come to a special pre-opening "tasting" at your restaurant. They will not be reviewing you—yet, which lets them off the ethical hook, so to speak.

Few are the people who, when passing the smiling woman with the clipboard from the restaurant's PR agency, want to find themselves off that list the next time a restaurant opens—particularly if it's a high-end, high-prestige operator, or if there's a hotshot chef involved. The thinking is: "Okay, I hate *this* place. But if I take too ferocious a dump on it, I won't be welcome at the *next* place—which might be really good!" Or . . . "I really enjoy being able to get a table on short notice at X (an existing, hard-to-get-into, fine-dining restaurant). I don't want to fuck that up!"

When it comes to yours truly, I confess to being hopelessly mobbed up. While I do not claim to "review" restaurants—or even write about them for magazines much anymore—I cannot be trusted or relied on to give readers anywhere near the truth, the whole truth, or anything like it.

I've been swimming in those blood-warm waters for a long time now. I'm friends with a lot of chefs. Others, whom I'm not friends with, I often identify with, or respect to a degree that would prevent me from being frank with a reader—or anyone outside the business. After all those years inside the business, I'm still too sympathetic to anybody who works hard in a kitchen to be a trustworthy reviewer. I'm three degrees separated from a lot of chefs in this world. I get a lot of meals comped. If I were to walk into one of Mario Batali's places, for instance, and see something unspeakable going on in the kitchen— animal sacrifice or satanic rituals, or something unhygienic or deeply disturbing, I'd never write about it.

I've been on both sides of the fence. Eager chef, looking to make "friends" out of journos or bloggers. And a bent, compromised writer— whose interests are way too commingled with his subjects for him to ever be truly trusted.

But for all the awful things I've seen and done, I've never stooped to . . . well . . . let's begin at the beginning . . . with a food writer, critic, and journalist who could, on balance, be considered among the very best: a lion among the trolls, an excellent writer of sentences, with remarkably good taste in restaurants, a refined palate, and decades of experience. But I digress. Let's get to the action.

I called Alan Richman a douchebag.

So, Richman, respected elder statesman of restaurant criticism, winner of an armload of James Beard Awards, and writer-reviewer for *GQ*, responded in keeping with his position as the "dean" of food journalism and in the time-honored tradition of his craft.

He reviewed the restaurant I worked at.

Actually, it was somewhat worse than that. He reviewed the restaurant I *used to* work at.

Though he acknowledged, by paragraph two of the gleeful takedown that followed, that he *knew* I hadn't worked at Les Halles in nearly a decade, he forged on, absolutely savaging everything from upholstery to lighting, service, and food. He did mention a dessert favorably, attributing its lack of awfulness to the probability that I had not contaminated it. It was a thorough critical disembowelment: the words "grubby," "acrid," "flavorless," "surly," "greasy," and "inedible" all making appearances in the same few paragraphs.

It's the customary practice of major media to devote their very limited restaurant review space to three categories of restaurant: (1) new endeavors brought to us by already critically acclaimed chefs, (2) the rarer discovery of a new chef's debut effort, or (3) a change of guard or concept at a well-known, already well-reviewed restaurant. Les Halles did not, by any stretch of the imagination, meet any of these criteria. At no time did Richman suggest why he might be reviewing a sixteen-year-old restaurant of limited aspirations. Whatever its virtues, Les Halles was not "hot" or particularly relevant to today's trends. The menu certainly hadn't changed in years—and there had been no change in chefs.

Nor did he mention anywhere in his scorching review what was surely the most cogent point: that only weeks earlier, I'd repeatedly called him a douchebag. In fact, I'd nominated him for "Douchebag of the Year" in front of a hooting audience of half-drunk foodies at the South Beach Food and Wine Festival (an award Richman won handily, I might add).

The award, only one of many honors handed out in a silly, half-assed faux ceremony (presenters wore shorts and flip-flops), was widely reported on the Internet. And I guess Richman's feelings were hurt.

Enough so that he was inspired to remove his bathrobe, brush the cat hair off his jacket, and head into Manhattan to review—after all these years—Les Halles. A steak frites joint.

Now, let me ask *you* a question: If I were to call you, say . . . an asshole? You'd probably call me an asshole right back. Or maybe you'd go me one better. You'd call me a *fucking* asshole. Or, better yet, get really personal: "A loud, egotistical, one-note asshole who's been cruising on the reputation of one obnoxious, over-testosteroned book for way too long and who should just shut the fuck up."

This would be entirely fair and appropriate, one would think. I call you a schoolyard name. You respond in kind. You acknowledge the insult and reply with a pithy riposte.

But not Richman. He is, after all, an impeccably credentialed journalist, critic, educator, and arbiter of taste. Not for him a public pissing contest with some semi-educated journeyman who called him a dirty name.

No. What this utterly bent, gutless punk does, metaphorically speaking, is track down my old girlfriend from junior high—whom I haven't seen in years—sneak up behind her, and deliver a vicious sucker punch.

That'll teach me, right?

It's the old "I can't hurt you—but I can surely hurt someone you love" strategy, made more egregious and pathetic by the simple fact that Richman, douchebag or not, is a fairly erudite guy, fully trained in the manly art of the insult. He *could* have nailed me directly. An option whose possibilities are only hinted at in his review when he makes a most excellent (and painfully funny) comparison of me to beefy, direct-to-video action star Steven Seagal. That was what you'd call a palpable hit. *That* hurt.

In order to better understand Richman's inappropriate and unethical coldcocking of my blameless former comrades, you need to go back, to examine what moved me to accuse this beloved titan of food journalism of epic douchebaggery in the first place—and ponder if even that description is adequate. Was it, perhaps, part of a larger pattern of behavior?

A year after the worst natural disaster in the history of the United States, New Orleans was a city still on its knees—1,836 people dead; 100 billion dollars in damages; untold thousands of its citizens dispersed, dislocated, traumatized; lifetimes of accumulated possessions, photographs, mementos gone forever. Worse, still, there was the realization by the residents of an entire major American city that their government, when push came to shove, just didn't give a fuck about them. The city was still in shock, whole neighborhoods stood empty, one hospital was fully functioning, and the restaurant industry—which had been among the first to return after the flooding and was desperately trying to hold on to its staffs—was down 40 percent in business. Or more.

And that is when Alan Richman comes along, having decided in his wisdom that *now* is the time for a snarky reevaluation of the New Orleans dining scene. He'd already determined that New Orleans pretty much deserved what it got. Inspired, perhaps, by the Tyson defense team, he launches right away into a key component of his argument. That "the bitch was asking for it":

> It was never the best idea, building a subterranean city on a defenseless coastline . . . residents could have responded to that miscalculation in any number of conscientious ways, but they chose

endless revelry . . . becoming a festival of narcissism, indolence and corruption. Tragedy could not have come to a place more incapable of dealing with it.

He suggests that bad character and loose morals have led directly to what happened to New Orleans. For one thing, they like food too much, he goes on to say. This from a man who, for decades, has made a living shoving food into his crumb-flecked maw—then writing about it in a way calculated to make us feel like we should care. And we *did* care. So it's monstrously disingenuous of Richman to now claim that, perhaps, we care too much:

It might sound harmless for a civilization to focus on food, but it's enormously indulgent. Name a society that cherishes tasting menus and I'll show you a people too portly to mount up and repel invaders.

Maybe I'm reading too much into this, but, here, is Richman *really* saying, "If only these fat fucks had laid off the dessert cart they could have outrun the flood?"

Having blamed the victims for the carnage—a direct result, he proposes, of their immoral and ungodly behavior—he seems to depict Katrina and the perfect storm of incompetence and neglect that followed as some kind of divine retribution, a punishment for libertinism.

Not yet done, he goes on to question if the food was ever any good in the first place—if New Orleans's famous Creole cuisine (or Creoles themselves, for that matter) ever existed. Not only is New Orleans not worth visiting now, but perhaps—perhaps—it sucked all along!

Supposedly, Creoles can be found in and around New Orleans. I have never met one and suspect they are a faerie folk, like leprechauns, rather than an indigenous race. The idea that you might today eat an authentic Creole dish is a fantasy . . .

What the fuck does "authentic" mean, anyway? Creole, by definition, is a cuisine and a culture undergoing slow but constant change since its beginnings, a result of a gradual, natural fusion—like Singaporean or Malaysian flavors and ingredients changing along with who's making babies with whom, and for how long. The term "authentic"—as Richman surely knows—whether discussing Indian curries or Brazilian *feijoada*, is essentially meaningless. "Authentic" when? "Authentic" to whom? But it sounds good and wise, doesn't it?

In the days following Katrina, chef Donald Link of the restaurant Herbsaint was one of the very first business owners to return to the city, the flood waters still barely receded, to slop out the ruins of his existing restaurant, and to—rather heroically and against all odds— open a new one. He staffed his place with anyone he could find, took on volunteers, and served food—whatever he could—in the streets, sending a timely and important message that New Orleans was still alive and worth returning to. Richman chose his restaurant to trash.

I should mention that I visited New Orleans a year *after* Richman's article. It was a city still struggling to get up off its knees. The vast dining rooms and banquet spaces of Antoine's, the beloved institution in the French Quarter, were mostly empty—and yet the restaurant soldiered on with nearly a full staff, unwilling to fire people who'd worked for the company for decades. Everyone I spoke to, at one point or another, would still tear up and start to cry, remembering lost friends, lost neighborhoods, whole lives swept away. It seemed sometimes like all New Orleans had had a collective nervous breakdown, their psyches shattered by first the disaster itself—and then, later, by a pervasive sense of betrayal. How could a country—their country—have let this happen, their neighbors left to huddle like cattle in a fetid, reeking stadium, or bloat and rot, day after day, in full view of the world?

It's the kind of scenario, the kind of special circumstances, one would think, where even the most hardened journalist would ask himself, "Do I really want to kick them when they're down?" Richman was not reporting on Watergate, after all—he wasn't uncovering a secret Iranian nuclear program. He was writing an overview of restaurants. About a restaurant town that survives largely on its service economy. At its lowest, most vulnerable point—right after a disaster unprecedented in American history. And not for the *Washington Post*, either, mind you. For a magazine about ties and grooming accessories and choosing the right pair of slacks.

But no matter. The truth must be served. Alan Richman *knows* what "authentic" Creole cuisine means. And he damn sure wants you to know it.

This, alone, was surely reason enough to qualify as a finalist for Douchebag of the Year, but there was also this—another column: Richman's "restaurant commandments," in which he imperiously (if rather wittily) laid out a compendium of things which He found annoying and which those restaurants hoping to stay in His good graces should probably take to heart. This kind of article is much loved by writers in the field of restaurants, particularly recognizable ones, like Richman, whose lives are no doubt made easier in their daily rounds once their likes and dislikes have been communicated to their eager-to-please victims ahead of time. Under commandment #19, Richman lists:

Show Us the Chef:

If dinner for two is costing $200, you have every right to expect the chef to be at work. Restaurants where the famous celebrity chef has taken the night off should post a notice, similar to the ones seen in Broadway theaters: "The role of our highly publicized head chef will be played tonight by sous-chef Willie Norkin, who took one semester of home economics and can't cook."

As an example of lazy, disingenuous food journalism, one could scarcely hope for a better example. And this kind of cheap populism is particularly galling coming from Richman, because he knows better. If anyone knows the chef is not in, is not likely to be in, and can't reasonably be expected to be in anytime soon—it's Richman. He doesn't live and work in a vacuum. He doesn't write from a cork-lined room. Like others of his ilk, he moves in a demimonde of writers, journalists, bloggers, "foodies," freeloaders, and publicists, all of whom know each other by sight: a large, ever-migrating school of fish involved—to one degree or another—in a symbiotic relationship with chefs. For years, he has observed his subjects being shaken down by every charity, foundation, "professional association," civic booster, and magazine symposium—as well as by some of his colleagues. Many times, no doubt, they have complained to him (off the record) directly. Countless times, I'm sure, Richman has gazed wearily across the latest Fiji water–sponsored chef clusterfuck, over the same tuna tartare hors d'oeuvres (provided by some poor chef who's been squeezed into service by whatever the concern of the moment is), seen the chef or chefs dutifully doing their dog-and-pony act. He also well understands, one would think, the economics of maintaining the kinds of operations he's talking about.

Yet he demands, and expects us to believe, that every time a table of customers plunks down $200 at one of Bobby Flay's restaurants, that Bobby himself should rush on over to personally wrap their tamales—then maybe swing by, give them a little face time over dessert. Thomas Keller, according to Richman's thesis, should be burning up the air miles, commuting between coasts for every service at the French Laundry *and* Per Se. Particularly if Richman is in the house.

The whole suggestion is predicated on a damnable fucking lie— the BIG lie, actually—one which Richman himself happily helped create and which he works hard, on a daily basis, to keep alive. See . . . it makes for a better article when you associate the food with a personality. Richman, along with the best and worst of his peers, built up these names, helped make them celebrities by promoting the illusion that they cook—that if you walk into one of dozens of Jean-Georges's restaurants, he's somehow back there on the line, personally sweating over your halibut, measuring freshly chopped herbs between thumb and forefinger. Every time someone writes "Mr. Batali is fond of strong, assertive flavors" (however true that might be) or "Jean Georges has a way with herbs" and implies or suggests that it was Mr. Batali or Mr. Vongerichten who actually cooked the dish, it ignores the reality, if not the whole history, of command and control and the creative process in restaurant kitchens. While helpful to chefs, on the one hand, in that the Big Lie builds interest and helps create an identifiable brand, it also denies the truth of what is great about them: that there are plenty of great cooks in this world—but not that many great *chefs*.

The word "chef" means "chief." A chef is simply a cook who leads other cooks. That quality—leadership, the ability to successfully command, inspire, and delegate work to others—is the very essence of what chefs are about. As Richman knows. But it makes better reading (and easier writing) to first propagate a lie—then, later, react with entirely feigned outrage at the reality.

Underlying Richman's argument, one suspects, is his real exasperation. Who *are* these grubby little cooks to *dare* open more restaurants? How *could* they be so . . . presumptuous as to try to move up and beyond their stations? Surely it is the writers of sentences, the storytellers—so close to poets—upon whom praise and riches and clandestine blow jobs should be lavished! Not these brutish, unwashed, and undereducated men whose names are known only because he, Richman, once deigned to write them down!

The line about "sous-chef Willie Norkin, who took one semester of home economics and can't cook," while entertaining from an ignoramus, is unpardonable coming from Richman.

The whole system of fine dining, the whole brigade system—since Escoffier's time—is designed so that the chef might have a day off. The French Laundry, Per Se—ANY top-flight restaurant's whole command-and-training organization—is built around the ideal of consistency, the necessity for the food and service to be exactly the same every time, whether the chef (famous or otherwise) is in or out. Richman knows full well that the chef, by the time his name is well-known enough to profitably write about, is more likely to be in the full reclining position on a Cathay Pacific flight to Shanghai than in the kitchen, when Richman next parks his wrinkled haunches into a chair in said chef's dining room. In any great restaurant, the food is going to be just as good without the chef as with—otherwise it wouldn't be great in the first place.

Richman's Commandment #19 is a fucking insult to the very people who've been cooking and creating dishes for him for years. What's worse is that, once again, this uniquely gas-engorged douche knows better. But rest assured that while he has no problem giving the stiff middle finger to the people who actually prepare his food, he will be sure to remain in good odor with the "celebrity" chefs he claims— on our behalf, no doubt—to be outraged by. He needs that access, you see. He likes the little kitchen tours, the advance looks at next season's menus, the "friends and family" invites to restaurants that have yet to open to the public, the occasional scrap of strategically leaked gossip, the free hors d'oeuvres, the swag bags, the extra courses, the atten- tion, the flattering ministrations of the few remaining chefs who still pretend that what Alan Richman writes is in any way relevant.

Not to single out Richman.

Using his position as a critic to settle personal hash puts him in the same self-interested swamp as those of his peers who use their power for personal gain. Take John Mariani, the professional jun- keteer over at *Esquire*, whose "likes and dislikes" (shower cap in his comped hotel, attractive waitresses, car service) are mysteriously communicated, as if telepathically, to chefs before his arrival. (Mother-fucker hands out pre-printed recipe cards on arrival, with instructions on how to prepare his cocktail of choice—a daiquiri.) This guy has been a one-man schnorrer for decades. He's been caught red-handed on numerous occasions—but his employers continue to dissemble on his behalf. What his editors fail to understand is that all the denials in the world don't change what everybody—and I mean *everybody*—in the restaurant business knows. Among his subjects, people don't won-der about this guy—and whether he's bent or not. They *know*.

Simply stated, this allows savvy restaurants in Cleveland or Chi-cago to essentially "buy" a good review—and national coverage. Just don't blow the gaff—as chef Homaro Cantu found out, to his displea-sure. It'll only fuck things up for everybody. After Cantu complained publicly of the way he had been treated by Mariani, making mention of the legendary wish list that preceded his arrival, *Esquire* editors made assurances that Mr. Mariani is directly responsible for no such list but artfully avoided the fact that a list most surely emanates from someone associated with him (a PR firm, perhaps?). But then the same delicate parsing of words is employed when Mariani is described as always paying for the meals that he reviews. Leaving to dangle the question of who pays for all the other meals, his transportation, lodging, and shower caps.

Over at the financial magazine *Crane's*, longtime reviewer Bob Lape was known to one and all in the industry as "Sponge Bob." It was not a term of endearment. He earned it—with hijinks like jacking up "friendly" chefs to provide food for his wedding. On the subject of the critic referred to as "Sgt. Pepper," I'll abstain. Let her go gentle into that good night. Like Richman, she did good work in her day. Maybe it helped to buy the boyfriend's pictures, maybe not. Maybe *all* of Jerry Kretchmer's restaurants really *were* that good. She was always, to her credit, an enthusiast first.

Richman, unlike many of his peers, generally knows what he's talking about. As a writer, he has all God's gifts: experience, knowledge of subject matter, a vocabulary—and the ability to put words together in entertaining and incisive fashion. Unlike the grifters, freeloaders, and pushovers who make up the majority of the food-and-dining press, Richman's is a discerning palate. But dumping on a place because you have a personal beef with the chef (past, present, or otherwise)?

Hell, the *Times* would fire your ass for that (or, at least, "promote" you to the "T" section).

In the film *Sexy Beast*, Sir Ben Kingsley's terrifyingly believable English gangster character frequently uses a pejorative common to the British Isles, a term that Americans must circumspectly refer to as the "c-word." The English and Irish bandy it about often—as, in their manner of usage and in their context, it does not refer hatefully or disparagingly to a part of the female anatomy. On the contrary, it is an unflattering (even, sometimes, an affectionately unflattering) noun describing a male person—often used in conjunction with the adjective "silly."

It implies someone slightly more odious than a twit, older and more substantial than a shithead, yet without the gravitas required to be called an asshole.

So, maybe I got it wrong.

Alan Richman is *not* a douchebag.

He's a cunt.

15

"I Lost on *Top Chef*"

Erik Hopfinger at thirty-eight, twenty years in the business, stood in front of the pass, a stack of dupes in his right hand, expediting to his cooks. It was Sunday morning in San Francisco's Marina District and Circa restaurant was full up with brunchers. The bar was crowded with them, sucking down all-you-can-drink mimosas.

He'd made a tactical error putting the "Benedict sampler" on the menu, he realized. Though wildly popular and a successful exercise in marketing, the dish had quickly become his nemesis. Customers could choose *two* of six different eggs Bennie preparations per order, allowing for over twenty different combinations of poached egg varietals and interchangeable components. The outcome was predictable: a simple four-top led easily to a dupe as long as your fucking arm. By the time the customer at position one had finished pairing the "Nova Benedict" with a "Mexi-Benedict" and substituted tenderloin from the "Bernaise" for the chorizo—and then swapped out regular hollandaise for the saffron hollandaise and asked for the eggs well done—and the doofus across the table at position three has done the same—but different—well, multiply this times four at one table and extrapolate for the whole main-floor dining room and mezzanine, and you've got yourself the kind of morning that any cook who's ever worked a busy Saturday-night shift, and followed that with an injudicious number of Fernet-Branca-and-ginger-ale shots, hates and fears in their bones.

The rest of the brunch menu was filled with slightly tweaked conventional-wisdom classics, a savvy but unimaginative variation on the standard document that experience tells you you absolutely *need* in order to fill your restaurant on a Sunday morning and afternoon. In addition to the obligatory eggs, there was a club sandwich of turkey and avocado, an equally inevitable "veggie club," skewers of tomato and mozzarella, French toast, roast beef hash, huevos rancheros—and sliders (albeit with black truffle and Brie)—and there was fried calamari and a lobster mac 'n' cheese and a fruit platter and the tragically inescapable "classic" Caesar salad. The addition of chicken to the Caesar being, of course, an option.

It says something about a person when you put chicken Caesar on the menu. You've crossed a line and you know it. It's the chef version of sucking Ron Jeremy's cock. If you do it late in your career, any notions of future stardom are usually pretty much out the window.

But Erik Hopfinger was already a star.

Arms crossed, front and center of a group of shorter, less menacing-looking chefs, his giant-size, bald, bullet-headed, heavily pierced, and tattooed image glowered at the world from buses, billboards, and the pages of glossy magazines everywhere. His was the principal face of season four of *Top Chef*, the best and most watched of the competitive cooking shows. Of the contestants, Erik had obviously been designated the "bad-ass." He was older, more experienced (in years, anyway), and with an imposing—if not threateningly transgressive—look; so much, one would imagine, had been expected of him on the show. You could tell that from how they'd photographed him for the posters: like the lead singer of a band—or a top-billed professional wrestler. (In fact, Erik looks like a bit of both.) The producers, I think it is safe to suppose, anticipated much drama from Chef Hopfinger over the course of a long and closely contested competition.

Unhappily for everybody, he barely made it through episode one.

I know this because I was a judge on that episode.

And he got sent home from the field of battle by episode three.

Today, though, he was still famous and, at the very least, among friends. In between the smart-looking couples at the large, oblong bar, heavily inked young men drank in groups of two and three. Fellow cooks. The home team. You could tell the cooks from the civilians by what they drank. Civilians drank the free mimosas. The industry types were deep into the Fernet shots. Somewhere in the dining room were Erik's best friend, his girlfriend—and his mom. He was getting paid good money for a five-day workweek (almost unheard of in the industry). And dinner service ended at the unbelievably early hour of ten p.m. so Circa could make the changeover to its principal business, which was the club/lounge thing.

"I couldn't get into auto mechanics," he said later, at the bar across the street, a pint of beer in his hand, watching the dust motes float over the beer taps in the late-afternoon light. He fell into a vocational cooking class instead.

Perhaps now is the time to picture him, an imposingly tall, wide, barrel-chested guy, silver hoop earrings in both ears, multiple rings, the goatee, the tats. He cultivates a shave-headed piratical look. But what doesn't come across in the photos is his sweetness. The voice doesn't really fit the appearance; his eyes dart away from you when he talks. He seems . . . shy. From within the hulking body and the designed-to-intimidate look—half pirate, half Aryan Brother—there's a vibe of a scared and damaged little boy, someone who might burst into tears at any moment. Which is to say he's a very likeable guy. You want—shortly after meeting him—to give him a hug.

At seventeen, he answered an ad in the local penny-saver and began washing dishes at the Chateau Continental in Briarcliff, New York.

"It was a two-man kitchen," he said. "Ugly Albanian dudes." They did about forty depressing covers a night, a mixed bag of delusionally transatlantic fare like Greek salad, beef bourguignon, and stuffed veal chop. He washed dishes, scrubbed pots, peeled potatoes, and did general scut work there for a year and a half before decamping for greener fields and more elevated social status at T.G.I. Friday's in Tarrytown.

"I started getting laid at Friday's," he said, by way of explanation. He made eleven dollars an hour, worked the grill station, drank for free—and by age eighteen had been rewarded for his high standards of burgerdom with a promotion to what would appear on later résumés alternately as "sous chef" and "kitchen manager."

Around this time, he fell into the professional orbit of friend and hockey buddy, Scott.

Scott was living a relatively high life over at Huckleberry's in Yorktown, which put even the sybaritic delights of T.G.I. Friday's to shame.

He had "a cool car and hot chicks," Erik remembered, an observation that led him to abandon Friday's for his friend's kitchen. He enthusiastically took the less prestigious but presumably more rewarding position of "fry monkey" at Huckleberry's. Asked to remember the menu, he foggily recalls chicken potpie, shepherd's pie, and tempura. With somewhat more clarity, he recalls being fired twice during the year and a half he worked there—and that he "fucked the whole staff."

Young Erik was now twenty years old. Examining the murk of his résumé, one would likely find one of those mysteriously soft, gray spots—all too common to cooks of his generation (and mine). What was actually a yearlong "hiatus" as a landscaper disappears, no doubt in between the happy days of wine and frolic at Huckleberry's and his next restaurant gig at the Thataway Cafe in Greenwich, Connecticut. Departure date at Huckleberry's moved forward a bit. Start day at

Thataway pulled back. In my case, whole years disappear in this way. One's younger years now a seamless record of full and (as important) *steady* employment. Or, depending on who's going to be looking at your résumé, T.G.I. Friday's or Thataway Cafe can be replaced by "traveling in France."

Unless—like Erik—you spend *three years* at the Thataway, "drinking and snorting" and cooking an unchallenging menu of burgers, chicken sandwiches, and flank steaks.

Sometime in the early '90s (the exact dates being characteristically hazy), Erik Hopfinger answered an ad and found himself working the pantry and grill stations at Eros on First Avenue in Manhattan. He describes it as the first good restaurant he'd ever worked in. The chef had worked at the Quilted Giraffe (a still important restaurant). They made their own charcuterie, roasted fish whole, on the bone, and grilled fresh sardines. Small things, one would think now—but relatively advanced thinking back then—and definitely a big deal for Erik. Nearly two decades later, he puts down his pint glass with a five-mile stare and remembers. It's the first time since we've started talking that he seems genuinely excited talking about *food*.

"Eros was super-new. I had never worked in the city and was totally overwhelmed. With the spices, the brines, the butchering—and the city itself. I think I took the challenge balls to the wall, you know? Putting in my first real shifts, arriving at two p.m. and working until two a.m. I never asked so many questions in my life."

"But, soon after this, you bugged out for fucking California," I challenge him. "You're learning stuff. It's just started getting tough, the first good food you've cooked in your life. Okay, maybe it's not the majors yet . . . but at least you've got a foot on the fucking *ladder*. And then you're *gone*? You screw the pooch for California? Why?"

"Scott," he answered. As if that explained everything.

"When I left for San Francisco, I felt a little shitty. But I was determined to be a chef and thought by being a New Yorker, I'd have a leg up on all those laid-back Cali dudes," he added in a statement I found unconvincing. The more likely explanation is simply that his bestest buddy was in San Francisco and said he should come out, that it was fun. So he did.

What is a reasonably certain matter of record is that Erik Hopfinger arrived in San Francisco in 1996 and became the sous chef at City Tavern. Not too long after, when the chef didn't show up on a Friday night, he says, he found himself in charge.

Two years later, he was the chef at Backflip, a hipster bar in a retro-cool motel in the Tenderloin District, where he started to get some attention—a nod for best bar food from the *San Francisco Chronicle*—and where he began to establish a career pattern of working fairly high-profile places that were as much bars (or lounges) as they were restaurants. It's also—and I'm guessing this on the basis of almost nothing—where he started to learn how to hustle, how to manage expectations, work the press, shape the beginnings of a public image of sorts.

Then there was Butterfly, a more ambitious venture into Asian fusion—and also a big bar scene.

Which is where I met him for the first time—an occasion I describe pseudonymously in *A Cook's Tour*.

I remember him, in 2001, with hair. Blond, at the time, I think. Comping me and my crew a meal and then inviting me back into his kitchen, where he unburdened himself of some staffing problems he was having. I believe I advised him to fire his sous chef. Was it Scott? My recollection is that he appeared to agree with my suggested course of action—before offering me a bump.

I saw him again a year or so later. At the House of Prime Rib. We got pretty drunk together and ate a lot of beef.

After Butterfly, there was something called Spoon. He alludes to a brief spell in a Mexican jail. (The name "Scott" appears again in this episode.) Then Cozmo's Corner Grill . . . before finally landing at Circa.

I hadn't heard anything more from him or about him until the producers of *Top Chef* called. Since I was an occasional guest judge, they wanted to know how well I knew this guy Hopfinger—as I would likely be facing him across the table in the coming season. They wanted to know if I could exercise my critical duties without any personal considerations coming into play.

I assured them that I could.

According to Erik, he'd attracted the notice of the *Top Chef* casting people at a "Battle of the Chefs" event held at a department store— one of those silly promotional clusterfucks much loved by restaurant publicists, as it makes them look like they're actually doing something. The chef gets to bust his ass giving away a lot of free food—and, presumably, the masses, having noticed his fine work, form a herd and gang-rush his restaurant. Usually, this kind of thing attracts a bunch of freeloading types. The kind of people who hang around department stores for free food, or because they have nothing better to do, are very rarely the kind of customer to come into your restaurant with friends and spend profligately on wine. But in this case, says Erik, it attracted two television producers. "One dude was kind of geeky. The other was a hot blonde. It was their first Fernet experience."

Curiously, he never had to cook for them.

They wanted to know:

"What do you think of Tom Colicchio?" (Correct answer: "I see him as the walking Buddha of chefdom.")

"What are your passions?" (Correct answer: "Cooking! And being a 'character' with a good backstory—prone to dramatic confrontations with fellow contestants!")

After he was told he'd made the cut, he went to the Horseshoe and got loaded, dreaming of his future fame.

Not too long after, Erik Hopfinger found himself boarded up and under guard with fifteen other contestants at an undisclosed location in Chicago, deprived of television, Internet, unsupervised telephone calls, and subject to a secret agreement so draconian as to be the envy of the NSA.

Now, I haven't read *my* copy of this agreement. But I seem to remember the figure "million" mentioned—along with "dollars" and vows of absolute confidentiality. And I'm guessing that both Erik and I are *still* somehow constrained from talking about specifics of security; any on-set instances of the use of controlled substances; which judges might or might not be smarter than the others; whether or not there are tumblers of gin and tonic under the judges' table—and so on. To speculate on such things would be irresponsible.

What *I* can assure you—without hesitation or qualification—is that the judging I've been witness to or part of, in five appearances as a judge, has always been straight. Meaning, no matter how much the producers of the show may *want* the contestant with the heartbreakingly tragic personal story (and amazing chesticles) to survive until next week, the worst cook *that particular week* goes home. On *Top Chef*—as long as Tom Colicchio is head judge—the best food that week gets you the win. The worst gets you the loss. It's the "what have you done for me lately" criterion at judges' table. Due to the fact that guest judges can't and haven't been witness to a contestant's previous efforts, past works do NOT factor into the final judgment. I feel sorry for the producers sometimes, imagining their silent screams as Tom reluctantly decides that the all-around better contestant, with the movie-star looks and the huge popularity with viewers, just fucked up too bad to make it to next week and has to go home.

Their lips mouthing, "Nooooooo! Not Trey!!! NOT TREYYY!!!" impotently in the control room as another beloved fan-favorite gets sent packing.

Judging is taken seriously by the permanent judges and guest judges alike. I've spent *hours* arguing with Tom, Padma, and guest judges—trying to reach a consensus on winners and losers. It is a thoughtful and considered process.

What should be stressed here is that what the contestants on *Top Chef* are asked to do is really, *really* difficult. Confined to quarters with strangers, separated from family and friends, they are asked to execute—on short notice—a bizarre progression of cooking challenges without benefit of recipes or cookbooks. Anything from "create a snack from this crap vending machine" to "make a traditional Hawaiian meal with unfamiliar ingredients" to "create a four-course high-end menu for Eric Ripert." And do it in the rain. Over portable field-ranges. The rigors of *Top Chef*'s unpredictable, high-pressure, occasionally loony, product-placement-driven challenges ("be sure to use X brand frozen pasta dinners in your final dish") would be brutal for any seasoned professional.

I'll tell you honestly that if *I* were a contestant? I *might*, maybe—if I was lucky, and only through a combination of years of experience, stealth, strategy, and guile—duck and dodge my way through a few weeks. I'd never make the finals.

What's fascinating to a professional watching the show is how other talented professional cooks and chefs are pushed to the limits of their ability. You can actually see them hit the ceiling, the place beyond which they just aren't prepared to—just *can't* go. And exactly *why*: a failure of the imagination, a failure of technique or strategy, maturity or experience. And yet—many times, you see contestants go *beyond* their previous abilities. You can see them dig down—or pull from left field and go higher than they've ever been before. This leads—all by itself—to fascinating drama for food nerds. The "best" chef—or the best all-around talent—doesn't necessarily win. The most technically skilled cook, or the most creative, often overreaches, chokes, makes a crucial and inexplicable error of judgment. Just like real life. *That's* what makes the show worth watching (to me, anyway)—that the chef left standing after all others have fallen represents the qualities you'd want of a chef in the real world: a combination of creativity, technical skill, leadership abilities, flexibility, maturity, grace under pressure, sense of humor, and sheer strength and endurance.

Erik Hopfinger came one thin hair away from getting snuffed right out of the box.

I was guest judge, along with Rocco DiSpirito and regulars Padma and Tom. The challenge was to re-create one of a list of midrange-restaurant cliché classics, like shrimp scampi, lasagna, steak au poivre, and duck à l'orange. The contestants drew knives to determine who got what. Erik got the soufflé.

Now, a soufflé can be a tricky thing under the best of circumstances. Most cooks learn to make them in school—and, unless they move on to become pastry chefs, are seldom called on to make them again. Ever. Because of their delicacy and time concerns, and 'cause they just haven't been in fashion, you rarely see a soufflé of any kind in a restaurant these days. Which means very few cooks—if suddenly called upon to make one *without a recipe*—could do so. Hell, even with a recipe, I'd guess the greater part of the cooking population would fuck the job up. Me? Maybe. And that's only because I spent six months doing almost nothing *but* making soufflés at the Rainbow Room early in my career (and they were a pretty leathery, unimpressive version, made from cement-like bechamel, cheap flavorings, and meringue). Even if you do everything right before you get your soufflé in the oven, there's still a whole lot of ways to fuck up: pull it out too soon, it deflates by service. Too late? It burns and hollows. Slam the oven door? Forget to correctly grease and sugar the mold? Thermostat fucked? Uneven heat in the oven? Or will the thing just sit too long while they reset the cameras or apply powder to a shiny judge? The soufflé is fraught with peril. And in a competitive, high-pressure situation like *Top Chef*—where even shit you *know* how to do in your *bones* can suddenly sense fear and go south on you—well . . . a soufflé is a death sentence.

From the relative comfort of my judge's chair, a freshly poured gin close at hand, I saw Erik draw the soufflé and knew the poor bastard had walked right into the grinder. He looked like he'd been punched in the stomach before he even started cooking.

In retrospect, he says now, *Top Chef* "looks a lot easier sittin' on the couch with a joint in your mouth."

What he came up with was a soufflé only in the most liberal interpretation of the word. It *did* come in a soufflé mold—intended, I could only guess, as an airier version of cornbread or corn pudding. But like a dog trying to cover its shit with leaves or dirt, Erik had literally piled on every trick—or trope—in the faux-Mex, Southwestern cookbook. The plate looked like the last shot of a *bukakke* video—filmed at Chili's. There was some kind of awful avocado jiz squirted all over the plate. Some other squeeze-bottled madness . . . and, worst of all, the "soufflé" itself had been buried under a fried garnish either crushing the fucking thing or ineptly concealing the fact that it had never risen in the first place. Looking down with no small amount of sadness at what he'd put in front of me, I could only compare it to the work of a first-time serial killer, hurriedly and inadequately trying to dispose of his victim under twigs and brush—inevitably to be discovered by the first passing dogwalker.

What saved him that week was another contestant's shrimp scampi. While Erik had thoroughly fucked up a hard task, she'd managed to make a hideous botch of a very simple one. Her twist on scampi involved three very basic, very simple elements—all of which she'd botched indefensibly. The shrimp was overcooked. The accompanying "flan" had curdled into an unappetizing, smegma-like substance. And she'd criminally oversalted the dish.

As happens sometime on the show, someone who failed utterly was saved solely by the fact that someone else sucked worse.

Two weeks later, the ax fell. He was sent home over a soggy corn dog.

"Did you ever belong on the show in the first place?" I ask him.

"No. I knew it all along." He stopped watching the show after he was thrown off.

Was he ever scared?

"What scares me," he says, "is growing up. Having kids. I'm deathly afraid of having kids. Probably 'cause I *am* a big kid." He drains his beer, examines the empty pint glass thoughtfully, and offers, "But that would probably make me a good father. I love Disneyland. The whole pirate thing. I love Disneyland. *That* makes me want to procreate."

Of his *Top Chef* experience, he has no complaints. "They didn't turn me into something I wasn't." And of his life and career in general? The good, the bad?

"I'm pretty happy with the way I've done things, where I'm at. I'm going down a good path. The quality of life is good. Hanging out . . . my friends, eating great food.

"Look," he says, "I love cooking food. I'm not pressing any culinary envelopes. I know that. There's a few sick fuckers like us who were actually meant to do this."

16

"It's Not You, It's Me"

A while back, I had the uncomfortable yet illuminating experience of taking part in a public discussion with one of my chef heroes, Marco Pierre White. It was at a professional forum, held in an armory in New York—one of those chef clusterfucks where the usual suspects gather once a year to give away, in the front lobby, samples of cheese, thimble-size cups of fruit-flavored beers, and wines from Ecuador. An unsuspecting Michael Ruhlman attempted to moderate this free-for-all—an unenviable job, as trying to "control" Marco is to experience the joke about the "six-hundred-pound gorilla" firsthand: he sits wherever he fucking *wants*, *when* he fucking wants to sit, and fuck you if you don't like it. Marco was the Western world's first rock-star chef, the prototype for all celebrity chefs to follow, the first Englishman to grab three Michelin stars—and one of the youngest chefs to do so. Every cook of my generation wanted to grow up to be Marco. The orphaned, dyslexic son of a working-class hotel chef from Leeds, he came up in an era when they still *beat* cooks. Years after famously handing back his stars at the peak of his career, he's now got more money than he knows what to do with, has had every woman he's ever wanted—and, as he likes to say, contents himself these days with the full-time job of "being Marco."

He may spend much of his time stalking the English country-side with a $70,000 shotgun, contemplating the great mysteries of the natural world, half-country squire and half-hoodlum, but he's paid his dues. He's a man who, if you ask him a direct question, is going to tell you what he thinks.

On stage that day, I asked, innocently enough, what Marco thought of huge, multicourse tasting menus—whether, perhaps, we'd reached the point of diminishing returns. I knew he'd recently had a meal at Grant Achatz's very highly regarded Alinea in Chicago—thought of by many as the "best" restaurant in America. And I knew he hadn't enjoyed it. I thought it was worthwhile to explore why not.

Achatz, it is generally agreed, sits at the top of the heap of the American faction of innovative, experimental, forward-thinking chefs who were inspired by the work of Ferran Adrià and others. I thought it was a provocative but fair question—particularly given Marco's own history of innovation, as well as his elaborate, formal, and very French fine-dining menus. He seemed to have had a change of heart on the subject of tasting menus—maybe even about haute cuisine in general—having insisted to me previously that all he wanted these days was a proper "main, and some pudding."

What I hadn't anticipated—and what poor Ruhlman certainly hadn't—was the absolute vehemence with which Marco hated, hated, *hated* his meal at Alinea. Without bothering to even remember the chef's name or the name of his establishment, Marco spoke of an un-named restaurant that was unmistakably Alinea as if Achatz had shot his favorite dog and then served him the still-steaming head. The way Marco went after him, dismissing all his experimental presentations and new cooking techniques with a contemptuous wave of the hand, came from a place of real animus. Warming to his subject, he went on and on—all of us blissfully unaware that Achatz himself, a beloved and respected figure in gastronomy, was sitting a few rows in—right in front of us.

The next day, there were hurt feelings and recriminations all around. Ruhlman, who'd worked on a book with Achatz and who is unrestrained in his admiration for the man and his food, found himself accused of treachery by loyalists and acolytes, pilloried for "allowing" such a thing as this public demonstration of disrespect. It's rather hilarious to imagine Ruhlman or anyone else trying to stop it—given Marco's fearsome reputation, rock-star ego, not to mention his intimidating size. The fact that Achatz had only recently survived a heroic battle with cancer of the tongue, having had to contend with the possibility of losing his sense of taste forever, added another layer of awkwardness to the whole affair. Ruhlman was shaken up by the whole thing. (It's pretty much par for the course with Ruhlman and me. I always manage to put him in the shit. Last adventure I involved him in apparently got him blackballed from a budding career at Food Network.)

The next day, at the same conference, Achatz reacted directly. He stood up and gave an impassioned and well-reasoned defense of the kind of cooking he does, associating himself, appropriately, with other pioneers of the form. It was an argument with which, in principle, I am in total agreement. That without experimentation, a willingness to ask questions and try new things, we shall surely become static, repetitive, moribund. Of all the chefs in the room, he hardly needed to explain why he was eminently qualified for the job.

Have I mentioned yet that Grant Achatz is probably a genius? That he's one of the best chefs and cooks in America? That his kitchen, just like Marco's old kitchen, is staffed with the very best of the best, the most fiercely motivated and dedicated cooks there are, the true believers, the SAS, the Green Berets of kitchen crews?

That it was Grant Achatz, then working with Thomas Keller at the French Laundry, who was co-responsible for the greatest single meal of my life?

Thing is, I, *too*, hated Alinea. In fact, I *despised* it.

Don't take this as a caution. If ever my *not* enjoying myself at a restaurant is a reason for *you* to go and decide for yourself, this is surely it. Alinea is a serious restaurant with a serious staff doing serious and important work.

But my meal there was one of the longest, least pleasurable meals of my life. Twenty minutes in, and I was looking at the little menu card, counting the (many) dishes to come, ticking off the hours, minutes, and seconds I'd have to remain before earning my freedom. I thought it lethally self-serious, usually pointless, silly, annoying, and generally joyless. It was, for me, a misery from beginning to end.

At the time, I was in the middle of a particularly mind-numbing book tour, and I found myself that night with a journalist who was actually thoughtful, interesting, and fun to be with. The possibility of a good and sustained conversation presented itself. And dinner—at one of America's most exciting new restaurants—seemed the perfect setting.

No.

At Alinea, every twenty minutes or so (too soon—but also not soon enough by a long shot), a waiter would appear at my elbow with some extremely distracting construction—a single eye-gouging strand of flexible wire from which one was invited to nibble; a plate atop a slowly deflating whoopee cushion, intended to gradually fart rosemary fumes or some such; a slab of pork belly, dangling senselessly from a toy clothesline—each creation accompanied by a lengthy explanation for which one's full attention was demanded.

With each course, the waiter, like a freshly indoctrinated, still cheerful Moonie, would hang there tableside, waiting for us to stop our conversation, before delivering a too-long description of what we were about to eat—and exactly *how* we should eat it. Half the time, I'd already popped the thing in my mouth and swallowed it by the time he'd finished with his act.

I sat there, sneaking looks at the little menu card to my right, silently ticking off each course as I finished it. There was one course—lobster, as I remember it—that was infuriatingly brilliant. It was also uncharacteristically restrained. I came away thinking, this guy, Achatz, with his skills and creativity, is going to rule the world someday; that when he moved past the form-over-function stuff on his menu, he, better than anyone, was suited for the Big Job, the next pope, the next Keller.

I am in the great minority in my assessment of Alinea. Many people whose opinions I respect believe it to be a truly great restaurant. In fact, my wife, usually a much, much harsher critic than I am, adores the place. On reading an early draft of this chapter, the mad bitch got on a plane, flew off to Chicago by herself, and dined—alone—at Alinea, curious to see what I was griping about. She had exactly the opposite experience I did. I believe she used the words "fantastic," "delicious," and "always entertaining" to describe her meal. "One of the best meals of my life," she snarled at me, on returning.

So . . . here's what I have to ask myself.

Am I just a mean, jaded prick? Or was Alinea really bullshit? Or is there some other, third path—a way to look at my reaction in a constructive fashion?

Let's face it: I am, at this point in my life, the very picture of the jaded, overprivileged "foodie" (in the very worst sense of that word) that I used to despise. The kind who's eaten way more than his share of Michelin-starred meals all over the world and is (annoyingly) all too happy to tell you about them. I am the sort of person whose head I once called for in the streets, the sort of person who—with a straight face—will actually whine about "too much foie gras" or "truffles—*again*?"

In short, I have become, over time, the sort of person who secretly dreads long, elaborate tasting menus. I've been denying it, to myself, but no longer. In fact, the only people I know who hate long, elaborate tasting menus more than me are chefs who *serve* long, elaborate tasting menus.

You might well ask at this point: "Well, uh . . . asshole. If your mind is poisoned against them—if you hate big tasting menus so fucking much, why go to Alinea? And why, why, why, then, go to Per Se? Why go to the Mother of Them All?"

It's a fair question, and I don't really have an answer.

It's true I walked in the door at Per Se with a sense of trepidation very different from the feelings of child-like awe I'd felt at the French Laundry all those years ago—when the twenty-course meal was all fresh and new. I'm a romantic, I guess. I wanted to believe that love conquers all.

Understand this: I respect no American chef above Thomas Keller.

I believe him to be America's "greatest" chef—in every sense of that word.

The single best fine-dining, white-tablecloth meal of my life was at his French Laundry.

I'm quite sure that it would be unlikely in the extreme that one could find better, more technically accomplished, generally gifted, harder-working chefs than the Laundry's Corey Lee or Per Se's Jonathan Benno (or whoever follows them in those positions).

I think that Keller long ago achieved that ideal state of haute nirvana where it matters not at all to the quality of food or service whether or not he is in attendance on any given night at any particular restaurant—and I'm happy for him about that. It is a testament to his excellence, his unwavering standards, and to the excellence of the teams and systems and institutions he's created, that this is so.

Per Se in New York City has four *New York Times* stars—along with three from Michelin. They deserve every one of them. You'd have

a very difficult time making the argument that there is a "better" restaurant in America.

So, why, I ask myself, did I come home from Per Se heartbroken
last night? And why, in the hours since, has an unarticulated, indefin-
able sadness hung over me—a cloud that followed me home, an evil
imp on my shoulder whispering terrible things into my skull? Like the
spare tire around my waist—something I just don't want to acknowledge.

Maybe if I creep up on this thing slowly—this spirit-destroying
guinea worm wriggling around inside me, threatening my happiness,
making me a bad person—maybe if I stab blindly at him with a cocktail fork, with a lucky shot I can reel the whole fucker out and resume
life as it was before.

Why are there voices in my head—making me ask . . . questions?
Like this one:

At the end of the day, would a good and useful criterion for evalu-
ating a meal be "Was it fun?"

Meaning: after many courses of food, sitting in the taxi on the way
home, when you ask yourself or your dinner companion, "Was that a
good time?" is the answer a resounding "Yes! Yes! My God, yes!"—or
would it, on balance, have been more fun spending the evening at
home on the couch with a good movie and a pizza?

Perhaps, given the expense and seriousness of the enterprise—and
the fact that, presumably, you had to dress for dinner—a fairer question
might be "Was it better than a really good blow job?" As this is the
intended result of so many planned nights on the town, would you—
having achieved touchdown before even getting *up* from the couch—
have then bothered to go out to dinner at all?

Okay. It's apples and oranges. How can you compare two completely different experiences? It's situational. It's unfair. It's like asking
if you'd prefer a back massage now—or a life without ever having seen
a Cézanne or Renoir.

How about this, then? Same situation. You're on your way home from the *menu dégustation* (or whatever they're calling it). You're sitting in the back of that same taxi, and you ask yourself an even simpler question:

"How do I *feel*?"

That's fair, isn't it?

Do you feel good?

How's your stomach?

Could what you just had—assuming you're with a date—be described, by any stretch of the imagination, as a "romantic" experience? Honestly now. I know you spent a lot of money. But look across the seat at the woman with you. Do you *really* think she's breathlessly anticipating getting back to your apartment to ride you like the Pony Express? Or do you think it far more likely that (like you) she's counting the seconds till she can get away for a private moment or two and discreetly let loose with a backlog of painfully suppressed farts? That what she'd much prefer to do right now, rather than submit to your gentle thrusting, is to roll, groaning and miserable, into bed, praying she's not going to heave up four hundred dollars worth of fine food and wine?

And you—are you even up to the job? Any thoughts of sexual athleticism likely disappeared well before the cheese course.

That's a fair criterion, right? Least you could ask of a meal—by classical standards, anyway.

To establish precedent, let's take Ferran Adrià's El Bulli in Spain—perhaps the longest and most famous of the tasting menus. After the full-on experience there—about five sustained hours of eating and drinking—I felt pretty good. I hung around drinking gin and tonics for another two hours—after which I could, I believe, have performed sexually and then happily gone out for a snack.

Le Bernardin in New York offers a "Chef's Tasting Menu" and I always feel fine after. Both meals are pretty carefully calibrated experiences. Laurent Gras's L2O in Chicago, Andoni Aduriz's Mugaritz in Saint Sebastian both take a modest and reasoned approach to the limits of the human appetite.

I mentioned chefs dreading tasting menus.

Consider the curse of Ferran Adrià. Not Ferran Adrià the chef, restaurateur, and creative artist. Ferran Adrià the diner—the "eater," as he puts it. Ferran Adrià the frequent flyer. Doomed to walk this earth subjected to every jumped-up tasting menu, every wrongheaded venture in "molecular gastronomy" (a term he no longer uses), the interminable, well-intended ministrations of every admirer in every city and every country he may go. Imagine being Ferran Adrià. Food and wine festivals, chefs' conferences, book tours, symposia. Everywhere he goes, there's no getting out of it: he either gets dragged proudly to what his local handlers see as his kindred spirit—or he's just *obliged*, when in Melbourne or Milwaukee or wherever, to pay homage to the local Big Dog, who's famously worshipful of him. There's no slipping in and out of town quietly without dissing somebody. He's *got* to go.

One twenty-, thirty-course tasting menu after another, one earnest but half-baked imitator after another, wheeling out the tongue-scorching liquid nitrogen, the painfully imitative, long-discarded-by-Adrià foams, the clueless aping of Catalonian traditions they've probably never experienced firsthand.

And all the guy wants is a fucking burger.

Ferran Adrià walks into a bar . . . it's like a joke, right? Only, I'm guessing, it's no longer a joke to him. Because Ferran Adrià *can't* walk into a bar—without six or seven freebie courses he never wanted showing up in front of him. When all he wanted was a burger.

Thomas Keller surely knows this pain. If the stories are true, when Keller goes out to dinner, an assistant calls ahead and explicitly orders the restaurant to *not*, under *any* circumstances, send any extra courses. There will be no unasked-for amuse-bouches. The chef does not want to see your interpretation of his signature "oysters and pearls." He's coming in for your chicken on a stick—which is quite good or he wouldn't be coming—so please, leave the man alone.

You're thinking, oh, the poor dears, great chefs all over the world wanting to stuff expensive ingredients in their faces . . . fuck *them*! But c'mon . . . Imagine, day after day, tired from long flights, one hotel bed after another, bleary-eyed, exhausted, craving nothing more complicated than Mom's meatloaf, a simple roasted chicken—and here it comes, *another* three-hour extravaganza, usually a less good version of what you do for a living every day. It's like being an overworked porn star and everywhere you go in your off-hours people are grabbing your dick and demanding a quickie.

Sitting here, wrestling with my reaction to last night's meal at Per Se, I look back again; I search my memory for details from that greatest meal of my life at the French Laundry. There were me, Eric Ripert, Scott Bryan, and Michael Ruhlman. Twenty-two-some-odd courses—most of them different for each of us. God knows how many wines. A perfect, giddily excited five hours in wine country, thoughtfully punctuated by piss breaks. No one could have asked for more of a meal. Every plate seemed fresh and new—not just the ingredients, but the concepts behind them as well. It was a magical evening filled with many magical little moments. Those memories come back first:

The silly expressions on all our faces at the arrival of the famous cones of salmon tartare—how the presentation "worked" exactly as it was supposed to. Even on the chefs and on Ruhlman, Keller's coauthor on the cookbook.

The surprise course of "Marlboro-infused coffee custard with panseared foie gras," a dish designed specifically for me—at the time still a three-pack-a-day smoker—an acknowledgment that I was probably tweaking for a butt around that time.

The "oysters and pearls" dish—how thrilled I was to finally taste what I'd only gaped at previously in the lush pages of The Book. How they did not disappoint—if anything, only exceeded expectations. The way the waiter's hands trembled and shook as he shaved a gigantic black truffle over our pasta courses. How he dropped it—and how, with a look, we all agreed not to tell.

The four of us, during another break before dessert, drunk and whispering like kids on Halloween in the Laundry's rear garden as we snuck up to the kitchen window and spied enviously on Keller and his crew.

After-dinner drinks in the garden with the chef. Dark by now—and very late, the restaurant closing down. The way Keller seemed to vibrate at another, slower, deeper pitch than every other chef I'd met. He seemed a happy yet still restless man, sitting there, surrounded by growing things, the place he'd built. I asked the famously workaholic chef if he'd ever consider taking time off—just doing nothing for a month—and he reacted as if I'd asked the question in Urdu, tilting his head and trying to make out what I possibly could have meant. I remember pulling away in our ridiculous rented prom limousine, knowing that I had had the best meal of my life.

But I remember now another detail, something I'd forced from my memory as inconvenient. That didn't fit in the picture I was painting for myself—of an idyllic five hours in wine country, a timelessly magnificent meal prepared by a chef I idolized.

I push myself to remember what came *after*—what happened after we pulled away in our silly white stretch. There was little revelry in the back of that car. I remember moaning and heavy breathing. A struggle to hold on.

We willingly and enthusiastically ate and drank too much—this is clear. But this, I'd argue, is what is expected when you order the grand tasting at the Laundry or at Per Se. That you will—or should, if you're sensible—prepare yourself in advance: maybe fast for a day.

Wake up early the morning of your dinner and stretch your stomach with water. And the following day must be planned for as well. There will—there *must*—be a period of recovery.

Is there something fundamentally, ethically . . . *wrong* about a meal so Pantagruelian in its ambition and proportions? Other than the "people are starving in Africa" argument, and the "250,000 people lost their jobs in America last month alone" argument, there's the fact that they must necessarily trim off about 80 percent of the fish or bird to serve that perfectly oblong little nugget of deliciousness on the plate. There's the unavoidable observation that it's simply more food and alcohol than the human body is designed to handle. That you will, after even the best of times, the most wonderful of such meals, *need* to flop onto your bed, stomach roiling with reflux, the beginnings of a truly awful hangover forming in your skull, farting and belching like a medieval friar.

Is this the appropriate end, the inevitable result of genius? Of an otherwise sublime experience?

Must it end like this?

And should it end like this? Struggling mightily to not spray truffle-flecked chunks into the toilet?

No one expects that anyone would eat like this every other day—or even every other month. But even as a once-a-year thing . . . shouldn't how you feel afterward be a consideration?

I should point out that there is a perfectly reasonable *nine-course* option. We chose to be gluttonous. But when you're fortunate enough to be at Per Se or at the French Laundry, you just don't want to miss anything. You eat way past the point of hitting the wall. Or I do, anyway.

Last night, the early evening light appeared, to my jaundiced eye, unkind to Per Se. This was not a good way for me to start the meal. A dining room is a stage set, an elaborate illusion, a magician's trick contained between four walls. Per Se's dining room is one of the most meticulously constructed and most beautiful such spaces in New York.

It looks out over Columbus Circle and Central Park. There is a wide "breezeway" of unused space between the kitchen and dining room, a luxuriously empty zone designed to serve as a peaceful, quieting transitional area where servers can have a few extra seconds to make the transition from kitchen reality to dining-room reality.

If cooking professionally is about control, eating successfully should be about submission, about easily and without thinking giving yourself over to whatever dream they'd like you to share. In the best-case scenario, you shouldn't be intellectualizing what you're eating while you're eating it. You shouldn't be noticing things at all. You should be pleasingly oblivious to the movements of the servers in the dining area and bus stations, only dimly aware of the passage of time. Taking pictures of your food as it arrives—or, worse, jotting down brief descriptions for your blog entry later—is missing the point entirely. You shouldn't be forced to think at all. Only feel.

I was noticing things. Which is bad. Before darkness fell, bathing everything in sleek, sophisticated obscurity, the servers' uniforms looked a little sad. Shiny in spots, and old. They looked like . . . waiters instead of the ambassadors of culinary Olympus I'd always thought of them as. A wall-mounted table at a waiter station drooped ever so slightly at an angle uneven with the floor. The wood trim on the furniture was almost imperceptibly but nonetheless visibly patchy, and the roses on the table the tiniest bit old, their petals starting to go at the edges. For one of two of the most notoriously perfect dining rooms in America, this was shocking. I felt sad and depressed and deeply ashamed of myself for noticing.

And maybe I was detecting a sadness, too, in the voices of the servers. Jonathan Benno, the executive chef, had announced a few weeks earlier that he would be leaving, and maybe I was only imagining it, but the exuberance, the top-of-the-world pride and confidence I encountered at the French Laundry and at previous meals at Per Se seemed lacking that night, replaced by something else.

There were goujons. Two tiny little cheese-filled pillows.

And the famous cones of salmon tartare. Just as pretty and just as delicious as ever. But kind of like an old girlfriend by now. The thrill was gone. No word is as dead as "tartare" these days, and I found myself wondering how chef Benno really felt about the things; whether those cones, once objects of child-like wonder to even burned-out fucks like me, were now prison bars of a sort—too beloved, too famous, too expected to ever be removed or replaced by any chef.

I had a pretty weak summer vegetable gazpacho, but my wife's sweet carrot velouté was bright and clean, hinting of tarragon and anise.

I got the French Laundry classic, "oysters and pearls," one of Keller's most well-known and admired creations from back in the day: a sabayon of "pearls" of tapioca with oysters and caviar. The servers absolutely lavished it with caviar at tableside. If it is possible to put too much caviar on a dish, it happened here. It seemed . . . disrespectful of the old girl to dress her up that much. I admit to actually tearing up when this dish was put down in front of me. Even then, early in the meal, I had this inexplicable sense that I might never see her again. Here was a true modern American classic—and a personal favorite, one I was really sentimental about. I felt I shared personal history with her—all the things you'd want your guest to feel about their food. But I was dismayed by the profligacy with which my server ladled on the caviar. It felt like they were saying, "We don't trust the bitch to go out like that anymore, we got to put on some more lipstick"—and I was offended for her.

Day-boat scallop sashimi with cauliflower fleurettes, sweet carrots, and pea shoots was flawless, impeccable—and everybody else is doing it, or something like it, these days.

Marinated Atlantic squid with squash-blossom tempura and squash-blossom pesto was vibrant and new—and quickly, it was good to be alive again.

A white-truffle-oil-infused custard with a "ragout" of black winter truffles was over the top in a good way, a happy tweak of an old favorite from The Book, joyously excessive rather than insecure about itself. It was rich, wintery, and pounded its flavor home without apology. My wife's coddled egg with *"beurre noisette"* and toasted brioche was even better, too rich, too good, and too much—in the best possible ways.

But it was the next course—a homemade "mortadella" with turnip greens and violet artichokes and mustard for me, and a *"coppa di testa,"* made with guanciale with cucumber and ravigote for my wife—that was the first truly thrilling moment of the meal. These were refined but still relatively austere versions of everyday Italian country staples, flavors relatively rough and forward—and it felt like the first time I'd tasted salted food all day. I found myself hoping that this was the direction of the remainder of the meal. This, I thought, was good. This . . . was great.

I was brought rudely back to earth by the smoke-filled glass domes approaching our table. An otherwise wonderful "corned" veal tongue in one and a hunk of pork belly in the other, ruined by a completely unnecessary impulse to dazzle. They'd used those little smoke guns that no chefs seem able to keep their hands off these days, to pump the smoke into the specially custom-made, hand-blown glass vessels, and they shouldn't have bothered. The veal tongue managed to shrug the smoke off with little negative effect—but it totally fucked up the pork belly. It pissed me off—a gimmick.

There was sorbet. Then quail. A Long Island striped-bass "shank." I had a riff on the legendary butter-poached lobster while my wife ate softshell crabs. All good and lovely to look at.

A pasta course presented us with tagliatelle on the one hand and spinach rigatini on the other, both absolutely heaped with truffles by our waiter. Again, I wanted to say, "What the fuck are you doing? It's *too much!*" but I sat mute as my delicately flavored pasta disappeared beneath a blanket of aromatic fungi. I was again kind of hurt—this time, personally—feeling suddenly like a stripper you drunkenly throw money at in the mistaken belief she'll like you better.

There was a flawless and impeccably sourced hunk of veal and then a much-welcome and—once again—thrilling shock.

A large, decidedly un-Kelleresque single plate (not four plates nesting on top of one another) covered with beautiful slices of heirloom tomatoes, a rough mound of stunningly creamy burrata in the middle, a drizzle of extraordinary-quality olive oil. The simplest, most ordinary fucking thing imaginable—particularly for my wife, who came over from Italy only a few years back. It was a course as "foreign" to my expectations of the Laundry or Per Se as could be. It was also the best and most welcome course of the meal. Both wake-up call and antidote to what preceded it.

There were desserts, a lot of them. And, for the first time, I had no difficulty making room for at least a taste of each. It's worth noting that it's always the pastry chef at degustation-style restaurants who gets fucked—which is to say, neglected—as the customers usually hit the wall long before that department gets its opportunity to shine.

What did I make of all this? I'm still asking myself this, the next day, still trying to come to grips with my feelings. Playing the whole meal through again in my head, trying to separate out what percentage of my reactions comes from being a jaded, contrarian asshole and what might be "legitimate" or in any way "meaningful" criticism.

Maybe I should think about Thomas Keller like Orson Welles. It doesn't *matter* what happens now—or what he does, or what I may think of his later projects. The man made *Citizen Kane*, for fuck's sake! He's cool for life. Un-deposable. He's The Greatest. Always. Like Muhammad Ali. Why nitpick?

Fact is, I *love* Keller's more casual restaurant concept: Bouchon. I like that he's expanded his empire—that he's successfully moved on, loosened his reins on any one place. I think it's good for the world and, I hope, good for him personally.

The more I think about last night, the more I keep coming back to that mortadella, and that coppa, then that gleeful kick of that plate of tomatoes and cheese—and let me tell you, that was some pretty good motherfuckin' cheese and some mighty good tomatoes.

As it should be with all great dining experiences, as I'd felt throughout those first, golden hours at the French Laundry, it seemed, all too briefly, that someone was talking to me, telling me something about themselves, their past, the things they loved and remembered.

Maybe this was Jonathan Benno, intentionally or not, saying:

"This is what I'm going to be doing next. After I'm gone." (It's worth noting that shortly after this meal, he indeed announced his own new venture, into high-end Italian.)

Or maybe I'm just too thick and too dumb to figure out what was going on.

Was this meal a harbinger of anything? A sign of the apocalypse? Meaningful in any way? Or not? I don't know.

What I know for sure is that they comped me and I feel like an utter snake in the grass.

If I didn't love that meal at Per Se, if I can't "get" what Grant Achatz is doing, does that mean anything at all?

Which brings me to David Chang. Whose relatively recent arrival on the scene—and spectacular rise—I'm pretty damn sure means a fuck of a lot.

17

The Fury

Build, therefore, your own world.

—Ralph Waldo Emerson

What took me to cooking was that there was something honest about it," says David Chang.

There is no lying in the kitchen. And no god there, either. He couldn't help you anyway. You either can—or can't—make an omelet. You either can—or can't—chop an onion, shake a pan, keep up with the other cooks, replicate again and again, perfectly, the dishes that need to be done. No credential, no amount of bullshit, no well-formed sentences or pleas for mercy will change the basic facts. The kitchen is the last meritocracy—a world of absolutes; one knows without any ambiguity at the end of each day how one did. "Good" and "evil" are easily and instantly recognized for what they are. Good is a cook who shows up on time and does what he said yesterday he was going to do. Evil is a cook who's full of shit and *doesn't* or can't do what he said he was going to do. Good is a busy restaurant from which the customers go home happy and everybody makes money. Evil is a slow restaurant from which the cooks go home feeling depressed and ashamed.

Nobody wonders, in a busy kitchen, if there is a god. Or if they've chosen the right god.

Except maybe David Chang.

"I run on hate and anger," says David Chang. "It's fueled me for the longest fucking time."

As usual, when I meet him, he's got an air of frantic befuddlement about him—as if he just can't figure out what just happened or what's probably going to happen. He has the demeanor of a man who believes that whatever *might be* coming down the pike, whatever locomotive is headed his way, it's probably not going to be a good thing.

"Dude," he says, "I just got a *spinal tap!*"

Two days earlier, he woke up with the worst headache of his life, a sharp, driving pain in his skull so ferocious that he raced off to the hospital, convinced he was having a brain hemorrhage. He seems oddly disappointed that the tests found nothing.

Other successful chefs tend to screw up their faces a little bit when you mention David Chang. Even the ones who like him and like his restaurants, they wince perceptibly—exasperated, perhaps, by the unprecedented and seemingly never-ending torrent of praise for the thirty-two-year-old chef and restaurateur, the all-too quick Michelin stars, the awards—*Food and Wine*'s Best New Chef, *GQ*'s Chef of the Year, *Bon Appetit*'s Chef of the Year, the three James Beard Awards. They've watched with a mix of envy and astonishment the way he's effortlessly brought the blogosphere to heel and mesmerized the press like so many dancing cobras. The great chefs of France and Spain—not just great ones but the *cool* ones—make obligatory swings by his restaurants to sit happily at the bar, eating with their hands. Ruth Reichl treats him like a son. Alice Waters treats him like a son. Martha Stewart adores him. The *New Yorker* gives him the full-on treatment, the kind of lengthy, in-depth, and admiring profile usually reserved for economists or statesmen. Charlie Rose invites him on the show and interviews him like A Person of Serious Importance. Throughout the entire process of his elevation to Culinary Godhead, Chang has continued, in his public life, to curse uncontrollably like a Tourette's-afflicted Marine, rage injudiciously at and about his enemies, deny special treatment to those in the food-writing community who are used to such things, insult the very food bloggers who helped build his legend—and generally conduct himself as someone who's just woken up to find himself holding a winning lottery ticket. If there was a David Chang catchphrase written on T-shirts, it would be "Dude! I don't fuckin' *know*!"—his best explanation for what's happening. He continues to flirt with—and then turn down—deals that would have made him a millionaire many times over by now. His twelve-seat restaurant, Momofuku Ko, is the most sought-after and hardest-to-get reservation in America. He is, inarguably, a star.

"He's not that great a chef," says one very, very famous chef with no reason, one would think, to feel threatened by Chang. Chang just hasn't been around long enough for his taste. From his point of view, and from his hard-won, hard-fought place on the mountaintop, the man just hasn't paid enough dues. "He's not even that good a cook," says another.

Both statements miss the point entirely.

Things are going well and yet Chang is characteristically miserable. "I continuously feel like I'm a fuck. When is this going to end?"

Love the guy, hate the guy, overhyped or not, the simple fact is that David Chang is the most *important* chef in America today. It's a significant distinction. He's *not* a great chef—as he'd be the first to admit—or even a particularly experienced one, and there are many better, more talented, more technically proficient cooks in New York City. But he's an important chef, a man who, in a ridiculously brief period of time, changed the landscape of dining, created a new kind of model for high-end eateries, and tapped once, twice, three times and counting into a zeitgeist whose parameters people are still struggling to identify (and put in a bottle, if possible). That's what sets him above and apart from the rest—and it's also what drives some other chefs crazy. Describing David Chang as a chef does both him and the word "chef" a disservice. David Chang is . . . something else.

In the unforgiving restaurant universe, having a good idea is one thing. Executing that idea is harder. If you're skilled enough and lucky enough to succeed in realizing that idea, the challenge becomes keeping it going, maybe even expanding on it, and ultimately (and most vitally) not fucking it all up somewhere along the way. Perhaps the most remarkable thing about David Chang's growing empire is that he did fuck it up. *Twice.* And that fucking up was—in each case—absolutely essential to his success. His first restaurant, Momofuku Noodle Bar, was supposed to be just that—a joint selling noodles. His second, Momofuku Ssäm, was a far more knuckleheaded concept—a place intended to sell Korean burritos. It was only when Chang and his team, looking certain doom in the face, threw up their hands and said, like a baseball team sixteen runs down in the second inning, "What the fuck . . . let's just do the best we can. Let's try and have *fun*," that he twice backed into the pop-cultural Main Vein. Noodle Bar got famous for everything BUT the noodles. And nobody orders the burritos at Ssäm.

He's famously consumed by his restaurants—and where the whole circus is going. See him on TV and you'd think the man shell-shocked, an impression he reinforces with shrugs and a guilty, confused-looking "who, me?" smile. But somebody's keeping the train on the tracks. And somebody's cracking the whip, too. He is subject to notorious rages. People who've seen them for the first time have described them as "frightening," "near cataleptic," and seemingly "coming from no-where." These episodes often culminate with Chang punching holes in the walls of his kitchens—so many of them that they are referred to, jokingly, by his cooks as design features. He suffers periodically from paralyzing headaches, mysterious numbnesses, shingles—and every variety of stress-related affliction.

He knows very well that he's walking a high wire in front of the whole world of food wonks—and that many of them, maybe even most of them, would be only too happy to see him fall face-first into a shit pile. It is a characteristic of a certain breed of high-end foodie elite that they secretly *want* the place they most love to fail. Killing what one loves is a primal instinct. "Discover" an exciting new place, a uniquely creative chef in an unexpected location. Tell all your friends, blog gushingly about it. Then, months later, complain that because of growing pains, or because "everybody goes there now," the young chef couldn't handle the pressure, or that, simply because of the passage of time, the whole thing is "over."

It's great to say you ate the best meal of your life at the French Laundry. It's a far rarer distinction to be able to say you ate at Rakel, Thomas Keller's failed restaurant in SoHo, "back in the day"—and even then, recognized his brilliance. When Rakel closed and Keller left the city, it made for an instant Golden Era, a limited-edition experience that *nobody* can ever have again at any price. Unlike England, where they often build you up just so they can enjoy the process of tearing you down, people who genuinely adore and appreciate what you do as a chef are, at the same time, instinctively waiting for you to fail. As well, there's the age-old syndrome common to fans of musicians with passionate and discerning cult followings. When the objects of adulation are crass enough to become popular, they quickly become a case of "used to be good." As a devoted music fan himself—the kind of music nerd for whom listening to *Electric Ladyland* on vinyl is pure crack, and who gets most excited when indie musicians few others have heard of come to his restaurants—Chang is familiar with this auto-destruct impulse. Other chefs under that kind of scrutiny—the guys who've been around longer, stayed on top year after year—tend to deal with the problem laterally, through a subtle combination of good intelligence work and a continuing attention to the care and feeding of those who might, someday, hurt them.

Chang tends to attack the problem head-on, telling any and all—probably before it occurred to them—that yeah . . . things are very probably going to turn to shit any minute now. Only way one can react to that is with a gnawing suspicion that one should Eat Here Now. Much of what makes David Chang such a compelling subject is the ease with which one can imagine him as the protagonist of a neat, Icarus-style morality play. It is hard to imagine, meeting him, that he will *not* crash and burn. One Web site even has a "MomoWatch," a regular newsfeed dedicated to tracking developments in ChangWorld—hour by hour, if need be.

The degree and kind of fascination with which his every move and utterance are observed and discussed is unique in the history of chefdom. Marco Pierre White's exploits as the first rock-star chef—and Gordon Ramsay's strategic evictions—were tabloid fodder. The people watching and writing about Chang are, for the most part, *smart* people, sophisticated about dining. They know exactly where to slip the knife if and when it comes to that.

How does he handle all this?

"Rage or fear . . . It oscillates. Rage I need to motivate me to try things that I can't ordinarily do—as I'm a lazy man. Fear—to keep pushing harder so we don't lose what we've accomplished."

He's persisted with one even more bold throw after another: a series of what would appear to be erratic, straight-outta-left-field choices—and yet everything works.

When Noodle Bar opened, chefs and cooks liked that there was a place where they could get a bowl of noodles from a crazy, surly, overworked Korean-American who worked (fairly briefly) for Tom Colicchio and, later, Daniel Boulud. They enjoyed watching him curse at customers; liked that, after receiving complaints about the scarcity of vegetarian options, he'd turned around and put pork in nearly every dish on the menu.

It's no accident that all of his restaurants seem designed exclusively for hungry chefs and cooks and jaded industry people. When they opened, they felt like manifestations of a collective secret urge. Everything from counter service to menus to music to the appearance of the cooks, the way one interacts directly with them, seemed to suggest to those within the business: "This is the way—this is how good, how much *fun* our business *could* be if only we didn't have to worry about fucking *customers*."

Now, non-industry people are clamoring to get in on the kind of dining experience that was once the perk of a debauched but exclusive elite. If the mark of a successful chef is, indeed, getting regular, honest-John diners to eat what chefs themselves have always loved to eat—the way they themselves like to eat it—then David Chang is a very successful chef. But in the process, he's democratized a dining sector that once required, for admission, burn marks, aching feet, beef fat under the nails, and blisters. For some, that's treachery of a kind.

At my first meal at Momofuku Ssäm, one particular dish slapped me upside the head and suggested that, indeed, something really special was going on here. It was a riff on a classic French salad of *frisée aux lardons*: a respectful version of the bistro staple—smallish, garnished with puffy fried *chicharrones* of pork skin instead of the usual bacon, and topped with a wonderfully runny, perfectly poached quail egg. Good enough—and, so far, not something that would inspire me to tear off my shirt and go running out in the street proselytizing. But the salad sat on top of a wildly incongruous stew of spicy, Korean-style tripe—and it was, well, it was . . . genius. Here, on one hand, was everything I usually hate about modern cooking—and in one bowl, no less. It was "fusion"—in the sense that it combined a perfectly good European classic with Asian ingredients and preparation. It was post-modern and contained my least favorite ingredient these days: irony. It appeared to be trying to "improve" or riff on an "unimprovable" and perfectly good bistro icon. Unless you're Thomas Keller, or Ferran Adrià, I usually loathe that kind of thing.

But this was truly audacious. It was fucking delicious. And it had tripe in it. So, for me, there was a moral dimension as well: anyone who can make something irresistibly delicious with tripe and get New Yorkers to eat it is, to my mind, already on the side of the angels. It was as if all my favorite chefs had gotten together and somehow created a perfectly tuned, super mutant baby food—in Korea. I felt I wanted all my high-end meals—for the rest of my life—to resemble this one: both complex and strangely comforting.

From the outside, Momofuku Ko looks like an after-hours club— or a particularly dodgy storefront cocktail lounge. There's no sign— only Chang's tiny, trademark peach logo next to an uninviting door. You could easily stand outside looking for it for ten minutes before realizing you were there all along.

Reservations for the twelve seats at the rather spartan-looking bar are legendarily difficult to get—in that the process is the most truly (and painfully) democratic in the world of fine dining. You can't call or write or beg or network your way into Ko. You log on to their Web site at precisely the right second and manage, you hope, against all odds, to get in your request for a reservation for exactly six days ahead. You do this only by beating out the thousands of other people who are doing exactly the same thing you are—at exactly the same second—not an easy feat. You get a seat at Ko only over time and through persistent effort. Beyond hiring a platoon of helpers to log on at the same time and attempt, simultaneously, to make reservations on your behalf—which might increase your chances—there is no gaming the system. It's a lottery. The same rules apply for all: food critics, friends—even Chang's parents. They had to wait a year to eat at their own son's restaurant.

The menu at Ko—a set menu of ten courses for dinner (and sixteen for lunch)—changes with the lineup, and the chefs' and cooks' moods, though it usually includes one of a number of takes on concepts that have already been tried, tested, and found to work. The creative process leading up to each finished dish is mysterious and ill-understood. The natural inclination of lazy journalists is, of course, to credit Chang exclusively—which only (and unfairly) invites disappointment when one realizes he's rarely present. As was intended from its inception, Peter Serpico is the chef at Ko—and that's whom you're likely to find there.

The creative process by which the final dishes at Chang restaurants are arrived at is an absolutely fascinating stream of daily e-mails between chefs and cooks. Preceded and followed by many, many testings and tastings. Five-word rockets detailing a sudden flash of inspiration, thousand-word missives detailing an experience, a flavor, a possibility—an experiment that *might* lead to something great, continuing back and forth. The hard drive on Chang's laptop—from what transcripts I've seen—contains a years-long conversation with some of the most exciting and creative minds in gastronomy. And it's not just employees weighing in. Somewhere in the ether is a record of some seriously deep fucking thinking about food. Something I'd suggest, by the way, that the Culinary Institute of America make a bid on now—for their archives.

Service at Ko is informal for a restaurant with two Michelin stars. There are no waiters. The cooks prepare the dishes and, after describing what you're about to eat—with varying degrees of either casual good cheer or perfunctory (if charming) indifference—they put the plate in front of you on the counter. Though there is a wine list, it is advisable to allow the excellent sommelier to pour pairings with each course. She knows better than you. But if you just want beer with your dinner? They've got that, too.

There are no tablecloths or place settings, per se. The musical ac-

companiment to your meal is likely to be The Stooges or The Velvet
Underground. The "open kitchen" looks more like a short-order setup
than a Michelin-starred restaurant. And the cooks . . . they look gloriously like cooks. The kind they used to hide in the back when company
came calling. Scruffy, tattooed, and wearing the same snap-front white
shirts you see on the guys behind the counter at a Greek diner.

I was finally, after many tries, lucky enough to get into Ko.

There was a tiny plate of oyster, caviar, and sea urchin to start,
three ingredients born to be together—followed by a dish of braised
eggplant, tomato-water gel, and eggplant chip, a combination I'd
hardly been dreaming of all my life (in fact, three ingredients I
thought I could happily do without). Intensely, wonderfully flavorful—the kind of happy surprise I seldom expect from a vegetable.
There was a dish of tofu and duck heart in homemade XO sauce,
which fell more predictably into the territory of things I love; a
"*chicharrone*/pork fat brioche" was a mercifully small portion of tasty,
tasty overkill (and basically evil—in a good way). I pretty much hate
scallops (too rich and too sweet for me). And I'm indifferent to pineapple (also sweet). But sliced diver scallops with pineapple vinegar,
dehydrated ham, and fresh water chestnut was yet another dish I
should have hated but ended up wanting to tongue the plate. There
was another uni dish—this one in chilled "burned" dashi with pea
tendrils and melon—which was simply brilliant. Then came a lightly
smoked chicken egg with fingerling-potato chips, onion soubise, and
sweet-potato vinegar—which tasted like something you'd only be
lucky enough to discover if you were getting stoned late at night with
Ferran Adrià—and you both found yourselves with the munchies.
Corn pasta with chorizo, pickled tomato, dried chile, sour cream,
and lime. Caper-brined trout with potato risotto, dill powder, glazed
red-ball radish, and baby Swiss chard must have been the end of a
very long and probably painful process. Also awesome . . . A frozen,
freshly fallen snow of foie gras with lychee, pine nut brittle, and ries-

ling gelée, if you close your eyes and imagine it, already makes perfect sense, doesn't it? By the time the lighter-than-air duck liver melted on my tongue, it was already an answered prayer. Deep-fried shortribs (I ask you: Who the fuck wouldn't love that?) with scallion, lavender, and baby leek finished me off with savory. Then desserts: peach soda with animal-cracker ice cream, which I didn't love so much, maybe because I have no happy childhood associations with either ingredient. Cruelly, I wasn't allowed to drink soda at my house (a fact about which I am still bitter), and animal crackers were, for me, a default sort of a cookie—the kind of thing somebody's addled grandma would give you, thinking that they were just what every kid loved best. The loathsome-sounding black-pepper ganache, black-pepper crumbs, macerated blueberries with crème fraîche, and olive-oil ice cream was, typically of my Momofuku-related experiences, a shockingly unexpected joy. In fact, it was one of the most memorable dishes of the night—in a night full of them.

Trying to figure out Chang's "style" is a challenge—as he does his best to present a moving target, and because his menus are so collaborative.

But one window into where it all comes from is the time he spent at Café Boulud with chef Andrew Carmellini. His job there was the amuse-bouche station—challenged to throw together an always-changing array of tiny and, hopefully, exciting bites of first-course freebies, mostly with ingredients at hand. The idea of the amuse being to "wake up" or "tease" the customers' palates in preparation for the more studiously composed dishes to follow. Fast, pretty, flavorful—and, most important, "amusing." Whoever's making the amuses is usually less constrained by a need to stay "on brand." There are fewer rules. You are more likely to be allowed to stray from France, for instance—in what is otherwise a strictly French restaurant—on the amuses. Whimsy is a virtue.

Because David Chang is an interesting guy doing interesting

things, and because, unusually for a chef with a lot to lose, he's both articulate and impulsively undiplomatic, people who get paid to write about food, or blog about food, or make television about interesting people are constantly coming round and poking him with a stick—in the not-unreasonable assumption that something quotable and, hopefully, even controversial will come tumbling out of his mouth. An off-the-cuff and only half-serious quip that he "hate[s] San Francisco—all they do is put fuckin' figs on a plate" can be easily conflated into weeks of blog posts and newspaper articles. Actually, with Chang, you don't even have to poke him. Just wait around long enough and he's pretty sure to drop a soundbite that will piss off somebody somewhere. Column inches, especially for print food writers, are harder and harder to fill with something "new" or relevant these days. As drearily limiting as writing porn is for someone who enjoys adjectives, and difficult as hell for those looking to keep up with the many-headed, quick-reacting blogosphere. For a food writer usually consigned to matters no more exciting than cupcakes, Chang-watching has become something of a one-man Gold Rush, a potentially life-giving font of hipness. There are those who grudgingly admire the guy and look to his next move to show them what to write about or talk about ("The Next Big Thing!"), and those who sense the injury just beneath the surface of Chang's public persona, the recklessness—and hurt—and want to write about that. And those like me, who straight-up love the very fact that he exists—but also can't help trying to psychoanalyze him.

"Why does everybody want to get inside his skull?" asks his friend and coauthor Peter Meehan. Though he knows the answer.

Unlike just about any other chef in the public eye, Chang wears his fears and his most deeply felt loathings right on his sleeve, for everybody to see.

What Chang would have you believe is that he really deserves neither the acclaim nor the success. He's been saying this to journalists quite disarmingly for some time, repeatedly pointing out his relatively minimal qualifications and experience—and insistently comparing himself (unfavorably) to other chefs. To what degree this is a pose is debatable. I'd maintain that just because he says it often doesn't mean it's not true.

"I didn't want any of this," he says. A statement, conversely, I do *not* believe for a second.

He's a former junior golf champion, after all, who quit the sport completely at age thirteen because, he's said, "If I can't beat the brains out of everyone, I don't want to play. It's not fun otherwise."

That doesn't sound like somebody who doesn't want things.

"Golf fucked me up in the head," he says, by way of explanation.

We're talking about God over skewers of chicken ass at Yakitori Totto on the West Side.

We arrived early, because they don't take reservations before seven at this traditional, Japanese-style yakitori joint—and because they tend to run out of the good bits early: chicken heart, chicken ass, chicken "oyster," chicken skin. You don't want to miss that stuff. We're drinking beer and talking shit and I'm doing a very bad job of what everybody else is trying to do—which is to figure out what David Chang is all about.

He was born into a Korean family of observant Christians, the youngest of four kids.

In his book, he describes his relationship with his father—and the beginnings of his relationship with food—thus: "I grew up eating noodles with my dad . . . On nights when it was just him and me, he'd make me eat sea cucumber along with the noodles. And the weirdness of eating them would be offset by the warm afterglow of pride I felt in being an adventurous eating companion to him." His father, who had first worked in restaurants after emigrating from Korea, warned him to stay away from the business.

It is my theory that the fact that Chang attended Jesuit High

School and then Trinity College, majoring in religion, is of vital significance to the emerging science of Changology.

"For me . . . it wasn't . . . enough," he says cryptically. "I used to give a shit about God . . . but if God were to exist, I'd rather burn in hell. If he failed, he failed by putting the message in human hands. I guess I'm pretty pissed at God. The Crusades . . . Pol Pot . . . Hitler . . . Stalin. The same time all these terrible things were happening, people were bowing their heads and thanking God before they ate."

Which begs the question: If you don't believe in God, why study religion?

"I just needed to figure out . . . I just wanted to know," he says, draining his beer a little sadly. "You know, I always thought you can never *disprove* faith. The Christian God seemed flawed. I mean, you only had one chance to make it into heaven."

He looks up from a half-eaten skewer of chicken, worried.

"What if you don't *get* the chance? At the end of the day, the heart of the matter is: what happens when you're dead? For me, the Christian ending just isn't . . . good enough."

He mentions the bodhisattva of Mahayana Buddhism, sentient beings who delay their own attainment of nirvana to become guides to those who have yet to reach it—as more worthy of emulation than the Christian saints.

I generally don't hear a lot of talk about Buddhist spirituality (certainly not over chicken meatballs and beer), and I'm still pondering what it must be like to get out from under the twin boulders of a father's love and expectations—and a God who turned out to be a disappointment. "I try to put my goals second to other people's goals," he says.

Which I wonder about—so I later ask his friend Peter Meehan.

"I'd like to say he's a fucking sweetheart," he says, asked simply if he'd describe Chang as a *nice* guy, "that he's compassionate. That he's generous. And he is. But it's, like, steel-jacketed love. It's hard-edged.

I mean, I've never woken up next to him, but I don't think there are a lot of tender and delicate moments with David. He's . . . *loyal* as shit. So if you're part of his brood and somebody harms you? You can count on him to be appropriately supportive and vengeful."

"Loyalty and honesty are really important things to me," says Chang.

He is, to say the least, unforgiving of those he feels have lied to him or let him down in the loyalty department.

His friend Dave Arnold has told him, "Your hobby is hating people," and, to be sure, he has a long and carefully tended—even cherished—list of enemies.

"I don't mind people saying they hate my guts," he says, warming to his subject. "Just have the balls to say it to my face."

"Don't try to be my fuckin' friend and then . . ." he trails off, remembering the "Ozersky incident." Josh Ozersky, at the time of his transgression, was an editor-correspondent for *New York* magazine's influential food-and-dining Web site, Grub Street. The root of his conflict with Chang, it is said, stems from the publication of a Momofuku menu—before Chang felt it ready for release. There had been, Chang insists, assurances that the document would be withheld.

Ozersky's "scoop" got him banned for life from all Chang restaurants. And when I say "for life," I'm not kidding. There is no question in my mind that buffalo will graze in Times Square—and pink macaroons will fall from the sky—before Josh Ozersky ever makes it through the door of a Momofuku anywhere.

"I hate Antoinette Bruno," says Chang. This was a wound inflicted early in his career, when the Momofuku thing was just getting going. Chang felt particularly vulnerable at the time, and the offense still burns, years later. Bruno is head honcho of Star Chefs, an outfit that, every year, organizes what Chang calls "a poor imitation of Madrid Fusion." After one of the events, Bruno found herself shooting her mouth off about how "overrated" she found this David Chang character, blissfully—and stupidly—unaware that she was talking with Chang's cooks at the time. "Opportunist. A fake. Not a good person. Sycophant. Dishonorable," says Chang, still genuinely angry just thinking about her.

"I fuckin' hate X," he says, talking about the saintly proprietor of a good-for-the-world restaurant, a pioneer of conscientious, sustainable food production. "It's like hating the Dalai Lama!" I protest. "How could you hate that guy? And he stands for everything you support!" (Chang is deeply involved with—and curious about—new avenues and new sources for sustainable, low-impact ingredients.)

"I fuckin' hate him so much it's unbelievable."

"But you love Alice Waters," I point out, as an example of someone far, far more dogmatic.

"Yeah, but Alice *means* well. She may not articulate as well as she could—but she's a nice lady who maybe just took too much acid back in the '60s. Plus . . . she's a mom figure to me. When I got sick, she was the *first* person to call. Before my family even."

He doesn't elaborate about Chef X beyond "He's weirdly manipulative."

And "I hate Y," another beloved figure in cuisine, the hugely talented chef-owner of an innovative restaurant specializing in a cuisine that might be called "experimental."

"But . . . but you worship Ferran Adrià," I say, "you're bestest pals with Wylie Dufresne, for fuck's sake"—arguing the inconsistency in idolizing them while utterly dismissing the other guy, a major acolyte. Why hate this guy?

"For his seriousness" is all he has to say. "Eating in a restaurant should be fun."

Anyway, he continues, "Ferran Adrià is a genius; [his work was] like Bob Dylan going electric. Nobody has quite fathomed the Ferran impact yet. It will last forever."

I begin to gather that Chang doesn't need a logical reason to hate a guy. In almost every case, it's in some way personal.

Though he has said he "hates" San Francisco—and San Francisco chefs—neither is true. Ask him to mention chefs he really admires, who he thinks are doing important work, and he invariably names David Kinch, Jeremy Fox, and Corey Lee. He will hear no evil spoken of Alice Waters, worships Thomas Keller, and hangs with Chris Cosentino. He's admitted envying the same Bay Area "figs on a plate" he's claimed to hold in contempt.

He's aware of the contradictions, maybe bemused by the fact that he's just as much at war with himself as with anybody else, bemoaning the lack of order and discipline and high standards in kitchens on one hand and, moments later, regretting the passing of the time when "the funniest motherfucker in the kitchen" was a hero. "That doesn't exist anymore . . ." he complains. "But, David," I say, "you would have *fired* the funniest guy in the kitchen for not being serious enough about your fucking standards."

He charges on nonetheless. "Take away Keller and a handful of others and there's nobody producing serious cooks," he says—before admiringly mentioning the story of a cook who "chops off a fingertip— they cauterize it on the flattop." I am forced to remind him that this is a practice they would probably take a dim view of at the French Laundry.

"I hate that cooking has turned white-collar," says a man who knows full well that, with every day and every new restaurant, he moves farther and farther away from ever working the line again.

So . . . whom does he *like?*

"I don't talk to anybody," he confesses sadly. And I almost believe him.

Then he admits, reluctantly, that he's actually got a few friends. Peter Meehan, the writer and journalist and coauthor of his cookbook, is a friend. From what I've seen, Meehan, a smart and decent guy, appears to serve as Chang's thermostatic regulator, his consigliere. Someone he can turn to and ask, "Is this a good idea?" or "Is this good for *me*?" and get an honest answer.

Wylie Dufresne, the heroically innovative chef-owner of WD-50, is a friend. Chang calls him his mentor. "He lives close. He's like an older brother." Dufresne is always spoken of with both affection and respect. You get the impression that if you were to complain about so much as an appetizer at WD-50 in Chang's presence, he'd never speak to you again.

The name of Ken Friedman—owner of the wildly successful Spotted Pig gastro-pub, the bar The Rusty Knot, and an expanding bundle of other establishments—comes up. After a storied career in the music industry, Friedman has had a similarly fast and stellar rise in the restaurant business. Chang seems to look on the way he's handled his life with a mixture of kinship, admiration, and envy.

"He's lived the most ridiculously good life . . . he [seems to have] just bumbled his way through. And a good guy."

Dave Arnold, the head of the French Culinary Institute's Culinary Technology department, theorist, and advisor to cutting-edge chefs, is also a friend. ("Dave Chang + Dave Arnold = Happy Chang," says Meehan.)

Asked for other examples of happy-making Chang activities, Meehan mentions beer, lots of steamed crustaceans—and an impassioned argument over New England transcendentalism as an effective palliative to the pressures of empire.

Chang describes himself as unhealthily obsessed with a hockey player, defenseman Rod Langway of the Capitals, because, he says, he was one of the last to play the game without a helmet. There is, perhaps, an important metaphor there for amateur Changologists seeking to sum up the young chef's career.

Peter Meehan says, "The most important thing about David is . . . that . . . restlessness, the willingness to throw it all overboard and start again, the drive to always do better, that there's a palpable, actual dynamism to his places, which is rarer than rare."

Regretful, I think, about the limited time he spent at Café Boulud and Craft, Chang idealizes the great New York kitchens of Lespinasse, Le Cirque, Gramercy Tavern, Le Bernardin, Daniel—places where entire generations of chefs grew up and learned their craft.

"Christian Delouvrier . . . I would have been miserable as fuck working for him. But there's something romantic about it as a cook."

Longingly—like a kid with his nose pressed to the glass—he looks back at the superheroes of previous generations of cooking. In an amazing e-mail, he described in elegiac terms a cooking event in Copenhagen, where he got to watch the great Albert Adrià at work.

"Albert is all fun and games until we get to the kitchen and he turns into a maniac. He puts on a chef coat for the first time in over eight months (porter shirt), explains why high gastronomy is dead to him . . . I think three hours went by as I watched him work, his brain churning away . . . What was sad and beautiful was that we were watching what will probably be the last time he cooks, like watching Michael Jordan retire . . . He plated everything solo, the whole room, guests . . . cooks . . . chefs, watch in reverence. And it was fucking delicious."

"I'm a geek of culinary history," he says. At Ssäm, he keeps a gallery of photographs of chefs he respects on the wall for his cooks to memorize. "A chef comes in? I *know*." (And he wants his cooks to know, too.) He mentions no-longer-living legends like Jean-Louis Palladin and Gilbert Le Coze like some talk about Golden Age baseball players, and asks me, "Do you have any *idea* who went through Bouley's kitchens? *Everybody!*"

He observes that the recent trend away from white tablecloth, crystal glassware, and classic high-end service and haute cuisine is both good and bad. "Good because of the proliferation of restaurants that are *not* fine-dining. But it's a double-edged sword—because that erodes the training ground that produces better cooks. And what restaurants *need*," he stresses, "is cooks."

"But, dude! It's *you* killing it," I could easily have pointed out. If anybody has pointed out the way out of fine dining—created a viable and worthwhile alternative to the old model—it's Chang. After seeing the success of Ssäm and Ko, why would any chef want to weigh down their operation with all the bullshit of stemware and linen service? However he might feel, Chang—if only by example—is helping to kill what he most loves. He's making his heroes—the names on the cookbooks on his office shelves—obsolete.

Above all others, he seems to respect Alex Lee, the one-time chef of restaurant Daniel. The standards and level of performance he saw there during brief visits made a huge impression on Chang. It's a template he constantly measures himself against—and he's never satisfied with the comparison. That Lee, in his late thirties, with three children, recently went to work in a country club was an understandable move for a family man facing forty. But it was a strangely devastating moment for David.

"I see that, and I think, I'll *never* be that talented—or have the work ethic of this maniac—and *he's calling it quits?!?!*"

Given his own repeated claims to mediocrity as a chef and as a cook, I ask him what he thinks he's *good* at.

"I've got a weird ability to think what the other person I work with is thinking," he says, and when I ask whether he's a better manager or a cook, he says, "The best cooks are like the pretty girl in high school. Gifted. Born to cook. They never had to develop other skills." He thinks for a moment. "I mean . . . Larry Bird was a *terrible* coach."

Which leaves me with the definite impression that, in his heart of hearts, Chang would have greatly preferred to be a virtuoso talent like Larry Bird (and a crappy manager)—instead of whatever it is he turned out to be.

We've wiped out three beers and a fair amount of chicken parts.

A cup in front of him bristles with bare skewers. Chang sighs and sits back in his chair.

"Everything has changed in five years. The only things that stay the same are the platonic ideals. Love. Truth. Loyalty. It was the prettiest thing when nothing is expected of you."

But everything *is* expected of David Chang these days. In only five years, Momofuku Noodle Bar begat Momofuku Ssäm, Momofuku Ko, Milk Bar—and now, moving midtown to take over the hotel space once occupied by Geoffrey Zakarian's Town, the open-any-minute Má Pêche. The *Momofuku* cookbook (at time of our meeting) is hitting the shelves any second with book tour to follow—and with it all come attacks of unexplained deafness, psychosomatic paralysis, the mystery headache. When will enough be enough? Chang *talks* about taking a year off.

When I ask Meehan about this later, he scoffs: "A year? No fucking way. He's too ambitious and has too many people he's accountable for. [He's] like those touring juggernauts—like the Grateful Dead—there's a vagabond tent city of people relying on those tours for their livelihood. If and when David walks away from Momofuku, it'll be for health reasons, or because he's leaving the kitchen for good." On the other hand, he considers, "If your hero is Marco Pierre White and you listen to enough Neil Young, there's significant appeal to burning out instead of fading away, right?"

It's so easy to see or hear about what torments David Chang that I have to ask . . . what's a *good* day for him?

Chang looks up and away, as if trying to remember something so remote he's not sure anymore if it ever existed.

"I get up in the morning and it's not a business meeting . . . I get to go to the market, say a Saturday, early enough so I can talk to the farmers and beat the crowds and the rest of the chefs who descend on Union Square. If I go later, a forty-five-minute excursion turns into a three-hour bullshit talkfest.

"I get to the restaurants and everything is clean, the sidewalks are clean, the awnings glisten with water . . . I run through all the restaurants, make sure the walk-ins are tight and all the day mise-en-place is clean and great. The cooks are pushing themselves, there's a sense of urgency throughout the late morning and evening. The low-boys [refrigerators] are clean.

"Front-of-the-house meeting. The servers show up on time and no one is hung over or bitching . . .

"I eat a bowl of rice and kimchi and maybe some eggs—or whatever is for lunch staff meal. Lunch service, the trailer comes in and I don't have to say anything to him. All I want is for the cook to season properly, to label things, and condense his mise-en-place. The cook never responds with a 'no'—just hauls ass. Everyone has a sharp knife and there is no attitude. No one burns themselves. Servers don't fuck up the tables, and I don't have to yell . . .

"I step downstairs to work on new dishes or butcher or clean veg. That's so relaxing. Working on a dish with those in the inner circle at the restaurant and via e-mail. I give some to everyone to taste . . .

"I get no e-mails that say, 'Dave, can we talk for a bit' (translation: 'Dave: I want a raise,' or 'I quit,' or 'I'm unhappy').

"I stop by Ko and Noodle Bar, make sure everything is copacetic, everything tastes the way it should, every station is clean, every cook trying to find a way to make their prep better and faster and more efficient . . . I can see them going over their mise-en-place over and over again to make sure it's right, I can *see* them asking themselves, '*Is there a better way to do this?*' I don't have to question anyone's integrity or commitment.

"Family meal is a perfect spread of fried chicken, salad, lemonade. The most important meal of the day. I shoot the shit with the boys . . .

"Get ready for dinner service. No VIPs, but we're busy. I stand in the corners of the various restaurants and watch. I avoid service at Ko like the plague, stop by Noodle Bar and see them hustling and tinkering, see a line of people waiting and see happy faces. I keep my hat down low so I don't have to talk to anyone.

"No equipment breaks, and the air-conditioning or the heat is working, there are no plumbing issues and the walk-in is fuckin' *cold*. No problems.

"I walk downstairs and see the new trail or new hire doing knife work, and they don't realize that I'm watching, and they do it the *right* way—which means the long and stupid way (which is cooking with integrity) . . . cooking or prepping something, with no one watching, realizing there are a million shortcuts but taking the hard road [without] any glory or satisfaction from one's peers. I see this and walk back upstairs, see that the restaurants don't need me at all, that they run better during service without me. That makes me smile.

"I walk back to Ssäm and Milk and stand in the corner and watch one of my cooks berate another cook for not pulling their weight. The level of accountability is so high that I can bolt at around ten p.m. on a Saturday night with some other chefs who maybe skipped work early, grab a drink with a friend or my girlfriend . . . maybe a late night of drinking. A bar with a great jukebox. A night of bourbon.

"Basically? A night of no problems and where everybody is busting their ass and doing their jobs. I don't have to yell."

Finished with his reverie, he adds, "This *used to* happen. No more . . . This is more hypothetical."

As Chang's answer has almost everything to do with work and little with play, a few days later I ask Peter Meehan what he thinks makes David Chang really and truly happy—if the wheels can ever stop turning, he relaxes, takes a deep breath of free air, nothing on his mind.

"I've seen it," Meehan says. "It's there. But he doesn't pursue it. His happiness is not a priority in his life. It's an incidental benefit, but he's not dead to it. Maybe, if someday he realizes that happiness can help him achieve his goals, he'll give a shit about it."

The waiter at Yakitori Totto comes over and reminds us we have to be out by seven. They need the table. Chang looks out the window, then back at me. "My great regret is I can't get drunk with my cooks anymore.

"I'll die before I'm fifty," he says, matter-of-factly.

18

My Aim Is True

Spanish is the language of the early morning in Manhattan. At the bagel place where I get my coffee, everybody, customers and counter help alike, are *papi* or *flaco* or *hermano*—or addressed by country of origin. Doesn't matter if Spanish is even your language. At this hour, it's what's spoken. It's how things are done. The Bengali shop owner, the few American suits—everybody addresses each other in one form or another of Spanish. That's who's up and working this time of the morning and who owns this part of the day: the doormen from the nearby apartment buildings, the porters, the nannies on the way to work, the construction guys sent out on a coffee run, the dishwashers and early-arriving restaurant help, they greet each other with the familiar nicknames. If they don't recognize a face, they ask, in Spanish, *"Qué país?"*

It's seven a.m. in the chilly, white-tiled bowels of Le Bernardin in New York City, where the language is also Spanish, and Justo Thomas is looking at seven hundred pounds of fish. A stack of Styrofoam crates packed with halibut, white tuna, black sea bass, mahimahi, red snapper, skate, cod, monkfish, or salmon, mostly unscaled, on the bone, guts still in, reaches halfway up the wall of his tiny workspace.

"The way they catch," he explains—meaning, on the bone, the way God made them, the way they came out of the ocean and the way that Le Bernardin insists on receiving them. Shiny, clear-eyed, pink-gilled, still stiff with rigor, and smelling of nothing but seawater. Everybody from outside the restaurant—the constant procession of deliverymen who bring cases of wine, vegetables, langoustines, octopus, uni, dry goods—they call him "Primo" ("first" or "number one"). Which seems to please Justo.

Le Bernardin is probably the best seafood restaurant in America. It's certainly the most celebrated: three consecutive four-star reviews from the *New York Times*, two-time winner of three Michelin stars, Zagat's best-rated restaurant in New York—every honor, award you could imagine—the best by any measure of assessing such things. Which means they don't cut fish at Le Bernardin like other restaurants. The standards are—to say the least—different. Expectations for a hunk of protein are . . . higher.

Justo is from the rural Dominican Republic. He was the middle brother of three in a family of eight kids (five sisters). His father was a farmer—growing coffee and coconuts. The family raised a few pigs for sale—and chickens for the table. As a child, Justo went to school, then helped on the farm after. His first job was as counter help at his uncle's pastry shop—six a.m. until ten p.m., every day. He never learned to bake.

He's now forty-seven years old, and he's been working in New York City restaurants for twenty years—first under conditions of questionable legality but quickly thereafter, as a permanent resident and then as a citizen. He's got three kids; the eldest, a twenty-year-old, in college. At Le Bernardin, he makes a flat salary that would be considered spectacular by industry standards—an amount in the neighborhood of what I made in my best years as a chef. Like all employees of the restaurant, he has full medical coverage. Once a year, he takes a four-week vacation back in the DR. Unusually for the restaurant business, Justo has no set hours. He leaves whenever he feels like it—which is when he's done.

He came to Le Bernadin six years ago, having heard good things about it when he worked across the street at Palio. "They didn't even say 'Good morning,'" he says, shaking his head.

"The chef treat everybody the same," he says, proudly, adding that he'd been looking for someplace with job security. "I don't like to jump around." And at Le Bernardin, unlike almost every other job in the restaurant industry, "I work by myself." In fact, Justo Thomas enjoys a degree of autonomy unheard of by his peers.

The room where he works is actually a ten-foot-by-five-foot dog-leg off the hallway through which deliveries are dragged or wheeled from the underground loading dock of the Prudential building on Fifty-first Street. Justo works right next to the steward's, Fernando's, tiny office, a few feet from the service elevator to the upstairs kitchen. He's got one worktable covered with cutting boards, a shelf stacked with clear plastic Lexan storage trays, a child-size overhead shelf where he keeps a small electronic scale and some needle-nose pliers. At the other end of the room is a two-basin sink. The walls, curiously, have been carefully covered with fresh plastic cling wrap—like a serial killer would prepare his basement—to catch flying fish scales and for faster, easier cleanup. The plastic will come down, of course, at the end of the shift. Justo likes things clean and organized.

Each pre-positioned plastic tray has been fitted with a drainage rack—so that the fish are raised up out of any liquid—and each rack additionally wrapped in cling wrap. Justo's knives—a not particularly expensive slicing knife (usually intended for carving roasts), a cheap stainless steel chef's knife, a severely ground-down flexible filet knife (barely a half inch left of blade), and another personally customized mutation with a serpentine edge—are laid out in a row at knee level on a clean side towel. Hanging on a nail behind him, there's a roll of bright red labels reading WEDNESDAY, which he will use on each and every tray of fish he cuts today—so the cooks upstairs know at a glance which portions to use first and from whence they came. He wears a bright yellow dishwashing glove on his left hand, as he doesn't like to actually touch the fish. Justo Thomas, one notices quickly when observing him, is something of a germophobe.

One gets the impression very quickly that the concept of cross-contamination has made a powerful—even terrifying—impression on him. When he wipes down his cutting board with a wet cotton side towel, he throws the towel away. Every time.

He is a man set in his habits. He has organized his time and his space the way he likes them. He has a routine, a certain way he likes to do things. And he never deviates.

"With Justo," says Le Bernardin's chef de cuisine, Chris Muller, just arriving for work, "it's all about *no wasted motion*." In a Buckaroo Banzai–like explanation of the universe ("Wherever you go . . . there you are"), Muller holds up one hand flat, representing a fish in Justo-Land, and says, "It's here . . ." then turns the palm over, like flipping a page, " . . . and then it's *there*." He holds my gaze for a split second as if I should understand that he's just revealed something profoundly important.

Every sous chef, line cook, pâtissier, and stagiere who walks by Justo on the way from the locker rooms, stops, smiles admiringly, and says, "Good morning, chef" (which is the way it's done at Le Bernardin—courtesy is a matter of policy—one says good morning to all of one's colleagues, regardless of position, addressing each and every one as "chef"), every one who passes by and sees me standing there with a notebook in hand has to linger for a second, to determine if I've *gotten it yet*, how phenomenally, amazingly, supernaturally fucking *good* Justo Thomas is at doing this job. They appreciate this better than I ever could, because when Justo goes on vacation, it will take *three of them* to cut the same amount of fish that Justo, *alone*, will scale, gut, clean, and portion in four to five *hours*.

It's not just that one man will cut seven hundred pounds of fish today, and a thousand pounds Friday, and do the same, more or less, every day, day after day after day. But that every single portion *must* be perfect. He is well aware of what's at stake.

"Every piece. It's the chef's *name*," he says.

He's not overstating the case. At Le Bernardin's level of success and visibility in the fine-dining firmament, it is no exaggeration to say that were a single order of monkfish to smell even slightly "off"—to hit the table, the result could explode across the Internet like a neutron bomb. The scrutiny of a place of Le Bernardin's particular long-standing preeminence atop the high-wire is ferocious. There are all too many people ready, upon hearing of even one such incident, to declare the restaurant "not as good as it used to be" or "over"; terms that are, for better or worse, the currency of influential food nerdism.

Let's put it another way: I graduated from the best culinary school in the country. I spent twenty-eight years as a professional cook and chef. I've cleaned and portioned *thousands and thousands* of fish in my time. The executive chef–partner of Le Bernardin, Eric Ripert, is probably my best friend in the world.

And I would *never dare* to put a knife to a piece of fish at Le Bernardin.

Ripert maintains an unofficial intelligence network that would be the envy of the CIA—solely for the purpose of Defending the Realm. If you are a food critic, a person of importance, anyone who could possibly hurt or impact the restaurant in a negative way, you are recognized within seconds of walking in the door. Your likes and dislikes are . . . known. Even if you're a journalist who's never been in the restaurant— but are likely to visit soon—and write about it, chances are, you will not, on arriving, be a completely unknown quantity. Ripert is an astonishingly plugged-in guy. Point is: he *has* to be.

So, Justo's not being disingenuous when he says he identifies each piece of fish with the name and reputation of his chef. That—at that level of fine dining—is The System, where every server, every cook has to look at every little detail as having the potential to bring down the temple. Everything—absolutely everything—must be right. Always.

If you're Justo Thomas, and you cut and portion fish for a living, you find it's necessary to do things in a certain order. He works in the same unvarying progression every day. Fernando, who receives and weighs the fish, always arranges it in the same order and configuration. The way Justo likes it.

"I like fish," says Justo without a trace of irony. "I eat a lot of fish."

He does not feel the same way about meat. He doesn't like it. "I don't trust the blood," he exclaims, almost shuddering at the thought. "I get cut? The blood get in me." Fortunately, he's not required to touch the stuff often. Perhaps out of sensitivity to Justo's phobia, the one beef dish on the menu—a Wagyu beef surf and turf—is portioned by the line cooks.

Today, halibut comes first. It's one of the easiest fish to clean: two fat, boneless filets, top and bottom on each side. You zip them off the central spine easily, the skin comes off in one go—and the meat portions itself—like cutting filet mignons off a tenderloin. A twenty-five-pound halibut takes Justo about eight minutes.

Cod is a different matter. It's delicate. Extremely delicate—and perishable. The flesh, handled roughly, will mash. The physiognomy of a cod is not suited to eventual portioning as the identical, evenly shaped squares or oblongs a three-star restaurant requires. But before I'm even fully aware of what's going on, Justo's got the filets off the bone—neatly stacked. He puts all the left-side filets in one stack—the right-side filets in another. With the inappropriate (one would think) slicing knife, he's drilling out absolutely identical cubes of cod (all the left-hand filets first—then the right-hand ones). If they're not identical, he quickly—and almost imperceptibly—squares them off, trims them down to uniform size and shape. The trimmings form a steadily growing pile off to the side, which will be joined throughout the morning by other trimmings, for eventual donation to City Harvest. Tail ends—or smaller but still useful bits, doomed to never be uniform but, in every other respect, perfectly good, form another pile—above and away from the uniform ones. After he finishes one stack, he lays them out in a plastic tray, in the order that they came off the fish. When the uniform, cookbook-quality left-hand sides and right-hand sides of fish have been arranged (never stacked on top of each other) in the plastic tray, he pulls down the little gram scale from the shelf above him and, at supernatural speed, starts pairing up oddball pieces. He needs only weigh one piece for reference. The scale goes back to its shelf and he squares off and pairs up the remaining pieces of cod—segregating them to the side in the tray. These will be used either as two separate orders for a tasting menu—or artfully positioned on plates as whole orders. The point of segregating them from the others is that when the cooks have two or more orders of cod for the same table, it will be easy for them to ensure that all the plates will look the same (either two smaller pieces of cod—or one brick). The whole system is designed for uniformity and ease—under worst-case-scenario circumstances, the user, after all, is presumably a very busy line cook in a hurry. When Justo's done loading the cod, he covers the portions with plastic wrap, slaps a bright red WEDNESDAY label on top, covers that with the clear plastic lid. He puts the scraps of cod for City Harvest on a small, plastic wrap–covered sheet pan below the work table. He wipes down his station completely with hot water. Presses the button for the elevator. Washes his knives and hoses out the sink, knowing that he has just enough time to do this while the elevator to the à la carte kitchen comes down—not wanting to waste a minute waiting. Then he takes the tray upstairs, opens the walk-in, and places the tray on the shelf in the same exact place that the cod of the day has always been placed and always will be placed. The cooks will be able to find it blindfolded, if necessary.

Le Bernardin is a seafood restaurant—and we are hip-deep in the stuff. Ice from the fish crates is melting onto the floor, and Justo is even now hauling an enormous mahi onto the cutting board. But it does not smell of fish in this place. There is not even the vestigial smell of seafood you get at even the best wholesalers or Japanese fish-markets. The fish is exquisitely fresh. Fernando is constantly mopping—around and below us—every few minutes with hot, soapy water.

Full crates come in, empties are dragged out, an ongoing process—almost organic. It reminds me of the opening passages of Zola's *Belly of Paris*, a supply train of horsecarts laden with food, stretching from market into the countryside and beyond.

Any piece of fish you are likely to see at your supermarket or fishmonger's would be sniffed out and thrown away immediately here.

"If it smells like fish, it goes back," says Justo. Fish obtained from regional sources is sent back if deemed inferior in any way. Fish from a high-end wholesaler in Maine is simply weighed and thrown out if not up to standards. They reimburse without question.

He attacks the mahi with his chef's knife, taking the filets off with two strokes. Elapsed time? Sixty seconds. Left-side filet goes to one side, right-side to the other.

By eight fifteen in the morning, Justo has finished the day's portions of halibut, cod, and mahi.

It's time for the skate, a fish he's not so fond of. He empties a big bag of large wings into the sink, about thirty-five pounds in all, and immediately starts washing them with cold water. Skate are slimy, delicate, highly perishable, and loaded with transparent bits of cartilage, which, if left inadvertently inside, could do serious damage to the inside of your mouth or throat. Picture an airplane with fat wings.

Top side of each wing is a thick filet. On the underside, another, thinner one. The perimeters of each wing bristle with little bones, and between the top and bottom filets is a barrier of thin, flexible, dangerously translucent, cartilagenous spokes, like the buttress of a church—and about as unpleasant to bite into.

Justo picks up the chef's knife.

"I sharpen myself. Once a week."

I can't help asking, "Once a week?"

For a guy as scrupulous as Justo, that seems like a long time to go between sharpenings. Cooks much less conscientious than he labor over their blades on a daily basis. The very essence of knife mainte-nance—a notion inextricably tied up with one's self-image as a cook—is that the sharper the knife, the better.

Not necessarily, explains Justo.

"I like medium sharp," he says, pointing out the cartilage of the skate as an extreme example of his principle. "Too sharp? You get part of the bone. When it's sharpened *correct*, it passes *over* the bone." With this, he grabs a large skate with his gloved hand, and, with the chef's knife, removes the fattest part of the flesh from the top of both wings. It *looks* like he's savagely and indifferently hacking at the things. One skate after another, he quickly and brutally removes only the fattest part of the top of each wing. The rest, the two unexploited filets on the underside of each fish, go straight in the garbage—along with about 70 to 80 percent of the total body weight of the animal: skin, bone, and cartilage.

One could be forgiven for asking about City Harvest—an orga-nization with whom Eric Ripert works very closely and actively raises a lot money. *Why don't they take that fish?* It's complicated, I gather. Simply put—and, I'm guessing, this is true across the board in similar fine-dining restaurants—there's nobody and no place and no time to winnow out every scrap of fish from every carcass, or even most of them. Even the most good-hearted restaurants just can't do it. City Harvest does not, it appears, have the facilities or the personnel to transport, hold, process, and prepare the more close-in leavings of New York's seafood restaurants. Fish like skate are, in any case, so extremely perishable that they'd likely be spoiled by the time any secondary team could get a knife to them. The way things work now, they don't even like to take the incredibly high-quality filet meat that Le Bernardin generates unless it's fully cooked first. The restaurant boils or steams the stuff before City Harvest takes it away. (They claim it makes the trucks smell bad otherwise.)

It occurs to me that a worthwhile endeavor for a charitable organization might be the creation of a flying squad of ex-convict or ex-substance-abusing trainee fish-butchers—who could pick up and quickly trim out every scrap of useable fish from contributing restaurants. They could probably feed a whole hell of a lot of people. If perishability is a problem, perhaps they could quickly puree the stuff on site—prepare and freeze Asian-style fishballs and fish cakes by the thousands. (Note to self: talk to Eric about this idea.)

What's left of Justo's work on the mountain of skate are two large piles of perfectly bone-free pieces of fish. One side, then another, Justo removes the skin with the flexible blade at a forty-five-degree angle, trims off any and all blood or pink color that remains, and evens off the shapes with the slicer into the appropriate thicknesses and dimensions. Most fish—like skate wing—naturally taper off and narrow at the outer edges and toward the tail. Which is fine for moving through the water. Not so good for even cooking. A chef or cook looks at that graceful decline and sees a piece of protein that will cook unevenly: will, when the center—or fattest part—is perfect, be overcooked at the edges. They see a piece of fish that does *not* look like you could charge $39 for it. Customers should understand that what they are paying for, in any restaurant situation, is not just what's *on* the plate—but everything that's *not* on the plate: all the bone, skin, fat, and waste product which the chef *did* pay for, by the pound. When Eric Ripert, for instance, pays $15 or $20 a pound for a piece of fish, you can be sure, the guy who sells it to him does not care that 70 percent of that fish is going in the garbage. It's still the same price. Same principle applies to meat, poultry—or any other protein. The price of the protein on the market may be $10 per pound, but by the time you're putting the cleaned, prepped piece of meat or fish on the plate, it can actually cost you $35 a pound. And that's before paying the guy who cuts it for you. That disparity in purchase price and actual price becomes even more extreme at the top end of the dining spectrum. The famous French mantra of "Use Everything," by which most chefs live, is not the operative phrase of a three-starred Michelin restaurant. Here, it's "Use Only the Very Best."

The rest? You do what you can.

Justo pairs off the last, irregular bits of skate, draping one atop the other. He catches one he doesn't quite like—a nearly imperceptible flaw. Most prep cooks in this situation would instinctively tuck the less beautiful one underneath a perfect one. Food cost. Food cost. Food cost. Not him.

"It's like wearing clean clothes with dirty underwear," he says—without a trace of humor. The unacceptable piece goes in the trash.

It's only eight forty-five and the skate are done. The table is washed again. Knives, too. The skate is brought upstairs. A large white tuna hits the cutting board next. He zips off the skin and shows me where there's a single, very soft but hidden bone. "Your knife too sharp? You cut through—you don't feel it."

City Harvest is getting a lot of very expensive product off of this fish. Near the tail, Justo sees something he doesn't like and quickly carves off about a quarter of it. The fish is butchered as if for a sushi bar. *No* dark membrane, no raggedy bits. Center-cut filet *only*. He quickly breaks the thing down into four pristine hunks of loin. Then, without hesitating, divides those pieces into appropriate shapes for further slicing into medallions. At no other point during the day does he look so much like a machine. Uniform pieces of identical-looking portions fall away from his knife like industrially sliced bread. Lined up in the tray, they are the same size, weight, and height. He's almost apologetic about the huge pile of perfectly good tuna left on the board, rejected for its size rather than its quality. After trimming, it's probably costing the restaurant about twenty-five dollars a pound.

"Hard to balance perfect—and waste," he admits.

Nine fifteen, and Justo unloads an appalling heap of monkfish into the sink.

Monkfish are one of the slimiest, ugliest creatures you'll find in the sea. They are also wonderfully tasty—once you slip off the slippery, membrane-like skin and trim away the pink and red.

"This knife only for monkfish," says Justo, producing a long blade that might once have been a standard chef's knife but which has been, over the years, ground down into a thin, serpentine, almost double-teardrop edge. Once the monkfish meat is cut away from the bone, one loin at a time, he grabs the tail ends and runs the flexible blade down the body, pulling skin away. With a strange, flicking motion, he shaves off any pink or red.

The quiet in the room is noticeable—and I ask him if he ever listens to music while he works.

He shakes his head vigorously. "For me—I like to concentrate." He says the distraction of music might cause him to cut himself, an outcome not so terrible for him, he suggests—but bad for the product: "I don't want to get blood on the fish. I don't play around. I work fast because I work relaxed. I got nothing else on my mind."

The monkfish is finished and safely stored upstairs at nine forty. There are two kinds of salmon to deal with now. One large wild salmon and eight thirteen- to fifteen-pound organically farm-raised salmon. Sustainability has become a major focus of Le Bernardin in recent years, and this particular farm-raised stuff is supposed to be very good. Justo prefers it. "The organic, the farmed is fatter. Better raw. The wild—too much muscle for me. Too much exercise." With the chef's knife, he cuts from collar down and lifts off the filets. He peels a little bit of the meat that clings to the spine off one of the farmed salmon and hands me a piece. It is, indeed, extraordinary. The skins are removed with a few rocking sweeps of the knife. But most remarkable is what he does with the pin bones. These are the tiny, tricky, nearly invisible little rib bones left in the meat when you take the filets off the fish. They have to be removed individually by yanking the little fuckers out with tweezers or needle-nose pliers, a process that takes most cooks a while. Ordinary mortals have to feel for each slim bone lurking just beneath the surface, careful not to gouge the delicate flesh. Justo moves his hand up the filet in a literal flurry of movement; with each bone that comes out, he taps the pliers on the cutting board to release it, then, never stopping, in one continuous motion, repeats repeats repeats. It sounds like a quick, double-time snare drum beat, a staccato *tap tap tap tap tap tap*, and then . . . done. A pause of a few seconds as he begins another side of fish. I can barely see his hand move.

I have never seen anything like it in nearly three decades in the restaurant business.

With the slicer, he lifts the grayish meat that runs along the back straight away from the pink, a very delicate operation, which he, of course, accomplishes in seconds. One whole side of the wild salmon is put aside for the chef garde-manger. Justo lines a half sheet-pan with cling wrap, drapes the salmon on the tray—then wraps the whole tray under and over three times with one long piece of film. The fish is trapped in there as snug as if it were laminated.

"That way, if I fall down," says Justo, "nothing gonna happen to the fish."

In about two minutes, all the remaining salmon are portioned into seventy-five- to eighty-gram slices. He hand-checks each slice a second time by lightly pinching them as they're arranged side by side in the tray. Once in a great while, he feels a bone he missed on the first pass and slips it out. Two slices of salmon will constitute an order. Laid out end to end, all pointing the same direction, the slices themselves look like little pink fishes swimming upriver, identical patterns of fatty swirls running through their flesh, lovely to look at, breathtaking in their uniformity.

At ten twenty-five, the salmon is on its way upstairs.

A young cook, seeing me, asks eagerly, "Have you seen him do the pin bones?"

"Yes," I say, nodding my head. "Yes, I have."

"First time I heard it, I thought he was tapping his foot," says the cook.

Justo grabs the first of eight large striped bass out of a crate, with thumb and middle finger hooked deep into the fish's eye sockets, not trusting the usual two-fingers-into-the-gills grab popular with fishermen. They're on their way upstairs by ten forty-five. Then it's twelve red snappers. It takes him ten minutes to take all the snapper off the bone and remove their skins. Once again, left sides are put together in one stack, right sides in another. He shows me why: when cleaning the right sides, the knife has to always be drawn in one direction when cleaning membrane and trimming belly; the left sides, the blade is pushed away to perform the same tasks—in the opposite direction. By sorting his fish as he does, Justo saves time and unnecessary movement.

A half hour later, the snapper is done. Only a tremendous shitload of black sea bass (Justo's least favorite) remain. They are, for easily discernible reasons, the hardest fish to clean: unlike much of what arrives, they are still covered with tough scales, guts still in—and bristling with nasty-looking and extremely dangerous spines.

Fernando, the steward, comes by with Justo's staff meal: a rather forlorn-looking plate of chicken salad, dressed green salad, and potato, with a bun. The plate is wrapped in plastic and placed unhesitatingly beneath Justo's work station—as it has surely been agreed, by unwavering routine and practice, that Justo will wait to eat until he's finished with his work.

He's saved the worst until the end. At Le Bernardin, fish is served without the skin, the black sea bass being the lone exception. Its skin is an important component of the final dish, adding vital textural and flavor notes—as well as looking really cool. This means that one can't do simply a serviceable job of removing the scales, assuming that, later, any that remain will surely come off with the skin. Every single one has to be carefully scraped off in the sink—away from the cutting board. Justo is very conscious of the transparent scales' propensity to fly across the room and cling undetected to the white flesh of the fish. One transparent scale clinging to one order of fish? That would be bad. So, he's got to carefully scrape off the scales—quickly, of course, avoiding the long and extremely vicious spines on the fish, which could easily penetrate his glove and inflict a painful and instantaneously infectious wound. Then filet off the meat, remove the pin bones (which are even trickier and more reluctant to come out than those in salmon), trim, and portion. It is of tantamount importance for Justo, when portioning, to keep in mind the intended cooking method and result: a still-moist, evenly cooked oblong of fish with a *very crispy* layer of skin on one side. If the piece of fish is too small, by the time the skin has crisped, the flesh has overcooked. Nature being what it is, no two fish are exactly the same, and the optimal size is not always available. It's up to Justo to make do.

It's twelve ten in the afternoon and Justo Thomas has finished cleaning and portioning seven hundred pounds of fish. He cuts a piece of cardboard from a carton and uses it to scrape out the fish scales from the sink. He hoses both basins down, washes his knives, the scale, and all exposed surfaces. He peels the cling wrap off the walls.

He's done for the day.

In six years at Le Bernardin, and in twenty years cooking in New York restaurants, Justo Thomas has—like the overwhelming majority of people who cook our food—never eaten in his own restaurant.

It's a central irony of fine dining that, unlike the waiters who serve their food, the cooks are very rarely able to afford to eat what they have spent years learning to make. They are usually not welcome, in any case. They don't have the clothes for it. Many, if not most, expensive restaurants specifically prohibit their employees from coming as customers—at any time. The reasoning is part practical and part, one suspects, aesthetic. One doesn't want a bunch of loud, badly dressed cooks laughing and talking in an overfamiliar way with the bartender while trying to maintain an atmosphere of sophistication—of romantic illusion. There is also the temptation to slip freebies to people one works with every day. From the point of view of any sensible restaurateur or manager, it's generally believed to be a bad thing. Once you let employees start drinking in their own place of work—even on their days off—you've unleashed the dogs of war. No good can come of it.

Le Bernardin's rules reflect this industry-wide policy.

But I figured I had some pull with the chef and asked him to make an exception.

A short time later, I took Justo Thomas to lunch at his own restaurant.

He arrives straight from his shift, having changed into a dark, well-cut suit and glasses with black designer frames, having left work by the service entrance and reentered by the restaurant's front door. It takes a second for me to recognize him.

He's nervous but contained—and very happy to be here. He's dressed right for the room, but his posture and gait are not of a person who lives in spaces like this. His coworkers in the kitchen are excited for him, he says, scarcely believing this is happening, and the floor staff appear happy for him, too—though they do their very best to conceal their smiles. From the very beginning, Justo is treated like any other customer and with the same deference—led to our table, his chair pulled out, asked if he'd care to order from the menu or if he'd prefer the kitchen to cook for us. When wine arrives, the sommelier addresses her remarks to him.

A little bowl of salmon rillettes is brought to the table with some rounds of toast. Champagne is served.

Ordinarily, when Justo goes out to dinner, he's with his family. They go to a roasted-chicken place or, if it's a rare special occasion, to a Spanish restaurant for steak and lobster.

When that happens, he does not drink. At all.

"I am always the driver," he says.

Though he is the middle brother, Justo has become, by virtue of his character and what he's achieved in New York, something of a patriarch. He owns a house in the Dominican Republic. He keeps the top floor for family use and rents out to tenants the first floor and an adjoining structure. His siblings tend to come to him for advice on important matters. His father, he says, taught him the lesson that one should "never let your family be afraid while you're alive."

He's the example for the rest—and he takes that responsibility seriously.

"Family first. Then my job," he says.

I am enormously relieved when he takes his first sip of champagne—and when he tells me he will indeed be enjoying, along with me, the wine pairing to follow. The kitchen has insisted on doing a tasting menu for their favorite son—and one must, under such circumstances, drink wine. I was concerned earlier. Justo has said that his idea of getting really crazy on vacation is (in between working on his house) taking his family to the beach, buying pizza for his daughter—and maybe having a beer. On a perfect day, he'll dance with his wife. He will have arranged for a taxi to take them home.

He has made similar arrangements today.

The first course is tuna, layers of thinly pounded yellowfin, layered with foie gras and toasted baguette. Justo enthusiastically cleans his plate—with a critical eye. He recognizes his work, though the cooks have pounded it to paper-thinness. It's a popular dish—and on the rare occasions when the dinner crew needs to pound more after he's gone for the day, he doesn't like it when they use his station. We're washing the tuna down with a Gelber Muskateller Neumeister from Austria.

"My cutting board is special," he explains.

Justo handles only fish at Le Bernardin. Oysters, langoustines, prawns, and sea urchin are prepared upstairs in the à la carte kitchen. So, though he's seen the pricey little boxes of plump, orange sea-urchin roe, stacked neatly in even rows, as he passed by, he's never eaten the stuff. We get a spiny shell each, the roe on beds of jalapeño-wasabi jam, seasoned with seaweed salt—finished at the last second by our server, who pours wakame-orange-scented broth over them.

"Kasumi Tsuru, Yamahai Gingo," says the sommelier, serving Justo sake.

"Delicious," says Justo, closing his eyes. "It's like . . . a dream. I don't want to wake up."

The next course is seared langoustine with a "salad" of mâche and wild mushroom with shaved foie gras and white balsamic vinaigrette—and it's one of the most goddamn delicious things I've ever put in my mouth. Small, elegant, lushly but not overly rich.

"When I get out of here—I don't want to brush my teeth," he jokes—but I know exactly how he feels. You want to keep this taste.

I lose track of the wines at this point. There are a lot of them—and a trilogy of ales, I think. Then more wines. But I do remember a bread-crusted red snapper with zucchini and mint compote coming our way.

An extraordinary poached halibut with braised daikon, baby radish, and turnips in a sesame court bouillon.

"You recognize your work?" I ask. I point to the perfect squares of evenly shaped protein on our plates. Justo just nods and smiles—a look of satisfaction on his face.

His last entrée is the crispy black bass with braised celery and parsnip custard in an Iberico-ham-and-green-peppercorn sauce. It's the fish he likes least to work with—saves until last, the ever-more-popular labor-intensive fuckers that have to be gutted, scaled, fileted, rid of their resilient little pin bones, then squared off just right so the skin can get exactly this crispy without overcooking the meat.

Justo looks particularly pleased to see his nemesis on the plate. Hopefully, all his work now makes some kind of tangible sense.

I find myself looking up at the enormous oil paintings on the dining-room walls. Scenes of fishermen and port towns in Brittany—where Maguy Le Coze, the founder and co-owner of Le Bernardin (along with her brother Gilbert), came from. Where it all started and where the inspiration began for a fish-centric temple of seafood. I wonder what Justo would think of Brittany—and if he'll ever see it. I find myself wanting to make that happen.

I ask him what he wants to do—when he retires someday—and he answers me with the things he'll do when he goes back home, mostly involving repairs, improvements, work. But what about when the work is done, I ask? If things could be . . . perfect?

"When I think everything is perfect I think I'm going to get sick," he says. "I'll think—What am I *missing*?"

What about the customers at Le Bernardin, I ask, referring to the older, obviously more comfortable patrons around us. Some of these people will spend more money on a single bottle of wine with dinner than even he—a well-paid man by most standards—will make in months. How does he feel about that?

"I think in life, they give too much to some people and nothing to everybody else," he shrugs without bitterness. "Without work we are nothing."

We linger over chocolate *pot de crème* and mascarpone creams and pistachio mousse.

Not visibly affected by the generous pourings of wine, Justo orders an espresso. Sits back in his chair, pleased.

"I got a good job. A good family. I live in peace."

19

The Fish-on-Monday Thing

I was genuinely angry most mornings, writing *Kitchen Confidential*. An unfocused, aim-in-a-general-direction-and-fire kind of a rage only exacerbated by the fact that my writing "regimen" (such as it was) consisted of a five thirty or six a.m. wake-up, a hurried disgorging of sentences, reminiscences, and hastily reconstructed memories from the previous night (this after a ten- or twelve- or fourteen-hour day in the kitchen, followed invariably by too much to drink and a topple into bed). I'd spit whatever words I had quickly onto the page—no agonizing over sentences for me, there wasn't time anyway—then off to work again: put on the sauces, cut the meat, portion the fish, crack the peppercorns, cook lunch, and so on. Three thirty, two quick pints down the street, back to Les Halles, either work the line or read the board, then off to Siberia Bar—or simply sit down with the remains of the floor staff for just one more—get drunk *en place*. Sagged down in the back right passenger seat of a yellow Chevy Caprice, legs twisted uncomfortably behind the bulletproof partition—that's where I did my best work, thinking about what I was going to write the next day. Window half-cracked and me halfway or fully in the bag, I'd think about my life as New York City rolled by outside.

As I lived then in Morningside Heights, on the Upper West Side, by the time I got home, my taxi would have passed through a near-comprehensive landscape of greatest hits, all my sorrows, all my joys—as I think the song goes. A densely packed checkerboard pattern of mistakes, failures, crimes, betrayals large and small. The occasional happy spot with good associations would make me smile weakly—before plunging me in the other direction as I'd recall how things got all fucked up, went wrong, or simply just came to . . . *this*. I was always glad to see the spot on Broadway where my then-wife and I had set up our books and records for sale, happy that I wasn't doing *that* anymore—and that there was no longer a need for either of us to adhere to that kind of unrelentingly voracious math. But I was still angry—in the way, I suspect, that mobs get angry: angry about all the things I didn't have and (I was sure) I would never have.

I'd never had health insurance, for one thing. Nor had my wife. And that scared the hell out of me—as getting sick was, on one hand, just not an option, and on the other, increasingly likely as we grew older. A sudden pain in the jaw requiring a root canal would hit the financial picture (such as it was) like a freight train. Total destruction. It would mean groveling. Beg the nice dentist in the filthy-looking office on the ground floor of a housing project to accept payment on the installment plan.

Car commercials made me angry, as I'd never owned a car—or so much as a scooter—and, I was quite sure by now, never would. Home ownership was a concept so beyond imagining as to be laughable. I was so far behind on rent, so ridiculously in arrears on income taxes, that on the rare occasion when I went to bed sober, I'd lie there in terror, my heart pounding in my ears, trying desperately to *not* think the unthinkable: that at any time, either landlord or government or the long-ignored but very much still-there folks at AmEx could take everything, everything away. That "everything" amounted only to somewhere between fourteen and four hundred dollars on a good day was cold comfort. It was only a combination of rent-stabilized apartment, a byzantine, slow-moving, and tenant-friendly housing court—and a wife who could work the system that kept a roof over our heads. And that streak of improbable good luck, too, could run out at any minute.

So, I was afraid. Very afraid. Every day and every night and every time I bothered to think about these things—which was a lot, because that's the way a responsible person with a job who *doesn't* have a drug habit was supposed to think about things: realistically. Frightened people become angry people—as history teaches us again and again. Facing "reality" after a lifetime of doing everything I could to escape it offered no rewards that I could see. Only punishment. No solution presented itself. I couldn't go back (that way was blocked for sure), and I couldn't go forward.

I'd quit heroin and I'd quit methadone and I'd stopped doing cocaine and stopped smoking crack—like everybody tells you to, right? And yet there I was, still broke and still frightened and in a deep financial hole I knew I would never climb out of.

And I was angry about that. Very angry.

I was angry with my wife—very angry, a long-festering and deep-seated resentment that year after year after year she didn't, couldn't, wouldn't *work*. Strong, smart as hell, with a college degree from a Seven Sisters school, solid white-collar experience, and she'd long ago just . . . stopped looking. In nearly two decades, after a promising start, nothing but a couple of short-term, part-time gigs stocking books and sorting in-house mail for near-minimum wage. It made no sense to me and I resented it bitterly. To be fair, it consumed me out of all proportion, with the kind of smoldering, barely repressed passive-aggressive anger that poisons everything around it. And that, sure as shit, didn't help the situation. Waking up and going to sleep with this basic fact—

and the way I then handled that resentment—was contaminating everything. I just couldn't get past it. I didn't get past it. And I made things worse—far worse—in all the drearily predictable ways. Underscore that sentence.

As partners in crime, we'd been—in my mind, anyway—a Great Couple. As solid citizens? Neither of us seemed to know how.

I was angry, too, that all my little-boy dreams of travel and adventure would for absolutely sure never come true—that I'd never see Paris as a grown-up or Vietnam, or the South Pacific, or India, or even Rome. From my vantage point, standing behind the stove at Les Halles, that much was perfectly clear. And, to tell the truth, I only became angrier when my boss, Philippe, sent me to Tokyo for a week to consult, because now I knew what I was missing. Which was—as anyone who's been lucky enough to see those places knows—*everything*. It was as if someone had opened a happy, trippy, groovy, and exotic version of Pandora's box, allowed me to peek inside, into another dimension, an alternate life, and then slammed the thing shut.

I'm sure that many middle-aged, divorced guys could describe a drunken snog with a female croupier in similarly lush—and even apocalyptic—terms. And any "epiphany" I had in Asia was, at the end of the day, already the subject of about a thousand not very good movies. I can only say that once I'd stumbled around Asia's impenetrably "foreign" streets, surrounded only by people whose language I would never understand, nostrils filled with strange and wondrous smells, eyes boggling at everything I saw, eating things I'd never dreamed could be so good . . . well . . . I was doomed. I would ultimately have done anything to get some more of that. (Not that anyone was offering.) I knew, too, somewhere deep inside, that sharing would be out of the question. That's a bad thing to learn about yourself.

I was angry, too, in the usual ways: with my mom for having me, for being stupid enough to love me. With my brother for not being a fuckup like me. With my father for dying.

And, naturally, I was angry with myself most of all (people like us always are, aren't we? It's a Lifetime movie almost anyone can star in)—for being forty-four years old and still one phone call, one paycheck away from eviction. For fucking up, pissing away, sabotaging my life in every possible way.

Five years earlier, after the kind of once-in-a-lifetime, freakishly lucky breaks that have been all too common in my life, the kind of thing most aspiring writers only dream of, I'd published two spectacularly unsuccessful novels that had disappeared without a trace, never making it into paperback. This, the general wisdom taught me, effectively finished me in publishing. About this—and maybe only this—I was actually *not* angry. It had been a nice ride, I'd felt, one on which I'd embarked with zero expectations. I'd kept my day job—never imagining I'd do otherwise. The whole enterprise had dropped in my lap, felt like a scam from the get-go, so I'd thankfully never suffered from any delusions of being a "writer." Two uninterrupted hours of sitting at an empty table in a Northridge, California, Barnes and Noble on a one-stop, crackpot and equally crack-brained, self-financed book tour had quickly disabused me of such notions.

When I sat down at my desk every morning to write *Kitchen Confidential* and began clacking away at the keyboard, I was both gloriously free of hope that it would ever be read outside of a small subculture of restaurant people in New York City—and boiling with the general illwill of the unsatisfied, the envious, and the marginal. Let it be funny for cooks and waiters—and fuck everybody else, was pretty much my thinking at the time.

Which worked out okay in the end, as I never could have written the thing had I thought people would actually read it.

So, the result was an angry book in a lot of ways—and, over time, that's what people have come to expect from me. The angry, cynical, snarky guy who says mean things on *Top Chef*—and I guess it would be pretty easy to keep going with that: a long-running lounge act, the exasperatedly enraged food guy. "Rachael Ray? What's up with *that*?!" (Cue snare drum here.) To a great extent, that's already happened.

But looking back at those hurried, hungover early mornings, sitting at my desk with unbrushed teeth, a cigarette in my mouth, and a bad attitude, what was I angry about that I'm *still* angry about today? Who, of all the people and all the things I railed at in that book, really deserved my scorn?

I certainly wasn't angry at Emeril. And the many dreamers and crackpots I wrote about who'd employed me over the years—whatever their sins—are certainly no worse characters than I'd been. In fact, I *loved* them for their craziness, their excesses, their foolishness—their shrewdness or guile, their wastefulness, even their criminality. In almost every case, their choice of the restaurant business as a lifestyle option had cost them far, far more than it had ever cost me.

I wasn't ever angry with any of the people who worked with me. Not in a lasting way. It was they, after all—all of them, heroes and villains alike—who'd kept me in the business all those years. I may have called waiters "waitrons" and joked about abusing them, but I had always believed that if somebody who worked with me went home feeling like a jerk for giving their time and their genuine effort, then it was *me* who had failed *them*—and in a very personal, fundamental way.

No. I instinctively liked and respected anyone who cooked or served food in a restaurant and took any kind of satisfaction in the job. Still feel that way. It is the finest and noblest of toil, performed by only the very best of people.

Okay. I *am* genuinely angry—still—at vegetarians. That's not shtick. Not angry at them personally, mind you—but in principle. A shocking number of vegetarians and even vegans have come to my readings, surprised me with an occasional sense of humor, refrained from hurling animal blood at me—even befriended me. I have even knowingly had sex with one, truth be told. But what I've seen of the world in the past nine years has, if anything, made me angrier at anyone not a Hindu who insists on turning their nose up at a friendly offer of meat.

I don't care what you do in your home, but the idea of a vegetarian traveler in comfortable shoes waving away the hospitality—the distillation of a lifetime of training and experience—of, say, a Vietnamese *pho* vendor (or Italian mother-in-law, for that matter) fills me with spluttering indignation.

No principle is, to my mind, worth that; no Western concept of "is it a pet or is it meat" excuses that kind of rudeness.

I often talk about the "Grandma rule" for travelers. You may not like Grandma's Thanksgiving turkey. It may be overcooked and dry—and her stuffing salty and studded with rubbery pellets of giblet you find unpalatable in the extreme. You may not even like turkey at all. But it's *Grandma's* turkey. And you are in Grandma's *house*. So shut the fuck up and eat it. And afterward, say, "Thank you, Grandma, why, yes, yes of course I'd *love* seconds."

I guess I understand if your desire for a clean conscience and cleaner colon overrules any natural lust for bacon. But taking your belief system on the road—or to other people's houses—makes me angry. I feel too lucky—now more than ever—too acutely aware what an incredible, unexpected privilege it is to travel this world and enjoy the kindness of strangers to ever, ever be able to understand how one could do anything other than say yes, yes, yes.

I've tried. Really.

I can cheerfully eat vegetarian food and nothing but for about five days at a clip—if I'm in India. And I'm open to the occasional attempts by the opposition to make their case.

Unfortunately, those attempts don't always end happily.

A very nice, truly sweet guy, the boyfriend of a producer I was doing business with a few years back, went out of his way—as gently and as undogmatically as possible—to bring me over to the other side, making it something of a personal mission to get me to acknowledge the possibility of a delicious all-vegan meal. Let me repeat that this was a nice guy, who'd made his choices for what was, I'm sure, a visceral abhorrence for meat. When he saw a pork chop on a plate, I have no doubt, what he really saw was a golden retriever that had died screaming. I'd seen the genuine love this man had for his dogs—the way the poor guy would just tear up at the mention of some awful shelter on the other side of the country. I couldn't find it in my heart to refuse him. I went out to dinner at what was said to be New York's premier fine-dining vegan restaurant, a favorite, I was assured, of Paul McCartney's (not exactly a selling point—but a measure of how earnest were his efforts to get me in the door). The food was expensive and painstakingly—even artfully—prepared, and, admittedly, it did not entirely suck.

Over organic wines and much convivial conversation, I even passed on a suggestion (via my dining companion) to "Sir Paul" that I thought might be helpful in his very public efforts to save cute animals. I ventured that if he seriously wanted to see a *lot* of the rarest, most beautiful, and most endangered animals live longer, healthier lives—and maybe even multiply and prosper—he should, I advised, buy a few million dollars worth of Viagra and Cialis, start spreading that stuff around for free where it mattered, with accompanying public service announcements, in the parts of Asia where they think bear's paw, rhino horn, and tiger dicks are good boner medicine. Unlike these stratospherically expensive traditional Chinese remedies—the end-products of an enormously profitable black market that rewards the killing and even slow torturing of endangered animals—Viagra will actually make your dick hard, and for cheap. Hand out a few million little blue pills to middle-aged Chinese dudes—maybe even throw in a hooker, to boot—I suggested, and you'll see some changed hearts and minds. Break a centuries-old pattern of truly monstrous and extreme cruelty to what are often the rarest and most beautiful of animals! (I was later told that he'd actually passed this idea along. A conversation I would like to see a videotape of someday.)

After a surprisingly serviceable meal, I felt pretty good about things. I'd been a nice guy, I thought, had made an effort to be open-minded. The meal hadn't sucked. We'd even managed to find some common ground.

But then, months later, the poor bastard sent me an e-mail asking (innocently enough) for some statement of support—I think, for the Humane Society. Now, I *like* the Humane Society for the most part. I may disagree violently with their policy on—and activities on behalf of—anti–foie gras legislation, but I do like cats and dogs. (I've adopted one shelter cat after another for much of my life.) I'm supportive of any effort to stop dog-fighting, to spay animals, and to prevent abuse of domestic animals.

I don't like circuses and, given the chance, would probably vote against the indenturing of elephants and lions and tigers, or any other animals they might want to stand on chairs or train to juggle. I frankly think Siegfried or Roy—whichever one of those guys got mauled by a tiger—got what he deserved. Tigers, to my way of thinking, *like* to maul people, they're certainly built for the job, and anything preventing them from doing that on the one hand—while tempting them with a German in a sparkly, cerulean blue suit on the other—is clearly animal cruelty. Somebody who abuses an animal for the sheer joy of it—or solely for purposes of entertainment—should receive, at very least, equal ill treatment.

I'll go further into PETA territory:

I would have preferred that Steve Irwin, "Crocodile Hunter"—regardless of his saintly conservationist prattle—had ended up as "Crocodile Chow." *That* would have been some rough but entirely appropriate justice. In my opinion, the loud, irritating little fuck was in the business of disturbing, poking, tormenting, and generally annoying animals, who would have surely been far happier had they never met him. And if Bindi Irwin lived in my neighborhood, by the way, I would have called Child Protective Services on her parents years ago.

So, contrary to my reputation, I'm like Saint Francis of Fucking Assisi compared to what you might think—a friend to animals large and small, feeder of strays, adopter of runt kittens. A man who, though opposed to vegetarian orthodoxy, is still a reasonable fellow, willing, at least, to listen to the other guy's point of view.

Until, that is, I got back from Beirut, fresh from a war zone, to find in my inbox an earnest plea for support from my vegan dining companion. The urgency of his tone as he described what was happening to stray cats and dogs somewhere grated on me badly. As I read on, I found myself becoming angrier and angrier—soon becoming furious.

I'd just seen a city not very much unlike Miami bombed back twenty fucking years, I answered in a lather of righteous indignation. From a shameful distance, I'd watched, every day, as neighborhoods filled with people were smashed to rubble. I'd woken up and gone to sleep to the rumble of bombs and rockets rolling through the floor of my otherwise comfortable hotel room. And then seen, up close, the faces of people who'd lost everything—and sometimes *everyone*—in their lives: the fear and hopelessness and confusion of thousands of people, packed onto landing craft with the few possessions they could carry, off and away to uncertain futures. For nothing. For the "best" intentions, I'm sure—they always are, aren't they? But, ultimately, for nothing.

I had come straight from that—to this: this message filled with whiny, plaintive outrage on the behalf of the strays of Denver or something like that. There were strays in Beirut, too, I spat out, beginning what I'd intended to be a measured, sympathetic response. Surely, I suggested, where *people* were being bombed, and *whole fucking neighborhoods* knocked down to rubble, some doggies got hurt, too? I went on, warming (if not overheating) to my subject, venomously musing that when whole fucking families get crushed in their homes, abandoned pets can become a problem. Having just flown from the tarmac of a floating refugee camp, I now surfed deliriously on a wave of bile. Expanding the scope of my observations to include other places I'd been and other things I'd seen in my travels, I pointed out—any vestige of measured civility gone by now—that it was, perhaps, worth noting as well that *anyplace* where people were treated like animals—stacked in shantytowns, favelas, communes, and hutments—that animals suffered first and worst. Nobody gives a fuck about cute doggies or cats, much less a fucking dolphin or a white rhino, for that matter, when 90 percent of your diet is fucking bread—when you're lucky enough to get it—or pounded manioc gruel. Where charred monkey on a stick (in fur) is a life-saving gift for a family, I spewed, all those neatly anthropomorphized animals we so love—like your fucking Yorkie (this was a low blow)—are seen as nothing more than bush meat. Sadistically putting the boot in, I gave examples of places where people are concerned that men in black vans might be coming at night to put hoods over their heads and take them away. Possibly for something they may have casually said, or a neighbor might have thought they casually said—or falsely reported they may have casually said.

I believe I might have mentioned Ceaușescu's Bucharest as an example. Plowing under an entire neighborhood and displacing its residents to build a pharaoh-scale palace, the megalomaniacal dictator had created an instant and frighteningly large population of abandoned dogs. Reproducing at an astounding rate, the desperate animals begat countless roving packs of terrifying and vicious feral dogs, wild, aggressive and hungry predators who knew nothing but the streets. Parts of Bucharest became, particularly at night, a potentially dangerous jungle—with all the dog-on-dog, dog-on-man, and man-on-dog violence imaginable. Embarrassed by this all-too-visible phenomenon, the people's representatives were urged to deal with the matter. The dogs were eventually hunted down and exterminated in great number. If the death of the "Genius of the Carpathians" and his wife is any example (thoughtfully videotaped and broadcast), one can only imagine how gently the dogs were dispatched.

I believe I ended my bilious and cruel masterwork of an e-mail with the image of the gentle and beloved bovines of India, revered, protected by a population of people who worship them as life-givers, divine. Wandering freely through the streets, always and famously with the right of way, they were free as well, I thought my friend should know, to starve slowly to death, to eat garbage already picked over many times by equally hungry humans, often settling on the discarded plastic bags ubiquitous to impoverished communities where hope is almost gone and municipal garbage removal is a some-times—if ever—thing. The plastic bags, of course, are indigestible, I explained, gradually becoming twisted and balled up in the cow's guts and eventually—after what is surely a long period of agonizing discomfort—killing them.

Leaving him with this awful image, I ended in FULL CAPS that given the inconvenient and annoyingly complicated relationship be-tween the conditions in which people live and his adorable animal friends, maybe he should start thinking about *people* first.

Granted, my reaction was on a par with suddenly taking a baseball bat to the barista who mistakenly used skim instead of soy milk on your latte, but I was really and truly angry. Not at my poor, unsuspecting friend, undeserving of such treatment (from whom I've never heard since). He just wanted to save a few animals, after all. It was just his bad luck that he'd asked *me* for help—and at a very bad time. I was angry at all the shit he made me think about.

And I'm still angry.

But I digress.

From the softer-edged distance of a changed and far more com-fortable life, I've searched for a root cause, a common denominator that might explain my seemingly rote, instinctive, reflexive scorn for anyone cooking on TV (or in films, for that matter) whom I see, somehow, as unworthy.

What has Guy Fieri ever done to *me*? Why should I care if something Sandra Lee made on her show came from a can—or arrived held aloft by celestial virgins on a cubic zirconium–encrusted sleigh straight from Tuscany or Provence or fucking Valhalla? What does it matter if Rachael can cook or not? People *like* her! What's my problem? So *what* if the contestants on *Hell's Kitchen* are transparently delusional and hopeless? I shouldn't get mad about it, right?

But I do.

Here's what I'd like to think.

Back when I started cooking—back in the heady, crazy, admittedly lower-standard days of the early 1970s, when it was all about speed, endurance, attitude, physical toughness, and the ability to work through every variety of self-inflicted punishment—people handled food differently. The distinction between the way a "professional" and a home cook handled food was easy to spot: the professional cook was rougher with his food. (Obviously, I'm not talking about Lutèce or the Four Seasons or the better restaurants of the day here.) The fact was, cooks tended to slap their meat around a little bit more than was absolutely necessary, to drop portions of fish onto the cutting board with an audible panache that fell something short of delicacy. Looking like you didn't give a shit—while cranking out food with the speed and efficiency and consistency of someone who did—was something of the fashion. You saw it in the rough, easy familiarity with which professional butchers took apart a primal section, the too-cool-to-be-bothered expression that said, "I could do this in my sleep."

Simply put, neither I nor the people I worked with—or admired—particularly "respected the ingredient," as chefs are likely to call it these days. We were frankly brutal with our food. I don't know exactly when that attitude changed in me—somewhere, I'm sure, around the time I started putting on airs and spouting shit from the Larousse. But over time, without my realizing it was happening, my attitude *did* change, hardening, eventually, into a deeply held belief that doing bad things to food, especially when one does them knowingly—or wasting perfectly good food, or, in general, disrespecting it—is fundamentally *wrong*, a sin (if such a thing exists), a violation of a basic contract with decency, with the world and its citizens. In a word: evil.

Traveling has only reinforced that feeling.

I'm sure that I'm not alone in feeling an almost physical pain when I see somebody cut heedlessly into an unrested steak. Most people I know who have cooked for a living will react with a groan or a wince if they see someone committing an easily preventable crime against food. But most of my friends don't actually get angry when somebody who knows (or should know) better massacres a perfectly good dish on TV.

I do.

I don't dislike Guy Fieri, I realized, after many viewings of his cooking shows, much soul-searching at my personal ashram, and many doses of prescription hypnotics. I just dislike—*really* dislike—the idea that somebody would put Texas-style barbeque inside a fucking nori roll. I was, and remain, angry that there are genuine pit-masters who've made a calling of getting pork shoulder just right—and sushi chefs who worked three years on rice alone before being deemed worthy to lay hands on fish—and here's some guy on TV blithely smashing those two disciplines together like junkers in a demolition derby. A pre-chopped onion is *not* okay, the way I look at it—no matter what Rachael or Sandra tell you. The shit in a can is not anywhere nearly as good—and almost always more expensive—than stuff you can often make yourself just as quickly. It's . . . it's just . . . wrong to tell people otherwise.

It is, of course, ludicrous for me to be insulted on behalf of strangers who would probably find my outrage completely misplaced, embarrassing, and probably even deranged. I don't claim to speak for them and am unworthy, in any case, of doing so. I'm just saying that some of the shit I see some people doing to food on television causes a physical reaction in some deeply buried reptile part of my brain—and that makes me angry. It makes me want to say mean things. It probably shortens my life every time it happens.

One might expect Thomas Keller, who famously insists on storing his fish in their natural "swimming" position, to feel this way about food being mistreated. But me? Where do I get off, one might well ask?

It's more an affliction than the expression of any high-minded ideals.

I watch Mark Bittman enjoy a perfectly and authentically prepared Spanish paella on TV, after which he demonstrates how his viewers can do it at home—in an aluminum saucepot—and I want to shove my head through the glass of my TV screen and take a giant bite out of his skull, scoop the soft, slurry-like material inside into my paw, and then throw it right back into his smug, fireplug face. The notion that anyone would believe Catherine Zeta-Jones as an obsessively perfectionist chef (particularly given the ridiculously clumsy, 1980s-looking food) in the wretched film *No Reservations* made me want to vomit blood, hunt down the producers, and kick them slowly to death. (Worse was the fact that the damn thing was a remake of the unusually excellent German chef flick *Mostly Martha*.) On *Hell's Kitchen*, when Gordon Ramsay pretends that the criminally inept, desperately unhealthy gland case in front of him could *ever* stand a chance in hell of surviving even three minutes as "executive chef of the new Gordon Ramsay restaurant" (the putative grand prize for the finalist), I'm inexplicably actually angry on *Gordon's* behalf. And *he's* the one making a quarter-million dollars an episode—very contentedly, too, from all reports.

The eye-searing "Kwanzaa Cake" clip on YouTube, of Sandra Lee doing things with store-bought angel food cake, canned frosting, and corn nuts, instead of being simply the unintentionally hilarious viral video it should be, makes me mad for all humanity. I. Just. Can't. Help it.

I wish, really, that I was so far up my own ass that I could somehow believe myself to be some kind of standard-bearer for good eating—or ombudsman, or even the deliverer of thoughtful critique. But that wouldn't be true, would it?

I'm just a cranky old fuck with what, I guess, could charitably be called "issues."

And I'm *still* angry.

But *eat* the fucking fish on Monday already. Okay?

I wrote those immortal words about *not* going for the Monday fish, the ones that'll haunt me long after I'm crumbs in a can, knowing nothing other than New York City. And times, to be fair, have changed. Okay, I still would advise against the fish special at T.G.I. McSweenigan's, "A Place for Beer," on a Monday. Fresh fish, I'd guess, is probably not the main thrust of their business. But things are different now for chefs and cooks. The odds are better than ever that the guy slinging fish and chips back there in the kitchen actually gives a shit about what he's doing. And even if he doesn't, these days he has to figure that you might actually know the difference.

Back when I wrote the book that changed my life, I was angriest—like a lot of chefs and cooks of my middling abilities—at my customers. They've changed. I've changed.

About them, I'm not angry anymore.

Still Here

There are songs I'll never listen to again. Not the ones that remind me of the bad times.

It's certain songs from long ago when everything, whether I knew it or not at the time, was golden. Those I can't abide. Those hurt. And what's the point of doing that to oneself? I can't go back and enjoy them any more than I did at the time—and there's no fixing things.

I was sitting in a restaurant fairly late one night, a neighborhood place my wife and I pop out to now and again. The dinner rush was over and the dining room was only half-filled with customers. We'd just gotten our drinks and finished ordering food when the woman at the next table said, "Tony," and pointed at her husband, the middle-aged man sitting across from her. "It's the Silver Shadow," she said.

It had been more than twenty years since I'd seen the Shadow, as I called him in *Kitchen Confidential*. And the picture I'd painted of him and the outrageous maelstrom of multiunit madness that surrounded him had not been flattering. I'd always liked the Shadow—no matter how bat-shit crazy things were in his kingdom, or how badly I'd fared there—and I was happy to see him again. I didn't know what happened with him in the intervening years, though I'd heard stories, of course. He now owns two very good, very sensibly scaled restaurants, one of them in New York and one in a very nice place—the kind where a person might take a vacation.

I didn't recognize this man, would never have connected him with his younger self. I remember the Shadow as looking like a well-fed, overprivileged grad student (though slightly older)—someone whose yearbook photo from high school one could easily imagine. He looked *good* now—though considerably older and maybe a little tired-looking. His wife looked the same. She'd looked gorgeous then—she looked gorgeous now. Though friendly during what could have been a far more awkward conversation about the book, she would casually refer to it as "fiction."

The Shadow was more circumspect. He talked about the reaction when the book came out. Everyone had recognized him right away, he said. His daughter might have told him about it first. "Dad, there's this book—about *you*!" He described reading it as "devastating." He said he cried. And, of course, I felt fucking awful. Like I said, I'd always liked the guy. I'd seen him guilty of a lot of really hubristic, lunatic shit back in the day—but I'd never seen him, unlike so many of his fellow mini-moguls of the time, deliberately fuck anybody over.

After dinner, I ran home and reread his chapter. Yes. There *were* machine guns in the bathroom . . . Yes. Cocaine was sold over the service bar. Representatives of a Sicilian-American fraternal organization did indeed come by on a weekly basis to solicit donations. The whole fleet of Shadow restaurants did seem, to even the casual observer, to steam full-speed ahead without anybody having any idea who—if anyone—was at the tiller. But as I did a quick fact-check of my version of the Shadow story, I realized that while I'd gotten the lurid details right, I'd sounded so—shocked, so outraged, so unforgiving of his excesses. I'd made the guy sound like an idiot—which he surely was not.

If the Shadow was ever guilty of anything, it was that he had been very much a creature of his time. Only on a much larger scale. Like I said to him that night, as we sat at our separate tables, reflecting on the past, "Hey. It was the '80s . . . We made it through. We're still here."

I'd like to say that that was a comfort to the man—or that it might have served as an explanation—even an apology. But I don't think so.

I *have*, on the other hand, seen Pino Luongo fuck people over many times. And enjoy it while he did it.

My chapter on Pino made him look like a son of a bitch—but it was *still* the nicest thing anyone has ever written about the guy. *He* seemed to think so. We've seen each other a few times since the book came out. He even asked me to write the foreword to his memoirs. I happily did, and, as a result, will never get a table at certain restaurants in town where his name—still—is never to be spoken. "I got fucked by Pino" is something I've heard from just about every Italian chef I know—usually accompanied by a smile and a shrug. It is worth mentioning that they are now, all of them, at the top of their profession. Most will acknowledge a connection between that early "learning experience" and their current success, maybe even a debt, to the former Dark Prince for teaching them the ways of this sometimes cold and cruel world.

From his once-dominating position at the top of the heap of Italian fine dining in New York City, Pino fell hard. A very ill-considered expansion put his whole organization into deep shit—from which, I gather, he had some difficulty climbing out. There was also the fact that now *everybody* does what Pino used to do. All the authentic, Tuscan-style touches, oily little fishes, little-known pasta cuts he struggled so hard to convince his customers to eat, are all over menus now. They're everywhere. As are survivors of his reign of terror.

Even though I was traumatized by my brief experience with Pino, it still hurts when I drive by the space where Le Madri used to be. What a wonderful restaurant that was. It represented the very best of Pino's nature. So many incredible people passed through those kitchen doors, whom I learned so much from so quickly. It was a magical place.

In the end, they tore the building down.

Pino now is often to be found at his restaurant, Centolire, on Madison Avenue. He greets customers in chef's whites—before disappearing back in the kitchen, where he often *cooks*.

It's a different Pino one encounters these days. A happier, more lighthearted version. Maybe because he is now unburdened by the weight of empire, he is free to be the more playful and child-like version of himself we saw on rare occasions back in the day. The one that would break through at the table for a moment now and again as he told a story or reached for a freshly grilled sardine.

Bigfoot is *not* Drew Nieporent—as so many people have suggested. I don't know why anyone would make a connection between the two, as they are as unlike each other as any two people could be. Drew is a romantic. Bigfoot is not. Anybody who ever worked with Bigfoot, drank in proximity to Bigfoot—or even brushed up against him in the '70s, '80s, or '90s—recognized him immediately in *Kitchen Confidential*. And, of course, he's still at it. He owns and operates a saloon in the financial district, where, I have no doubt, he is, at this moment, staring at some tiny design feature trying to figure out how to make it work better—or sorting through the dissembled parts of an ice machine, figuring out how to fix it himself so the crooked fucks who usually do these things can't gouge him. He's gazing innocently at some applicant for a waiter job with guileless-looking eyes and pretending to be a little less intelligent than he is, savoring the moment when he can spring the trap. He's sitting at the bar, measuring the distance between peanut bowls, or contemplating some new menu gimmick or just enjoying being Bigfoot as much as his nature will allow. He has, after all, no choice in the matter.

To this day, there are bars in the West Village where the guy behind the stick has been there twenty years or more. Find one of those one quiet afternoon, sit down, and have a pint or two—and, after a few, ask the bartender to tell you some Bigfoot stories. He'll have plenty of them.

My old sous chef, Steven Tempel, left New York for Florida, worked briefly for a corporate dining facility (how he passed the piss test I can only guess), left that job, married his longtime, long-suffering sweetheart, had a son, split with his wife, and moved to the small Upstate New York town of Speculator, where he opened a bar and grill named Logan's—after his son. Though one of the best, most capable cooks I ever worked with, Steven had always said from the beginning that his highest ambition was to open a diner, so, in some sense, his dreams—of all the characters in the book—have come true.

I visited the Logan's Web site to see what he'd put on his menu, secretly hoping to see some vestige of all those menus, all those restaurant kitchens we'd worked together. Steven had always been unapologetic about how low-rent his culinary ambitions were—and I vividly recall the kind of food he'd eat or prepare for himself to eat, even when we were surrounded by caviar, fresh truffles, and soon-to-be-endangered animals. But I still held out some foolish hope that some sign of all those times—with Pino, at Supper Club, Sullivan's, One Fifth—would peek through from in-between the quesadillas, chicken wings, and burgers on the Logan's menu. I smiled and was pleased to see an incongruous osso bucco on the home page (as Steven's had always been very good), but when I clicked on the current menu, it was gone, the scroll down an unbroken litany of very sensible sports-bar classics. No vestige of the former Steven in evidence. Which was, of course, just what I should have expected. He had never been sentimental about food. And certainly never been apologetic about *anything*.

Almost alone among the people I knew and worked with and wrote about in *Kitchen Confidential*, maybe it was Steven—the guy who never looked back—who figured it all out.

Last I saw the guy, Adam Real Last Name Unknown had an honest job with a company selling prepared stocks and sauces. Strange thing for a baker of his talents to do, but by then it was strange that he had any job at all, so thoroughly had he burned his bridges. And he held that position—whatever it was—for what was, for him, quite some time, maybe a year or two, before disappearing back into the netherworld of what Steven describes to me as "doing the unemployment thing." Naturally, the prick still owes me money.

I'm sure there's some neat moral or lesson to be learned from the Adam Real Last Name Unknown story. The idiot savant who made the best bread any of us had ever tasted. The self-sabotaging genius who couldn't and wouldn't allow himself to succeed. The lost boy—among many lost boys. I'll always remember him crying when his cassata cake started to sag. If anybody ever needed a hug, it was Adam. Unfortunately, he would have stuck his tongue down your throat or picked your pocket if you'd tried. Like with all the true geniuses—there's rarely a happy ending.

My old chef, "Jimmy Sears," who may or may not be John Tesar, just opened his own place, Tesar's Modern Steak and Seafood in Houston—

after successful (for him) runs in Vegas and Dallas. Then, two months later, he left his own restaurant. Tesar was probably the single most talented cook I ever worked with—and the most inspiring. Walking into Bigfoot's kitchen one day and finding him holed up "incognito" as the new (and ridiculously overqualified) chef was a pivotal moment for me. His food—even the simplest of things—made me care about cooking again. The ease with which he conjured up recipes, remembered old recipes (his dyslexia prevented him from writing much of value), and threw things together was thrilling to me. And, in a very direct way, he was responsible for any success I had as a chef afterward. It was he, after all, who took me along to Black Sheep, and then Supper Club.

Just as I was inspired and swept along by John's strengths, I was a direct beneficiary of his weaknesses and foibles. When he fucked up, I stepped up. When he left Supper Club, I had my first chef's chef job in a decade.

It was John who first hired Steven and Adam (a mixed blessing, to be sure). And it was John who helped introduce me to a far more skilled pool of chefs and cooks than I'd been used to—like Maurice Hurley (who'd work at Le Bernardin, then run over after his shift to do banquets for me at Supper Club), his brother Orlando, Herb Wilson, Scott Bryan, a whole graduating class of guys who'd worked together out in the Hamptons—or come up with Brendan Walsh at Arizona 206.

Looking back at a lot of the people I've known and worked with over the years, I see a common thread starting to reveal itself. Not universal, mind you, but there all too often to be a coincidence: a striking tendency among people I've liked to sabotage themselves. Tesar pretty much wrote the book on this behavior pattern: finding a way to fuck up badly whenever success threatens, accompanied by a countervailing ability to bounce back again and again—or, at the very least, survive.

. . .

My old pal, role model, and catering partner from Provincetown, whom I referred to as Vladimir, disappeared off the face of the earth back in the '80s. I've heard he went back to school, went into computers or something. Though a photograph of him looking like a Mexican bandit adorns the front covers of countless thousands of copies of *Kitchen Confidential* all over the world, I have not heard a peep out of him, and he has not, to my knowledge, ever tried to contact me. He, unlike everybody else, got out—not too long after the time period I covered in the chapter titled "The Happy Time." Vladimir (real name, Alexey) was older than us—and maybe he recognized what we didn't yet: that the way we were going, times wouldn't be that happy for long.

Those songs, from those days, from those first years working in New York—though I heard them first in the early days of heroin addiction—that honeymoon period when it's fun and exciting and oh so . . . bad to be a junkie, they still hit hard, a mix of exhilaration and loss: "Mad World," by Tears for Fears, The Bush Tetras, dFunkt, James White & The Blacks, early Talking Heads, Grandmaster Flash's "The Message," The Gap Band—all the background noise of that time. Those songs will always be a bit dangerous. Music to score by.

My chef and high school buddy, Sam, went fully down the rabbit hole with me—starting in the early '80s. He's on that cover, too, standing there with us, leaning against a wall, all of us holding our knives defiantly. It just took him a lot longer to climb his way out. He did some time in a federal prison—which, he says, saved his life. Clean and sober for some time now, he sells meat in California. Maybe you've seen him in such shows as . . . mine.

. . .

Beth Aretsky, the self-named "Grill Bitch," after a long career in professional kitchens, came to work as my assistant, basically running my life for me when things got so crazy and complicated after *Kitchen Confidential* and the TV thing and I found myself the kind of person, suddenly, who needed such things as an assistant. She was my right hand, enforcer, and confidante for ten years—and, occasionally even my bodyguard. On book tour one time, when I was menaced by an overaggressive vegan, she slapped him up against a wall with a forearm to the neck. She has walloped overly liquored, overly friendly female fans with the occasional blunt objects as well. Beth married a man she'd been seeing periodically for years and years in the Caribbean—and the two promptly had a baby girl together. She left the service for a more secure, parent-friendly position a year ago—one where, presumably, martial art skills will not be required.

Les Halles Tokyo, the excuse—the purpose—for my first trip to Asia, my first, mind-blowing experience on the other side of the world, closed down shortly after. I will always be grateful to Philippe Lajaunie, the owner, for giving me that life-changing experience—and sharing it with me. People say, and I can well believe, that he is a difficult man to do business with. Strangely enough, even when I was doing business with him as owner of Les Halles, we never actually talked business. He is the best of traveling companions. Relentlessly curious, tireless—and totally without fear.

José de Meirelles, his former partner and the guy who hired me at Les Halles, has gone on to other things, taking sole control of the very successful kosher French brasserie Le Marais, in New York City's diamond district—and opening a Portugese/Spanish-style tapas place (since closed). Les Halles Washington, DC, closed its doors, and Les Halles Miami changed ownership. Thank God, the way I look at it. They were always, in my experience, a drag on the reputation and finances of the mother ship on Park Avenue—and the successful downtown branch on John Street. I still love those two restaurants, still swing by whenever I can, and am much relieved that their bastard cousins in the hinterlands have stopped being a problem.

Tim the waiter still holds court in the dining room of Les Halles on Park, milking his notoriety for everything he can. If you go to dinner there and inquire of me, he will tell you that you just missed me, that I'm in Thailand having a sex change, or in a Turkish prison, or dog-sledding the Antarctic. Anything but the truth—which means I probably haven't been around for quite some time.

The kitchens of Les Halles, finally, and deservedly, are now being run by Carlos Llaguna Morales, who started cooking on the fry station many years ago. He is a fantastic cook—far better than I ever was—and, to my surprise, a much better organizer. The dark recesses of Les Halles' old cellars are now sparklingly clean and bright, compared to my time. The food handling and control systems, a whole different story. And though the kitchen is the same size, with the same number of cooks, the dining room has expanded into the space that used to house the deli next door, nearly doubling the number of seats. Where, in the old days, we considered a night of three hundred and fifty dinners to be a Monster, they now do as many as six to seven hundred.

In 2007, I got the bright idea that I'd go *back* to Les Halles and work my old station. The Tuesday double shift, no less—where I used to come in at eight a.m., set up, cook the line for lunch, then slam straight into dinner, behind the stove the whole time. That the dining room had gotten so much bigger and busier, and that I'd gotten so much older, didn't really occur to me until the date was nearly upon me. I'd figured that it would make good television.

As the implications and likely outcome began to dawn on me, I struggled to find a solution, a distraction, some way to mitigate what could very well be a public butt-fucking of historic proportions.

So I invited Eric Ripert out for dinner and plied him with high-end tequila (which is something of a weakness of his), and when he was in suitably good spirits and nicely relaxed, the time was ripe. I suggested he join me for a rollicking good time cooking together at Les Halles. It'll be fun, you know . . .

The result is something I'm very proud of. I managed (just) to bully my way through the night (a not very busy one, by current Les Halles standards). It was hard. Very hard. Made harder by the fact that I could no longer read the dupes. When I'd try and slip on my reading glasses, by the time they reached my nose, they were invariably smeared with grease. My knees were creaky, to say the least. But my moves were still there. I could still—if just barely—do it. But at the end of the night, I knew that to do it again tomorrow—as any real cook would have had to do—was out of the question.

Eric, to my surprise, was smooth. I'd hoped that he, who'd never in his life worked in a turn-and-burn joint like mine, who'd never had to hustle out hundreds of plates—much less grill steaks in such quantities and at such speeds—I figured he'd be thrown for a loop. But no. He made it through elegantly, his uniform as snow-white at the end of the shift as when he'd begun. It was enraging. He does, to this day, however, complain bitterly about how "understaffed" the kitchen is at Les Halles. That it's "inhuman" to pump out so many meals with so few cooks. And "impossible." He won't let go of the subject, either.

I'm proud of the television show that came out of it—because it demonstrated in specific, realistic, and very visual terms not just how a busy kitchen works, but how fucking *hard* it is; how much it requires of a person, the kind of teamwork, the kind of endurance, the mindset, choreography, and organization—and what it takes away.

When people ask me if I ever miss it, my answer is always the same.

No. I don't.

I know people want me to say yes. Yes, of course I miss it. But I had enough. I had twenty-eight years of it, I tell them, twenty-eight *years*. I was forty-four years old when *Kitchen Confidential* hit—and if there was ever a lucky break or better timing, I don't know about it. At forty-four, I was, as all cooks too long on the line must be, already in decline. You're not getting any faster—or smarter—as a cook after age thirty-seven. The knees and back go first, of course. That you'd expect. But the hand-eye coordination starts to break up a little as well. And the vision thing. But it's the brain that sends you the most worrying indications of decay. After all those years of intense focus, multitasking, high stress, late nights, and alcohol, the brain stops responding the way you like. You miss things. You aren't as quick reading the board, prioritizing the dupes, grasping at a glance what food goes where, adding up totals of steaks on hold and steaks on the fire—and cumulative donenesses. Your hangovers are more crippling and last longer. Your temper becomes shorter—and you become more easily frustrated with yourself for fucking up little things (though less so with others). Despair—always a sometime thing in the bipolar world of the kitchen—becomes more frequent and longer-lasting as one grows more philosophical with age and has more to despair about.

You're basically done—or on your way to being done. Your brain knows it. Your body knows it—and tells you every day. But pride persists.

What I do miss, I tell them, and will *always* miss, is that first pull on a cold beer after work. *That* is irreplaceable. Nothing approaches that. That's the kind of satisfaction no bestseller can ever beat—no television show, no crowd, no nothing. That single moment after a long and very busy night, sitting down at the bar with your colleagues, wiping the sweat off your neck, taking a deep breath, with unspoken congratulations all around—and then that first sip of cold, cold beer. It tastes like victory. Happy waiters, flush with tips, are ringing out, the cooks look pleased with you and with each other, and you remind yourself that nothing came back the whole night.

Maybe it's Curtis Mayfield, "Superfly," that comes on the sound system then—put on by a sympathetic bartender—or "Gin and Juice" (also for the old folks), or something the moment somehow, by collective will, requires: "Gimme Shelter" or The Stooges' "Dirt." Songs from some other time—not this one—songs that will always mean something to somebody present, but maybe you had to be there.

You look at each other with the intense camaraderie of people who've suffered together and think,

"We did well tonight. We will go home proud."

There are nods and half-smiles. A sigh. Maybe even a groan of relief.

Once again. We survived. We did well.

We're still here.

ACKNOWLEDGMENTS

Many thanks to Kim Witherspoon, Dan Halpern, Karen Rinaldi, Peter Meehan, Mandy Moser, Chris Collins, Lydia Tenaglia, the entire zeropointzero production and post-production crew, and the truly incredible Laurie Woolever.

Thanks, Tony Bourdain